Great Natural Areas in Eastern Pennsylvania

Great Natural Areas in Eastern Pennsylvania

Stephen J. Ostrander

STACKPOLE
BOOKS

Published by
STACKPOLE BOOKS
5067 Ritter Road
Mechanicsburg, PA 17055
www.stackpolebooks.com

Printed in the United States of America

Cover design by Tracy Patterson
Maps by Kevin Patrick

First Edition

10 9 8 7 6 5 4

Library of Congress Cataloging-in-Publication Data

Ostrander, Stephen.
    Great natural areas in eastern Pennsylvania / Stephen J. Ostrander.
    — 1st ed.
        p.   cm.
    Includes index.
    ISBN 0-8117-2574-X
    1. Natural areas—Pennsylvania—Guidebooks.   2. Parks—Pennsylvania—Guidebooks.   3. Pennsylvania—Guidebooks.   I. Title.
QH76.5.P4088   1996
333.78'09748—dc20   95-40286
                                                          CIP

ISBN 978-0-8117-2574-3

To my family,
who gave me the love and opportunity
to pursue this dream

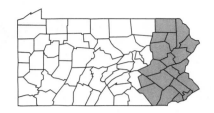

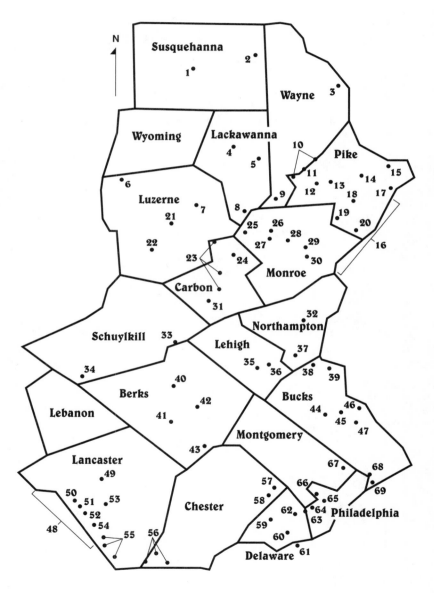

N

Susquehanna
1
2

Wayne
3

Wyoming   Lackawanna   10   Pike
4   15
5   11   14
6   9   12   13   18   17
Luzerne   25   26   19   20
21   7   8   28   29   16
22   27   30
23   24   Monroe
Carbon
31

Northampton   32
Schuylkill   33   37
Lehigh   35   36   38   39
34   Bucks
40   46
Berks   42   44   45   47
Lebanon   41
Montgomery
43   67   68
Lancaster   49   69
50   53   57   66   65
51   58   62   64   Philadelphia
48   52   54   59   63
55   56   60
Chester   61
Delaware

Contents

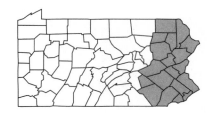

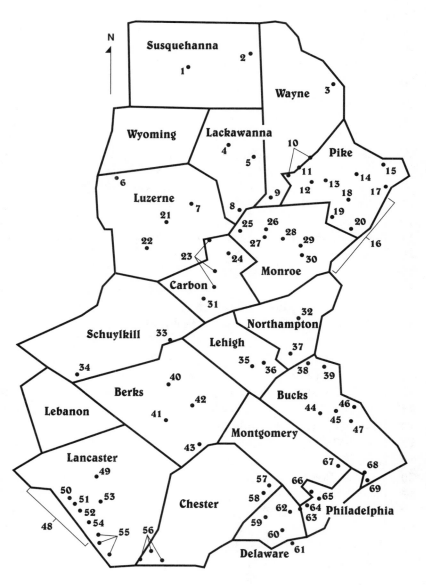

N

Susquehanna
1 • 2 •

Wayne
3 •

Wyoming

Lackawanna
4 •
5 •

10
Pike
11 •
12 • 13 • 14 • 15 •
17
18 •
19 •
20 •
16

Luzerne
6 •
7 •
21 •
22 •
8 •
9 •
25 • 26 •
27 • 28 • 29 •
30 •
Monroe

23
24 •
Carbon
31 •

Schuylkill
33 •

34 •

Berks
40 •
42 •
41 •

Lebanon

Northampton
32 •
37 •
Lehigh
35 • 36 •
38 •
39 •

Bucks
44 • 46 •
45 • 47 •

Montgomery
43 •
67 •
68 •
69 •

Lancaster
49 •
50 •
51 • 53 •
52 •
54 •
48
55
56

Chester
57 •
58 •
59 •
62 •
60 •
61 •
Delaware

66
65 •
64 •
63 •
Philadelphia

Acknowledgments

Writing a book is a euphoric journey for me. Like every literary voyager, I am indebted to the kindness of strangers—the many people who helped me with research or simply gave me directions. I am especially thankful for the help given by naturalists, information specialists, and staff at natural areas. This book is partly the product of their labor and love. I am also indebted to the many scientists and writers whose studies and books on Pennsylvania's natural history proved invaluable.

Several people deserve special praise: Dan Devlin, chief of resource planning, Bureau of Forestry, who helped me gather information on the natural history of state forest preserves; Ellen Hearn, Poconos Office of The Nature Conservancy, and Jim Thorn and his associates at the Pennsylvania Chapter of The Nature Conservancy, Philadelphia, who shared their knowledge and resources; long-time friend Lawrence Barth, who let me use his home as a staging ground for some of my expeditions; and Sally Atwater at Stackpole Books who steered me through the rough rapids of book publishing.

Introduction

I want you to know, right up front, that I am a writer with a mission. I want this book to arouse your curiosity, so that you get out and explore the natural wonders of eastern Pennsylvania. Consider it the first step of an ambitious adventure to recapture lost treasure. To save the land, you must understand it. To understand it, you must be in it.

More practically, this volume serves as a travel and natural history guide. It points you to many of the state's natural attractions that are well worth visiting, and tells you what is so special about them. The selections in this book present a brief picture of the natural history of eastern Pennsylvania. It is not a complete list, certainly. I had to draw the line somewhere.

Natural areas, or nature preserves, are places for preserving wildlife, especially endangered species and habitats, and for showing off natural beauty. Here, natural processes continue without interference by humans. William Shakespeare was right when he wrote, "One touch of nature makes the whole world kin." In nature preserves, we accept natural processes and biological diversity, a discovery that will help us respect human diversity as well.

Nature preserves may be better understood by knowing what they are not. Most are not designed for big crowds. Many offer visitors little more than a hiking trail and parking for one car. Rest rooms, if they exist, are often primitive. Drinking water is best carried in a canteen. Picnicking, camping, rock climbing, fishing, hunting, boating, ball playing, bike riding, and swimming may be prohibited in preserves, though facilities for these activities are usually nearby. Plant gathering, flower and berry picking, mushroom harvesting, and rock collecting are not allowed either. In most places, you may not stray from the trail, play a radio, climb a tree, snooze in its shade, or skinny-dip. Assume that state hunting and fishing laws apply in all sites that allow these activities. Check on special restrictions at each location.

Most of the natural areas included in this book are open to the public year-round, and are free. These places include a national wildlife refuge, state forest natural areas, state game lands, state and county parks, preserves owned by land conservancies and electric companies, nature centers, arboretums, historic sites and privately owned sites. At multipurpose locations, the text focuses on the natural wonders. Valley Forge National Historical Park, for example, has unique geological and botanical stories in addition to the historical one.

Most preserves have year-round charm. Spring is the best time to view wildflowers and migratory birds. Summer displays nature's full abundance, but it's not the best time to see forest birds and animals or geological formations. Pennsylvania's autumn colors rival those of New England. Fall is a good time for birding and wildlife observation. Winter is quiet and bare, and it's the best time to view geological formations.

Wildlife, of course, does not punch a precise clock. Though I note the presence of black bears in a preserve, for example, it does not mean you will see them during your visit. I saw none of these noble beasts in my travels, but evidence of their residence—claw marks and scat—was enough to assure me of their existence.

Sites deemed off limits by the managing agency are not included in the book. These areas either protect extremely fragile environments and endangered species or have visiting restrictions. The status of imperiled plants and animals is given in parentheses. *Endangered* species are those in danger of extinction unless their habitat is restored. *Threatened* plants and animals are experiencing rapid population decline and habitat degradation. They may be abundant in one place but declining throughout their range. Species restricted to small areas, endemic (exclusive to a locality), or disjunct (separated from the main population) are considered *rare*. Those species deemed *at risk* may suffer a decline in population if their habitat is stressed.

Wildflowers often have more than one common name. To avoid confusion, I have included the taxonomic name for wildflowers, and for shrubs when necessary. Since most trees and ferns have just one common name, their scientific names are not given.

When going to a natural area, dress appropriately, and wear sturdy footwear. Wearing summer shorts to a bog or canvas tennis shoes on a boulder-strewn trail may not make for an enjoyable experience. A sturdy stick can help you avoid falls, slips, and injuries.

Pesky insects can spoil summer hikes. Use environmentally safe insect repellent, and wear lightweight long pants and a full-brim hat to reduce insect attacks. (Put repellent on the hat, too.)

Take along drinking water even for winter hikes, and toilet paper, especially if you bring children. If nature calls, dig a small hole, then cover it.

Carry out all litter. Do not smoke, play radios, talk incessantly, shout, run, or jog on foot trails. These activities disturb other visitors and frighten wildlife. Slow, quiet, and alert hikers always see the most wildlife.

Though you are not likely to get lost, it is always good to obtain a trail map before hiking. Do not stray from the trail, especially in a remote location.

The maps in this book are your escorts. Sometimes, getting to a preserve is half the fun.

Best Picks

ALL-AROUND FAVORITES
Every preserve has its charm, but these charmed me. Your top ten may differ.
- Hawk Mountain Sanctuary
- Ricketts Glen State Park
- Delaware Water Gap National Recreation Area
- Kelly's Run Preserve
- Lost Lakes Preserve
- Tannersville Cranberry Bog
- Bruce Lake State Forest Natural Area
- Tucquan Glen Preserve
- Ringing Rocks County Park
- Hickory Run State Park

BIRDING HOT SPOTS
These are rewarding locales for bird-watchers.
- Hawk Mountain Sanctuary
- Susquehanna Overlooks
- John Heinz National Wildlife Refuge at Tinicum
- Delaware Water Gap National Recreation Area
- Honey Hollow Environmental Education Center

TOP WILDFLOWER PRESERVES
These sites are especially colorful in spring and summer.
- Bowman's Hill Wildflower Preserve
- Shenk's Ferry Wildflower Preserve
- Jacobsburg Environmental Education Center
- Delaware Water Gap National Recreation Area
- Serpentine Barrens
- Tannersville Cranberry Bog
- Tyler Arboretum

BEST SCENIC OVERLOOKS
Enjoy the view, but watch your step!
- Delaware Water Gap National Recreation Area
- Susquehanna Overlooks (Chickies Rock, Pinnacle Rock, Susquehannock State Park)

- Hawk Mountain Sanctuary
- Long Eddy Preserve
- Susquehanna Riverlands

GREAT GEOLOGICAL SITES
Waterfalls, gorges, and rock spots.
- Ricketts Glen State Park
- Delaware Water Gap National Recreation Area
- Bushkill Falls
- Ringing Rocks County Park
- Hickory Run State Park
- Lehigh Gorge State Park
- Tannersville Cranberry Bog
- Wissahickon Valley

SOLITUDE AND SILENCE
Places where you can get away from it all.
- Bruce Lake State Forest Natural Area
- Serpentine Barrens
- Pennel Run State Forest Natural Area
- Trout Run Preserve
- Devil's Hole

BEST OUTINGS FOR CHILDREN
When your kids tire of nature centers, take them to these special places.
- Valley Forge National Historical Park
- Ringing Rocks County Park
- Hawk Mountain Sanctuary
- Tannersville Cranberry Bog

BEST EASYGOING STROLLS
Wide, smooth, flat trails and never boring!
- Valley Forge National Historical Park
- Wissahickon Valley (Forbidden Drive)
- John Heinz National Wildlife Refuge at Tinicum
- Lehigh Gorge State Park
- Bowman's Hill Wildflower Preserve
- Tyler Arboretum

Woodbourne Forest and Wildlife Sanctuary

Some ancient hemlocks in this forest may predate Christopher Columbus's arrival in the New World. This virgin wood, the largest of its kind in northeastern Pennsylvania, is what Penn's Woods was like before it belonged to William Penn.

In the 1940s, a plant thought to be extinct, Oconee bells *(Shortia galacifolia),* turned up in South Carolina. The land's former owner planted the rare white flower here. Amazingly, the plant flourished in this high northern clime. Today it grows in a small colony beside a community of pink lady's slippers.

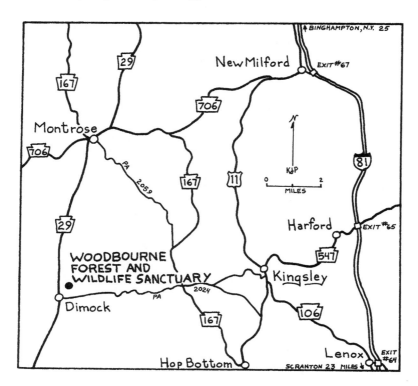

Ownership. Pennsylvania Chapter of the Nature Conservancy.

Size and Designation. This forest preserve, encompassing 648 acres, has been proposed for designation as a national natural landmark.

Nearby Nature Attractions. Florence L. Shelly Preserve and Salt Springs State Park.

Features. A three-quarter mile, yellow-blazed nature trail visits part of the virgin hemlock forest, an alder swamp, a maturing second-growth woods, and meadows. Look for trail guides in the registration box at the south end of the parking lot. The trail is open daily from dawn to dusk. To protect the sanctuary, pets, camping, campfires, smoking, and picnicking are prohibited.

The sanctuary's resident naturalist lives in the home north of the parking lot. Guided tours, nature programs, and other events usually begin here. Occasionally the naturalist leads small groups deep into the forest or to Cope Pond. Groups of eight or more should schedule tours in advance by contacting the naturalist at Woodbourne Forest and Wildlife Sanctuary, R.R. 6, Box 6294, Montrose, PA 18801, telephone (717) 278-3384.

Geology. Woodbourne sanctuary is situated on the Allegheny Plateau at an elevation of about 1,600 feet. The colder climate at this altitude hosts flora and fauna common in the boreal swamp forests in Canada.

The rill that drains from the alder swamp flows into Meshoppen Creek, a feeder of the Susquehanna River. Beavers dam the stream to raise the water level in the swamp to improve their habitat.

Parallel layers of sandstone and shale underlay the sanctuary. This bedrock originated as sediment at the bottom of a shallow sea 365 to 405 million years ago. At least three glaciers passed over this spot during the ice age. Each ice mass removed younger rock and bruised the older layers.

Cope Pond and the 16-acre alder swamp started as blocks of ice that broke from the last withdrawing glacier 12,000 years ago. These chunks eventually melted into ponds and small lakes. Decayed vegetation now gives the water in these wetlands its brown color.

Wildlife. Woodbourne has an abundance of habitats and wildlife. There are 11 distinct habitats here, with more than 300 species of plants, 31 mammals, and 145 birds.

The best way to explore the sanctuary is to follow the nature trail guide, which describes some of the plants and animals you may see. Trees along the trail include white ash, bitternut hickory, basswood, red maple, yellow birch, red oak, eastern hemlock, black cherry, and American beech.

The old-growth hemlock-hardwood forest contains trees more than 400 years old. In the Pocono Mountains and Delaware River Valley, hemlocks must gather in cool ravines, but here the climate is cold enough for them to spread out on flat terrain. Other northern species, such as hobblebush and striped and mountain maples, grow in the understory.

Lichens (a fungus and an alga living cooperatively) on rocks might be a century old. Twenty-two varieties of ferns have been counted here, including interrupted, sensitive, lady, Christmas, New York, spinulose wood, hay-scented, cinnamon, royal, marsh, Clinton's, crested, and Boott's. The royal fern rises six to eight feet from hummocks in the swamp; the delicate and diminutive New York fern prefers open areas at the edge of the swamp.

Wildflowers bloom in the spring and summer. In the swamp, look for flat-leaved pondweed (*Potamogeton robbinsii*, PA rare), turtlehead *(Chelone glabra),* and wild calla *(Calla palu tris).* In the moist forest, you may find jack-in-the-pulpit *(Arisaema triphyllum),* wood sorrel *(Oxalis montana),* starflower *(Trientalis borealis),* goldthread *(Coptis groenlandica),* corn lily *(Clintonia borealis),* painted trillium *(Trillium undulatum),* Canada mayflower *(Maianthemum canadense),* sharp-lobed hepatica *(Hepatica acutiloba),* and several kinds of violets (*Viola* spp.).

Deer feed heavily on the hobblebush *(Viburnum alnifolium),* jewelweed *(Impatiens pallida),* and shining club moss.

Dense carpets of sphagnum moss floating on Cope Pond support the insect-eating northern pitcher plant *(Sarracenia purpurea)* and round-leaved sundew *(Drosera rotundifolia).* At the pond's edge grow a community of pink lady's slippers *(Cypripedium acaule)* and the unusual colony of Onconee bells. Cope Pond and the alder swamp are home to the forked clubtail, an imperiled dragonfly.

During the summer, the noisiest creature in the treetops is the red-eyed vireo. The solitary vireo, American redstart, and Canada, black-throated green, black-throated blue, magnolia, and yellow warblers nest in the sanctuary. Also look for the scarlet tanager, rose-breasted grosbeak, rufous-sided towhee, eastern bluebird, indigo bunting, northern waterthrush, hermit thrush, and winter wren, which favors upturned roots for nests. The wood duck, great horned and barred owls, ruffed grouse, yellow-bellied sapsucker, yellow-shafted flicker, and pileated, hairy, red-bellied, and downy woodpeckers may be seen here.

Snowshoe hares and river otters (both PA at risk) find refuge in the preserve, along with the southern bog lemming, starnose mole, mink, raccoon, and jumping mouse. The work of the beaver is evident along the trail—gnawed stumps and girdled saplings.

Nine species of salamanders, including a forest dweller called the purple salamander, survive in the preserve. Other residents include the American toad, spring peeper, green frog, bullfrog, and gray tree frog.

History. The Cope family donated Woodbourne Forest to the Nature Conservancy in 1956. The preserve functions as a wildlife sanctuary and nature education center.

Florence Shelly Preserve

Thompson Wetlands Preserve

At dusk on a magical November day, you might see a mink scamper across this ice-covered bog and then see it dive into water the same color as its brown-black fur. And you may hear, if you're lucky, the hoot of a great horned owl from its perch atop a dead tree.

Ownership. The Pennsylvania Chapter of the Nature Conservancy.

Size and Designation. 358 acres. Thompson Wetlands has been designated an exceptional value watershed by the Pennsylvania Department of Environmental Resources.

Nearby Nature Attractions. Salt Springs State Park and Woodbourne Forest and Wildlife Sanctuary.

Features. The trail from the Ireland Road parking lot leads to a two-story observation deck overlooking Plew's Swamp. Trails branching from the path off PA 171 go to Plew's Swamp and the ten-acre Weir Pond. Because of the fragility of wetland plants, visitors must stay on the trails, which stay open from sunrise to sunset every day.

Guided tours are available from Cathy Shelly, P.O. Box 25, Thompson, PA 18465. Also contact the Pennsylvania Chapter of the Nature Conservancy, 1211 Chestnut Street, 12th Floor, Philadelphia, PA 19107, telephone (215) 963-1400.

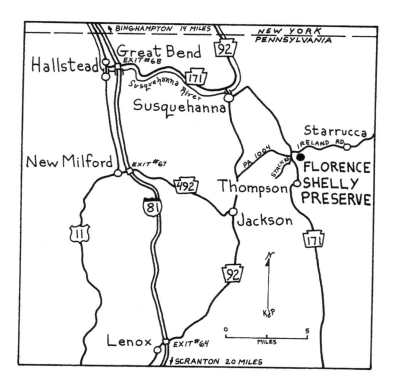

Geology. Plew's Swamp and Weir Pond trace their origins to the Wisconsinan glacier. As the glacier withdrew, about 12,000 years ago, blocks of ice broke off. Meanwhile, meltwater deposited glacial sediment, or till, around the ice chunks, creating basins. As the ice melted, ponds and lakes were formed.

Plew's Swamp was a pond before filling with sediment and vegetation. Technically, it is a fen, rather than a bog. (Swamp is a catchall term for most wetlands.) A bog's only water source is precipitation, whereas stream or spring water refreshes a fen and delivers nutrients. Fens have an outlet, allowing water to flush them out. Most bogs, however, do not release water, except via evaporation. A rill known as Black Spruce Run replenishes Plew's Swamp and Weir Pond.

Wildlife. Black Spruce Run delivers enough nutrients for a fragile red alga *(Batrachospermum vagum)* to blossom in Plew's Swamp. Fourteen kinds of sphagnum moss are found here. This water-absorbing plant grows in thick mats. At Weir Pond, the sphagnum mats grow outward from shore. Two carnivorous plants inhabit the mats: the northern pitcher plant *(Sarracenia purpurea)* and round-leaved sundew *(Drosera rotundifolia).* Cattails and sedges ring the pond, and pink swamp roses *(Rosa palustris)* bloom in the summer.

Plew's Swamp has an abundance of trees found in northern bog environments: tamarack, black spruce, balsam, and eastern hemlock. Snags become perches and homes for several animals. The preserve also has meadows, pine and spruce plantations, sugar maple, bigtooth aspen, red maple, yellow birch, and a vast shrub thicket on former farmland.

In the spring hepatica *(Hepatica americana)*, spring beauty *(Claytonia virginica)*, various trilliums *(Trillium* spp.), jack-in-the-pulpit *(Arisaema triphyllum)*, pink lady's slipper *(Cypripedium acaule)*, and other wildflowers decorate the forest floor. The preserve protects 375 plant species.

A large herd of deer finds protection here. Unfortunately, they have eaten everything in their reach and created a browse line. Piles of fish scales on swamp hummocks and logs suggest the presence of river otters (PA at risk). Black bears and coyotes are seen occasionally, and box turtles inhabit the woods. Several rare dragonflies hover above the swamp.

As many as three dozen species of warblers arrive in the spring. (Guided bird walks begin at 6 A.M.) Wood ducks, and sometimes broad-winged hawks, nest here. The black duck, Canada goose, and other waterfowl inhabit the waters. The great horned and barred owls also live here, and two fields are mowed to encourage bobolinks to stay.

History. Between 1979 and 1985, Dr. Robert M. and Florence L. Shelly donated three parcels of land to the Nature Conservancy. They formed the nucleus of the preserve, also known as the Thompson Wetlands Preserve. The conservancy's purchase of an additional 72 acres increased the acreage under protection.

Long Eddy Preserve

Water seeping from an ancient sandstone cliff nourishes a tiny wildflower called miner's lettuce, which is found in only four places east of the Rocky Mountains. Just how the plant got to the Allegheny Plateau remains a mystery. The rugged wildness of the terrain along with preservation efforts enable it to thrive here. Bald eagles have been spotted at the preserve, and river otters may be seen on the banks of the Delaware River.

Ownership. The Pennsylvania Chapter of the Nature Conservancy owns 122 acres. Another 566 acres is protected under a conservation easement granted by the landowners.

Size and Designation. The 688-acre preserve hugs the

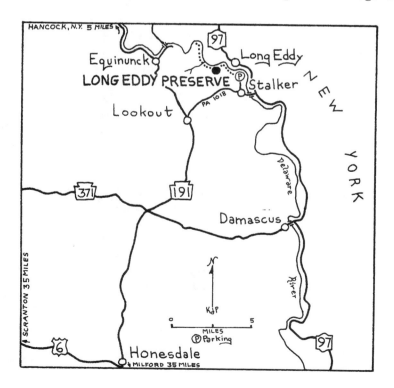

southern shore of the Delaware River for about 1.5 miles. The 73-mile stretch of the Delaware River from Hancock, New York, to Mongaup, New York, was designated a national scenic and recreational river.

Nearby Nature Attractions. Lacawac Sanctuary, Lehigh Pond Preserve, and Lake Wallenpaupack.

Features. Hike on the jeep trail about 1.5 miles to the bright orange signs marking the conservancy's property. The trail leads to a dramatic waterfall and continues beyond the western boundary line of the preserve. A round-trip walk from the parking lot to the waterfall is roughly four miles. To avoid trespassing and harming wildlife, stay on the trail. The terrain is extremely steep in places. Don't risk injury by climbing the slopes (the footing is not as solid as it looks) or the slippery waterfall.

For canoeists the conservancy's land begins a little upstream from the waterfall. Leaving the canoe to hike up the falls is prohibited. Paddlers will find a launch nine miles upstream at the Buckingham access off PA 191.

For more information, contact the Pennsylvania Chapter of the Nature Conservancy, 1211 Chestnut Street, 12th Floor, Philadelphia, PA 19107, telephone (215) 963-1400.

Geology. In this forested region, the Delaware River has sculpted a steep, snaking canyon through the ancient bedrock of the Allegheny Plateau. Below the topsoil lie horizontal layers of sandstone, conglomerate, and shales in various shades of gray, red, and green that date back 350 million years (Devonian Period).

The terrain slopes precipitously to the river. Boulders broken from the bedrock by erosion clutter the hillside and slide slowly toward the river. On them grow moss, ferns, and lichens, which hasten their erosion. Some house-size boulders topple trees on their journey, and a few fall into the river.

The unnamed cascade drains a small pond above the bluff and drops in steps more than 400 feet over a distance of less than 1,000 feet. Spring water also drips from cracks and washes down the slope into the river.

The Wisconsinan glacier last passed over the site 12,000 years ago, depositing boulders on the uplands atop a layer of glacial till (gravel, sand, and silt) derived from the local bedrock. Water pouring from the melting ice sheet engorged the Delaware River Valley and speeded up erosion of the valley.

Wildlife. You are not likely to see miner's lettuce (*Montia chamissoi,* PA endangered) from the trail. A handful of colonies survive on the wet, acidic cliffs, about a dozen feet above the river. Please don't go looking for them. Although they are common in bogs and swamps in the Rocky Mountains, their rarity in this part of the country makes them hard to identify, and climbers may accidentally step on them.

Loggers spared the forest owned by the conservancy because the slope was too steep for their equipment. This northern hardwood and conifer forest boasts stands of hemlock, sugar and striped maples, beech, and basswood. Only a few trees become giants. Most topple down the hillside before reaching maturity.

Wildflowers are abundant here because deer, though present, do not forage much on the steep slopes of this old-growth forest. Look for trilliums and saxifrages, Dutchman's breeches *(Dicentra cucullaria)*, and jack-in-the-pulpit *(Arisaema triphyllum)*.

Sugar maple, beech, yellow birch, and black cherry, along with some hemlock, cover the rim of the slope. Here also are a beaver meadow and a few clearings resulting from earlier logging.

Birds spotted here include the bald eagle (PA endangered), osprey (PA endangered), great blue heron, various hawks, kingfisher, and ruby-crowned kinglet. River otters (PA at risk) may be seen along the Delaware River.

History. The conservancy purchased the land for this preserve and obtained the conservation easement in January 1990.

Rabbit Hollow Wildlife Sanctuary

There *are* rabbits here; on a cool summer evening, though, you are just as likely to see deer bounding away.

Ownership. Abington Township.

Size and Designation. 16 acres.

Nearby Nature Attractions. Archbald Pothole and Lackawanna State Park.

Features. Walk south 200 yards on Miller Road to reach what was once a path on the sanctuary's western edge. The path has vanished beneath vegetation, but the spot is still the best place to

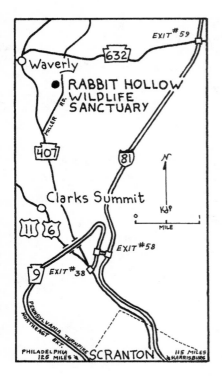

enter the preserve. From here follow the slim paths made by deer.

Because parking is limited, large groups are discouraged. There are no rest rooms or drinking water at this site.

For more information, contact the Chairman, Board of Supervisors, Abington Township, Waverly, PA 18471, telephone (717) 586-0111.

Geology. Rabbit Hollow is a typical hollow—a shallow valley drained by a creek. Ackerly Creek, once dammed to create a small pond, now flows freely into a pond in a neighboring township. Rabbit Hollow lies on the Allegheny Plateau.

Wildlife. Rabbit Hollow has three botanically rich habitats: a hillside of evergreens and hardwoods, meadows, and a swamp. Sawgrasses, sedges, and rushes abound in the swampy center of the preserve, bordered by thickets of willows and dogwood. The yellow flag *(Iris pseudacorus)* brightens this spot in the summer.

In open meadows grow grasses like wild oats (an important food source for animals) and blue-eyed grass *(Sisyrinchium angustifolium),* actually an iris with blue-violet flowers and a twisted stalk.

Eastern hemlock, spruce, scotch and white pines, American beech, oak, hickory, and black walnut rise on the drier slopes, along with mulberry, privet, quaking aspen, staghorn sumac, American elm, white ash, red and sugar maples, hawthorn, black cherry, honey locust, and white, yellow and gray birches. Wooded areas favor wildflowers like blue cohosh *(Caulophyllum thalictroides),* spring beauty *(Claytonia virginica),* hepatica *(Hepatica americana),* and mayapple *(Podophyllum peltatum).*

Other plants at Rabbit Hollow include spotted jewelweed *(Impatiens capensis),* buttercup *(Ranunculus acris),* common cinquefoil *(Potentilla simplex),* bittersweet nightshade *(Solanum dulcamara),* speedwell *(Veronica officinalis),* moneywort *(Lysimachia nummularia),* New York and sensitive ferns, and hair cap, white cushion, and shiny flourish mosses.

The Louisiana waterthrush, Cooper's hawk, wood thrush, belted kingfisher, swamp sparrow, pileated woodpecker, gray catbird, and red-winged blackbird have been observed here.

Rabbits are numerous, as the thickets provide them with excellent cover. Other inhabitants include the white-tailed deer, squirrel, woodchuck, and chipmunk. Ackerly Creek supports a small trout population.

History. The property was donated to the Pennsylvania Chapter of the Nature Conservancy in 1975 and was dedicated a preserve in 1977. Ownership was transferred to Abington Township.

5

Archbald Pothole

The Archbald Pothole was formed by a torrent of water tumbling 200 feet down a glacial crevasse. The mad current stirred rocks and pebbles at the bottom, scooping the deepest pothole in the world.

Ownership. Pennsylvania Department of Environmental Resources, Bureau of State Parks.

Size and Designation. The state park is 150 acres.

Nearby Nature Attractions. Rabbit Hollow Wildlife Sanctuary, Spruce Swamp State Natural Area, and Lackawanna State Park.

Features. The world's largest pothole lies just a few paces from the parking lot. It is the main (and only) attraction in the park. An enclosed deck lets you peer into the 38-foot-deep pothole. Be careful, and hold on to your camera tightly. Park officials fish out a few cameras every year.

There are picnic tables and rest rooms on the grounds. Hiking trails wander through woods on strip-mined land and are not especially scenic. Hunting is allowed in designated areas.

The park is open from 8 A.M. to 9 P.M. during the summer, and from 8 A.M. to sundown other times. For more information, contact Lackawanna State Park, Pennsylvania Department of Environmental Resources, P.O. Box 251, Dalton, PA 18414, telephone (717) 945-3239.

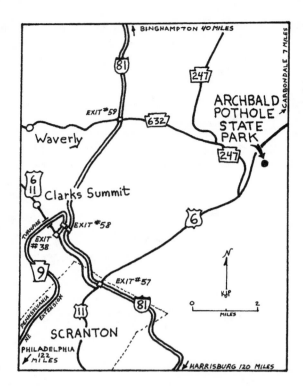

Geology. Potholes are round holes scoured into bedrock, usually deeper than their diameters. They are common features at waterfalls or turbulent rapids, and they also appear near the fronts of glaciers, where meltwater plunges off the steep face of the ice or through a crevasse. Since there is no evidence of a nearby stream or waterfall, Archbald Pothole was formed near the edge of a glacier, probably through a crack, during the ice age, 15,000 to 18,000 years ago. The pothole's size indicates that the glacier must have parked at this spot for a long time.

Note the bedrock layers of the pothole—coal at the bottom, and shale and sandstone at the top. The gray shale is especially well polished. The hole tapers like a flowerpot, from 42 feet to 24 feet across at the top to 14 feet to 17 feet at the bottom. A close look reveals that the walls are undulated, or ribbed, a result of the scouring action.

East of the pothole, miners removed anthracite coal from a surface mine. The coal seam slants into the earth at a 45-degree angle. Miners talked of another large pothole, roughly 100 yards from the first one, but this natural wonder remains hidden, if it existed. Road construction, strip mining, or some other human disturbance may have destroyed it.

Wildlife. Hunters bag deer, wild turkey, ruffed grouse, pheasants, and squirrels in the oak forest surrounding the pothole. Chestnut oak outnumbers the red, black, and scrub oaks. Black cherry and sassafras thrive here, too.

Scheduled reclamation of the strip mine will regrade the terrain to its original contour and seed the ground with native plants.

History. Coal miners discovered the pothole in 1884. While digging a coal seam, they found a column of rounded stones which they removed to empty the pothole.

Since its discovery, scientific and conservation groups have urged that the pothole be preserved as a geological wonder. The pothole became a protected attraction when the state park opened in 1961.

Ricketts Glen State Park

Twenty-two majestic waterfalls plunge down a verdant, hemlock-lined gorge. Trails along the glens allow you to follow the waterway as it gracefully cascades down the series of falls to the valley floor below.

Ownership. Pennsylvania Department of Environmental Resources, Bureau of State Parks.

Size and Designation. The state park totals 13,050 acres of which the Glens Natural Area makes up 2,000. The Glens Natural Area is listed on the National Registry of Natural Landmarks.

Nearby Nature Attractions. Nuangola Bog Preserve, Seven Tubs Natural Area, Susquehanna Riverlands, and Francis Slocum State Park.

Features. Eighteen waterfalls entice you to wander down Ganoga Glen and Glen Leigh, a three-and-a-half mile course that could take a full day, depending on how long you linger at each cascade. The Ganoga Glen Trail is a mile-long hike past ten waterfalls to Waters Meet. Here you can take the short Kitchen Creek Trail to see three more cascades, then backtrack to the confluence. The Glen Leigh Trail takes you past eight more waterfalls. Add three miles to the journey if you take the Kitchen Creek Trail from

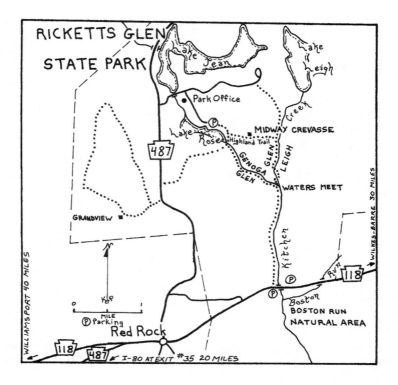

Waters Meet to view Adams Falls in the Boston Natural Run Area. Alternately, you can walk the half-mile Evergreen Trail to see Adams Falls. Pick up a trail map at park headquarters.

The trails are challenging, becoming steep, narrow, rocky, and slippery in places. This is a series of waterfalls plunging down a gorge, which means that to view them, you not only have to hike down into the gorge, but you also have to hike back up—and it's a long climb. Don't hurry. You will want to take time to admire every waterfall anyway, and each stop lets you catch your breath. Benches are at Waters Meet for hikers who get weary.

An additional half-mile hike to Grand View, elevation 2,449 feet, gives you a panoramic view of the Allegheny Front. The trail also leads to a fire tower standing near the junction of Luzerne, Sullivan, and Columbia counties.

Hikers can traipse along 25 miles of trails here. The park has swimming, boating rentals, fishing, hunting, cabins, camping, picnic areas, an amphitheater, a refreshment stand, rest rooms, drinking water, snowmobiling, ice skating, and sledding. Pick up a recreational guide when you enter the park.

For more information, contact the Pennsylvania Department of

Environmental Resources, Ricketts Glen State Park, P.O. Box 130, R.D. 2, Benton, PA 17814, telephone (717) 477-5675 or (800) 63-PARKS.

Geology. The waterfalls in the Glens Natural Area tumble down the Allegheny Front, an escarpment marking the edge of the high Allegheny Plateau to the northwest and the Appalachian Mountains to the southeast. North Mountain and Red Rock Mountain stand on the rim of the Front.

Ganoga Glen and Glen Leigh cut a Y-shaped gorge into the escarpment and plunge down cascades in a 1,000-foot descent over two and a quarter miles. They merge at Waters Meet to form Kitchen Creek, which then courses south through Ricketts Glen and tumbles over Adams Falls in the Boston Run Natural Area.

The Wisconsinan continental glacier formed the waterfalls 15,000 years ago. The ice mass spilled over the Allegheny Front three miles west of the state park and flowed southeastward across the valley in front of the escarpment. When the climate warmed, torrents of meltwater from the retreating glacier hastened erosion and created the cascades. The glacier also left behind lakes and swamps on the plateau. Today Kitchen Creek is fed by Ganoga Lake, Lake Jean, and tributaries.

The falls range from 11 to 94 feet high. Though each cascade is unique, it is classified as either a "wedding cake" or a "bridal veil" waterfall.

The wedding cake variety tumbles down rock steps and usually broadens at the bottom. The F. L. Ricketts Falls in Glen Leigh is a perfect example. Here the water flows over thick layers of sandstone.

Bridal veil falls wash straight down over a ledge. The harder top layer, called caprock, resists erosion better than the softer, less resistant layer beneath it. The spray and backwash of the waterfall erodes away the softer layer and forms a recess. Eventually, the heavy caprock, having lost its foundation, breaks off into the stream. At Ricketts Glen, gray sandstone serves as the caprock above red shale. Harrison Wright Falls, just below Waters Meet, is a bridal veil falls.

Adams Falls in Boston Run Natural Area is a series of three spills dropping over sandstone, shale, and siltstone. Plunge pools lie beneath the middle and lower falls. Potholes in the narrow gorge resulted from the scouring action of gravel caught in swirling eddies.

Above the falls, the Highland Trail passes the Midway Crevasse, a crack between two huge chunks of conglomerate rock. Frost that wedged its way into natural fractures split the rocks from a nearby ledge and continued to break up the rock.

Red Rock Mountain is composed of red shale and sandstone. Here you may find the fossilized burrows of ancient lungfish, which tunneled into the mud of riverbeds during dry periods.

Wildlife. Hemlocks toppled by a storm near Adams Falls were found to be more than 900 years old. Boston Run Natural Area protects some of the oldest hemlocks in the state, as well as a grove of ancient white pines.

Upstream along Kitchen Creek, there is another stand of venerable hemlock as well as yellow birch and American beech. Beeches need moist soil and level ground, because their roots spread out rather than sink deeply. Like hemlocks, beeches are shade tolerant. Unfortunately, the elm spanworm, a moth larvae, has been doing damage to the beeches at Ricketts Glen. Red and sugar maples also grow here, and some oaks rise on the higher ground.

Few wildflowers or shrubs live in the shady glen. You might see jack-in-the-pulpit *(Arisaema triphyllum)* near the streambank, though silvery and maidenhair spleenworts, liverworts (near the cascades), beech, and Boott's, spinulose wood, and common polypody ferns are more common. Highbush blueberry shrubs surround Lake Rose, now more a swamp than a pond. Several varieties of dragonflies enjoy this moist habitat. Elsewhere, mountain laurel blooms.

On the plateau summit, look for the black-throated blue warbler and hermit thrush, which has a flutelike song. Between cascades, listen for woodpeckers rapping. The hairy woodpecker may be the most common. White-breasted and red-breasted nuthatches hop on tree trunks. The evening grosbeak and white-throated sparrow nest here, and ruffed grouse and wild turkey inhabit the woods. Mallard ducks, Canada geese, and other waterfowl may be seen at Lake Jean.

Lake Jean is too acidic for trout, but it supports largemouth and smallmouth basses, sunfish, pickerel, perch, and muskellunge.

The white-tailed deer, black bear, fox, raccoon, and squirrel live here. From time to time, a bobcat (PA at risk) is sighted. Several varieties of dragonflies can be seen at Lake Rose.

History. Col. Robert Bruce Ricketts, for whom the park was named, was a hero at the Battle of Gettysburg. After the war, Rickets bought 80,000 acres of timberland in northeastern Pennsylvania, including the land now making up the state park.

Ricketts was charmed by the waterfalls on Kitchen Creek and forbade lumbering there. He named the falls after family members and American Indian tribes and terms. He built a trail to the cascades between 1889 and 1893. In 1914, Ricketts stocked the area with deer, the ancestors of today's large deer herd.

After Ricketts's death, his firm, the Central Penn Lumber Company, sold 40,000 acres to the Pennsylvania Game Commission between 1920 and 1924. That sale, however, did not include the glens, Lake Jean, or Ganoga Lake. In 1942, the state bought 1,261 acres—the falls and glens—from Ricketts's heirs. Additional tracts were purchased, and park facilities opened in 1944.

The U.S. Department of the Interior added the Glens Natural Area to the National Registry of Natural Landmarks in 1969.

7

Seven Tubs Natural Area

Meltwater pouring over a glacial precipice 12,000 years ago gouged a line of smooth tubs in gritty sandstone. Few places have this many glacier-formed potholes in a row.

Ownership. Luzerne County Recreation and Parks Department.

Size and Designation. 527 acres.

Nearby Nature Attractions. Ricketts Glen State Park; Nuangola Bog Preserve; Susquehanna Riverlands; Frances Slocum, Lehigh Gorge, and Nescopeck state parks; and the Lehigh River, a state-designated scenic river.

Features. A paved trail leads from the parking lot to the tubs of Wheelbarrow Run. Wheelchairs can negotiate this trail to a bridge across the ravine. Stairs descend to a pool below the tubs. Surprisingly, no signs warn hikers of the

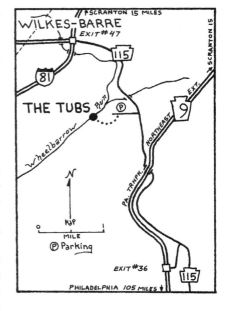

risks of climbing the rocks around the tubs. These rocks are slippery from water and algae. Be wary of loose rocks and roots, which could cause you to lose your footing.

For more information, contact the Luzerne County Recreation and Parks Department, Hunlock Creek, PA 18621, telephone (717) 675-1312.

Geology. Twelve-thousand years ago, a continental ice sheet covering the area, the Wisconsinan glacier, began to thaw. Torrents of meltwater and debris ranging from boulders to silt spilled over the edge of the glacier like a waterfall, fell into crevasses in the ice, or plunged down holes on the glacier surface. The swirling currents and spinning debris scoured a series of tub-shaped potholes in 350-million-year-old sandstone and conglomerate bedrock. Some of the potholes measure 30 feet in circumference and 20 feet deep.

Wheelbarrow Run winds through a narrow gorge known as Whirlpool Canyon. This is not a large canyon like those in the West, but its small size does not subtract from its intricacy and beauty.

The brook continues to polish the rock. Below the tubs, the run slides into a shaded pool, a perfect place to cool your feet on a July afternoon. Beyond that, the run empties quietly into larger Laurel Run, which has carved a scenic and precipitous gorge.

On the rocky gorge ledge, notice how erosion and weathering have broken the bedrock into slabs along bedding planes.

Wildlife. The tubs are shaded by hemlock and yellow, gray, and black birches. In other parts of the preserve, white, red, chestnut, and bear oaks are predominant, along with tulip tree, red and striped maples, bigtooth and quaking aspens, sycamore, American beech, white ash, slippery elm, sassafras, black gum, witch hazel, flowering dogwood, staghorn sumac, and white, red, and pitch pines.

About 60 kinds of wildflowers have been observed, including pearly everlasting *(Anaphalis margaritacea),* wild lettuce *(Prenanthes alba),* jack-in-the-pulpit *(Arisaema triphyllum),* closed gentian *(Gentiana andrewsii),* pink lady's slipper *(Cypripedium acaule),* self-heal *(Prunella vulgaris),* small round-leaved orchis *(Orchis rotundifolia),* and harebell *(Campanula rotundifolia).* Trailing arbutus *(Epigaea repens),* mountain laurel *(Kalmia latifolia),* sheep laurel *(Kalmia angustifolia),* and blueberry also thrive here.

Birds observed here include the whippoorwill (dwindling in numbers), saw-whet owl (becoming a rarity), barred owl, rufous-sided towhee, yellow-shafted flicker, brown thrasher, and eastern wood pewee. Gamebirds such as ruffed grouse and wild turkey have become residents.

Mammals include the black bear, deer, long-tailed weasel, red and gray foxes, opossum, and brown bat. Laurel Run supports brook trout and crayfish.

History. The preserve is composed of land from several estates. A utility donated 92 acres to the Pennsylvania Chapter of the Nature Conservancy in 1980, which then transferred the title to the Luzerne County Recreation and Parks Department.

8

Spruce Swamp State Forest Natural Area

Spruce Swamp seems to have missed the frontier wars, land disputes, logging, and forest fires that befell the rest of the Lackawanna State Forest. This forest, born in the postglacial period, continues to thrive, however, and black spruce and tamarack still prevail in this chilly habitat. Solitude can easily be found here.

Ownership. Pennsylvania Department of Environmental Resources, Bureau of Forestry.

Size and Designation. Spruce Swamp, designated a state forest natural area, is a 97-acre section of Lackawanna State Forest.

Nearby Nature Attractions. Archbald Pothole, Gouldsboro and Hickory Run state parks, and Rabbit Hollow Wildlife Sanctuary.

Features. The trail, an easy-to-follow logging road, heads north from Tannery Road. Spruce Swamp is on the right as you begin the hike. Narrow deer trails lead to the edge of the mire but disappear in the wetland. The logging road eventually reaches an electric fence marking the state forest boundary on the left. Stay on the logging road until you reach the blue blazes of the Sunday Trail on the right; follow this trail into the forest. Generally, the Sunday Trail journeys southeast through the preserve and joins Tannery Road east of the parking lot. (En route, you will pass the trailhead and blazes near a fire lane on Tannery Road.) You can trace the trail to its end or double back.

Tannery Road is not maintained in the winter. Visit Spruce Swamp between midspring and midautumn. Picnickers can use the Thornhurst Picnic Area, east of the preserve off Tannery Road. This section of Lackawanna State Forest is shown on the public use

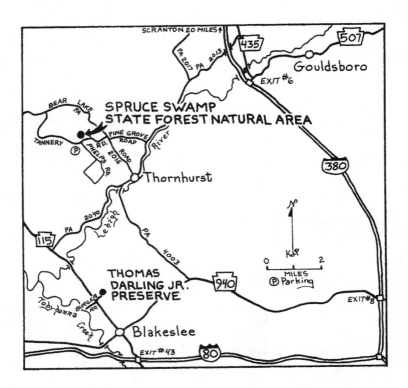

map for Delaware State Forest. To get a map, contact the Pennsylvania Department of Environmental Resources, Bureau of Forestry, Division of Forest Advisory Services, 400 Market Street, 3rd Floor, P.O. Box 8552, Harrisburg, PA 17105-8552, telephone (717) 787-3444.

Geology. Spruce Swamp originated as an island of ice that split from the retreating Wisconsinan glacier 12,000 years ago. The ice melted into a basin and formed a pond. Over time, sediment from surrounding ridges and encroaching vegetation transformed the pond into a bog.

The preserve lies on the western side of the Pocono Plateau. Sandstone, conglomerate, and shale underlay the swamp. Slabs of 380-million-year-old rock are strewn along the Sunday Trail.

Wildlife. Because of its elevation—1,800 feet—the climate at Spruce Swamp matches that of Canadian latitudes. Consequently, plants common in those boreal regions also thrive here. The boreal (northern) swamp is a rarity in the Poconos. Human development in the region has reduced the number of these fragile habitats to a handful.

Black spruce prevails in this cool, wet, and acidic environment. This conifer has short, bristly, blue-green needles and small inch-long cones. Tamarack, hemlock, and red maple also form the canopy. The tamarack, or larch, is deciduous and sheds its needles.

Shrubs like labrador tea (*Ledum groenlandicum,* PA rare), blueberry, and cranberry, as well as sedges and sensitive and cinnamon ferns, grow in abundance and make the swamp impenetrable to humans. A mixed forest of chestnut and white oaks, hemlock, red and sugar maples, and yellow birch surrounds the swampy spot.

The black bear, bobcat (PA at risk), coyote, mink, deer, porcupine, ermine, four species of squirrels, four kinds of shrews, and eight types of bats inhabit Lackawanna State Forest.

Observers have counted 180 species of birds in the state forest, including the bald eagle (PA endangered), northern harrier (PA at risk), eight kinds of owls (two of them imperiled), ten sparrows, four swallows, twenty-three warblers, and hairy, pileated, red-bellied, and red-headed woodpeckers.

Also living here are seven species of frogs; eleven salamanders; fourteen snakes, including the diminutive eastern worm snake and the venomous timber rattlesnake; and seven turtles, including the musk, snapping, and spotted.

History. This region, rich in game, was contested for more than 100 years. Susquehannock Indians lived in this area until they were overwhelmed by the Iroquois nation in 1675. Shawnees arrived around 1700, followed by the Wanamies, Mohicans, and Lenni Lenape, the last settling in 1742. Most native travelers followed the single-file Pechoquealin and Wechquetank trails, which merged a mile west of Shades Glen to form the Wyomong Path. Part of the Pechoquealin Trail crosses the state forest.

White settlers also fought over the land. King Charles gave it to Connecticut in the 1660s, but the same spot was handed to William Penn in 1681. Neither titleholder moved to colonize the area for nearly a century. Then, in 1762, the Susquehanna Company of Connecticut dispatched 119 armed men to prepare the tract for settlement. (The resident Lenni Lenape had temporarily vacated the area.) They cut down trees, built some cabins, cleared land, and went back to Connecticut to recruit emigrants. The next year, the Lenape returned to find Connecticut Yankees in their valley. Twenty-two settlers died in the ensuing frontier war. Indians were killed too. The remaining whites fled.

The Connecticut claimants returned in 1769 and routed squatters called Pennamites, settlers representing Penn's title. The

Pennamites regained control in 1770 but were booted out by the Yankees the following year. This tug-of-war continued until Connecticut gave up its claim in 1783. Still, Ethan Allen, leader of the Green Mountain Boys during the Revolution, was promised 4,500 acres in 1786 if he could wrest control from the Pennamites. He was unsuccessful. During the Revolution, Maj. Gen. John Sullivan drove the Iroquois and British from the area, and settlement resumed in the 1780s.

Logging boomed in the 1830s. Lumber was needed for buildings, coal mines, and railroads, and bark for tanneries. By 1880, however, the Thornhurst logging and tanning industries had declined. Most of the timber had been cut or ruined by forest fires, and one tannery had burned to the ground. Landowners forfeited their titles when taxes went unpaid, so the commonwealth picked up the land.

The land was left to regenerate. In the 1930s, workers for the Civilian Conservation Corps built the forest roads that lead to Spruce Swamp and other sites. Other government-funded conservation corps have participated in projects here. Spruce Swamp became a state forest natural area in 1993.

9

Lehigh Pond Preserve

The Lehigh River begins its journey at this pristine pond, which was formed at the end of the ice age. Sphagnum moss and a dense thicket of rhododendron and other shrubs ring the pond. This wild refuge hosts the state-endangered bald eagle and the river otter, at risk in the state, as well as six rare plants.

Ownership. Pennsylvania Game Commission.

Size and Designation. State Game Lands 312, in which the pond is situated, measures more than 4,000 acres.

Nearby Nature Attractions. Gouldsboro and Tobyhanna state parks; Spruce Swamp, Pine Lake, and Bruce Lake state forest natural areas; Lacawac Sanctuary; Lake Wallenpaupack; and Devil's Hole.

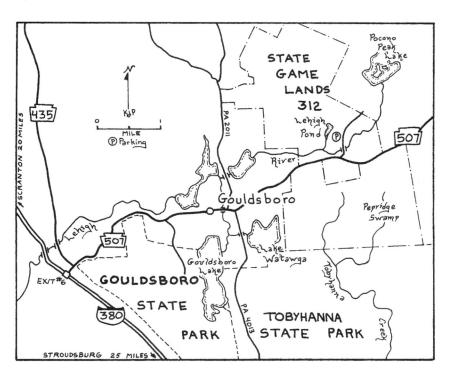

Features. The trail from the parking lot is discernible for about a mile, then it disappears. The shrubs encircling Lehigh Pond stop even the most determined hiker from reaching the shore.

Hunting is allowed here, and the Pennsylvania Game Commission has a helpful map of the area. For more information, contact the Pennsylvania Game Commission, 2001 Elmerton Avenue, Harrisburg, PA 17110-9797, telephone (800) 228-0789 (regional office).

Geology. Lehigh Pond is a glacial kettle hole lake. Twelve thousand years ago, a block of ice broke off the Wisconsinan glacier as it was retreating northward. Sediment-laden meltwater deposited gravel, sand, and other debris around the chunk of ice, which melted into a basin formed by the accumulated glacial sediments and its own weight. Other wetlands in the preserve—Big Sampson and Pepridge swamps—and nearby lakes and ponds had similar glacial origins. Over the years, Lehigh Pond has filled with sediment from surrounding ridges and vegetation and has shrunk to just 15 acres.

Pepridge Swamp, located in the southeastern corner of the refuge, is the headwater of Tobyhanna Creek, a tributary of the Lehigh River. At Easton, the Lehigh River pours into the Delaware River.

According to the Nature Conservancy, these wetlands stabilize the flow of the Lehigh and Delaware rivers by absorbing water during floods and releasing it during droughts.

Wildlife. Lehigh Pond was identified as a primary preservation site in a U.S.–Canada conservation pact called the North American Waterfowl Management Plan. It offers an excellent habitat for migratory and nesting waterfowl, notably the black duck, wood duck, and mallard. The osprey and bald eagle (each PA endangered), as well as the common snipe (PA at risk) and rails (some species imperiled) also visit the preserve. Songbirds flock to the forests surrounding the swamps. River otter and snowshoe hare (each PA at risk), black bear, beaver, and deer also reside here.

Several protected plants thrive in the wetlands. These include species typical of the Canadian wilderness, such as labrador tea (*Ledum groenlandicum,* PA rare) and hairy-fruited sedge (*Carex asincarpa,* dwindling in number). Black spruce, tamarack, bog laurel (*Kalmia polifolia),* and sheep laurel (*Kalmia angustifolia)* mature in the swampy spots. Wild cranberries, wetland orchids, and insectivorous flora like the northern pitcher plant *(Sarracenia purpurea)* bloom here too.

A dense tangle of great rhododendron encircles much of Lehigh Pond. On the higher ground, along the hiking trail, eastern hemlock, American beech, red maple, yellow birch, and black cherry form the canopy. Ferns, club mosses, and mushrooms decorate the forest floor. Also look for beechdrops *(Epifagus virginiana),* a brown-stemmed parasitic plant growing beneath beech trees.

Except for some logging in the forest (note the moss-covered stumps) and construction of a power line, the area has remained largely undisturbed.

History. Lehigh Pond owes its preservation to Thomas Darling (see Thomas Darling Jr. Preserve) and others who explored and recorded its unique botany several decades ago. In the early 1990s, the Pennsylvania Chapter of the Nature Conservancy, the Wildlands Conservancy, and Ducks Unlimited purchased nearly 4,000 acres. The Pennsylvania Game Commission got the title to the land. The acquisition protects nearly 40,000 acres of contiguous state-owned land made up of state parks and state game lands.

10

Lake Wallenpaupack

Ledgedale Natural Area
Shuman Point Natural Area

Thousands of summer outdoors enthusiasts head for the cool waters of Lake Wallenpaupack, a crooked lake that zigzags for 13 miles across the Pocono Plateau. Ledgedale and Shuman Point natural areas, one at each end of the lake, offer glimpses into the area's natural heritage.

Ownership. Pennsylvania Power and Light owns both natural areas.

Size and Designation. Shuman Point Natural Area (including Beech House Creek Wildlife Refuge) encompasses 360 acres; Ledgedale Natural Area, 80 acres.

Nearby Nature Attractions. Delaware Water Gap National Recreation Area; Delaware State Forest; Promised Land State Park; Bushkill Falls; Little Mud Pond Swamp, Bruce Lake, Buckhorn, Pennel Run, Pine Lake, and Stillwater state forest natural areas; Lacawac Sanctuary; Lehigh Pond, Carr Pond, and Long Eddy preserves; and the Delaware River, a national scenic river.

Features. Shuman Point and Ledgedale natural areas are just two of many recreation sites along Lake Wallenpaupack.

En route to Shuman Point Natural Area, stop at the visitors center on US 6. Open daily from 9:30 A.M. to 9 P.M., the center has exhibits on wildlife, hydroelectric power, and an American Indian canoe found in Lake Wallenpaupack. Nearby are the Mangan Cove boat access and lake overlook (off PA 590), Wilsonville campground and public swimming beach (US 6), and Caffrey campground (west of Shuman Point).

The three-mile Blue Trail loops through Shuman Point Natural Area. The path was the main road to Wilsonville before the dam flooded Wallenpaupack Creek. Expect a couple of steep hills. The trails are open for snowmobiles in the winter. Two miles of shoreline are accessible to anglers, and hunting is allowed.

Across PA 590, Beech House Creek Wildlife Refuge attracts

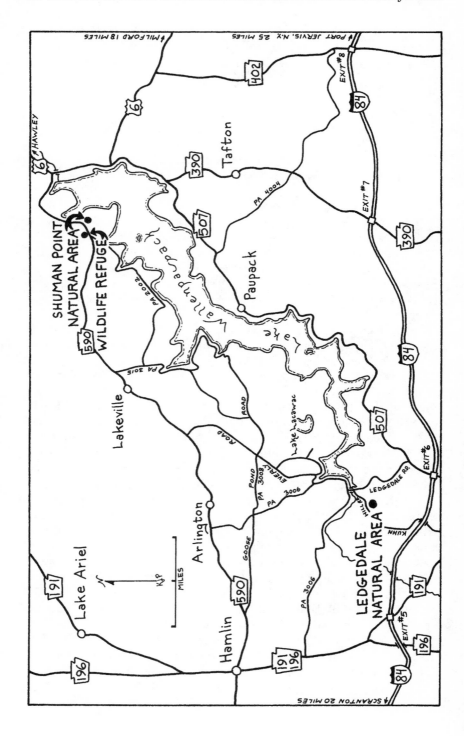

waterbirds, beaver, and other marsh animals. An unmarked path traces the edge of the 60-acre marsh, though at times it is swamped.

Four trails (old logging roads) wander through Ledgedale Natural Area. The longest path, the Lenape Trail, begins at the parking lot on Kuhn Hill Road and connects with the Ledgedale campground via the Moosewood Trail. The Ironwood campground is a few miles east of Ledgedale, off PA 507.

For more information, contact Lake Wallenpaupack Superintendent, Pennsylvania Power and Light Company, Box 122, Hawley, PA 18428-0122, telephone (717) 226-3702.

Geology. In the final days of the ice age, 12,000 years ago, torrents of water from the melting Wisconsinan glacier created Wallenpaupack Creek. The raging current cut through layers of ancient bedrock on the Pocono Plateau and emptied into the Lackawaxen River, a tributary of the Delaware River.

The bedrock exposed in lake ledges consists of sandstone and red shale that originated 380 million years ago during the Devonian Period.

During a mountain-building epoch that formed the Appalachians, this area lifted up and became part of the Allegheny Plateau. Glacier-born streams like Wallenpaupack Creek have been etching the plateau for many millennia.

Lake Wallenpaupack, created by a dam at the eastern end, has a surface area of 5,700 acres. Its deepest channel is 60 feet.

Wildlife. Shuman Point protects one of the last undeveloped woods along Lake Wallenpaupack. Stone walls on the site mark the boundaries of old farm fields.

Look for husky white pine, bigtooth aspen, gray and white birches, shagbark hickory, shadbush, and chestnut, pin, and white oaks. Red maple stands in moist soil, and eastern hemlock prefers the shady sites. American chestnut trees still sprout, but the bark fungus that wiped out their ancestors will take these before they mature.

At Shuman Point, deer tracks outnumber human footprints. Quiet hikers may observe fox, ruffed grouse, wild turkey, and black bear. Woodland birds, including warblers, nest in the treetops.

Beavers maintain the marsh environment at Beech House Creek Wildlife Refuge by constructing dams to slow and widen the flow of the creek. They dwell in dome-shaped lodges of branches and mud. Here you may see the river otter (PA at risk), mink, raccoon, mallard and wood ducks, great blue heron, and various hawks.

Ledgedale Natural Area lies on forested land that was logged between 1910 and 1920. Some giant specimens still remain, however, because of their inaccessibility. Towering eastern hemlocks stand in clusters throughout the preserve and shade a small wood-land pond near the center. Red and sugar maples, yellow and black birches, wild cherry, some oaks, and white pine also grow here. Great rhododendron thrives in the southeastern corner. Various ferns include the common polypody, which springs from pits and cracks in boulders.

Hikers may encounter white-tailed deer, red and gray foxes, ruffed grouse, and black bear.

History. The Lenni Lenape lived in camps along Wallenpau-pack Creek, which in Lenape means "the stream of swift and slow water." A Lenape dugout canoe at the visitors center was unearthed during construction of the dam.

For more details on the history of the Wallenpaupack Valley, see Lacawac Sanctuary.

Lacawac Sanctuary

The pristine waters of half-moon-shaped Lake Lacawac and the solitude found at the sanctuary refresh the soul.

Ownership. The Lacawac Sanctuary Foundation.

Size and Designation. The 478-acre preserve is listed on the National Registry of Natural Landmarks.

Nearby Nature Attractions. Tobyhanna State Park; Long Eddy and Lehigh Pond preserves.

Features. Free guided tours are held on Saturdays at 10 A.M. from May to October. The tour is the best way to visit this gem. The guide will explain the unique natural and geological histories that make this sanctuary a national landmark.

You can also wander on the mile-long Maurice Broun Self-Guided Nature Trail, named for the first curator of Hawk Moun-tain Sanctuary and former Lacawac Sanctuary board member. Pick up a trail guide at the trail entrance. Rest rooms and drinking water are not available at the sanctuary.

For more information, contact the Lacawac Sanctuary, R.D. 1, P.O. Box 518, Lake Ariel, PA 18436, telephone (717) 689-9494.

Geology. Lake Lacawac is the southernmost glacial lake on the continent, and it is said to be the purest. It is situated about 250 feet north of man-made Lake Wallenpaupack.

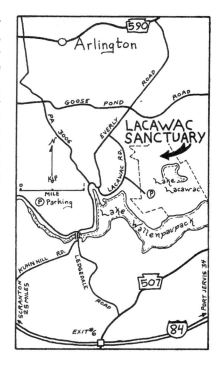

Lake Lacawac originated at the end of the ice age, 10,000 to 15,000 years ago, as the last ice mass, the Wisconsinan glacier, was shrinking northward. At this spot, a huge chunk of ice broke off the glacier and settled on the bluff above the Wallenpaupack Creek, which had been created by the glacier's erosive power.

Meltwater pouring off the glacier contained sediments that built up around the ice chunk. Eventually, the climate warmed, and the ice melted into a bowl formed by the sediment and its own weight.

A quarter mile south of the lake are steep sandstone and red shale ledges rising above the Wallenpaupack Valley. They originated as fine sediments that eroded off highlands to the east and settled in a shallow sea 380 million years ago. During the mountain-building period that formed the Appalachians, this area was lifted up and became part of the Allegheny Plateau. The soils derived from these rocks are acidic, which explains the abundance of hemlock, rhododendron, and other acid-loving plants.

The 52-acre lake is a eutrophic, or aging, lake due to accumulating vegetation and sediment. It is half its original depth and a third smaller in surface area. Lacawac is ideal for field experiments because it is an unpolluted eutrophic lake; lakes tainted by sewage and other contaminants lose oxygen and age faster.

Wildlife. Prevailing northwesterly winds determine the distribution of plants along the lake. The wind creates waves that lift clay and sandy sediment from the lake bottom and deposit them on the eastern and southern shores. Cattails and golden club—and little else—thrive on these sandy, wave-swept shores. The calmer northwestern shore is covered with a sphagnum moss mat with pitcher plant *(Sarracenia purpurea),* round-leaved sundew *(Drosera rotundifolia),* pickerelweed *(Pontederia cordata),* and fragrant water lily *(Nymphaea odorata).* The floating heart (*Nymphoides* *cordata,* PA threatened) and arrow arum *(Peltandra virginica)* are also among the three dozen aquatic plans rimming the lake.

Other plants include pearly everlasting *(Anaphalis margaritacea),* enchanter's nightshade *(Circaea canadensis),* king devil *(Hieracium pratense),* boneset *(Eupatorium rugosum),* cancer root *(Orobanche uniflora),* an unusual shrub called labrador tea (*Ledum groenlandicum* PA rare), and lady, rattlesnake, crested shield, fragile, and interrupted ferns.

Trees include birch, maple, oak, pine, aspen, tamarack, eastern hemlock, tulip tree, shagbark hickory, American beech, and witch hazel.

Huge lichens called rock tripe live on the inaccessible rock ledges overlooking Lake Wallenpaupack. Some are six inches or more in diameter and are believed to be a century old.

Seventy-seven species of birds have been sighted, including the bald eagle and osprey (each PA endangered), northern harrier (PA at risk), northern goshawk (PA rare), scarlet tanager, pileated woodpecker, cedar waxwing, American goldfinch, northern oriole, great blue heron, and ten kinds of warblers.

Deer have overbrowsed on wildflowers and tree seedlings. Other wildlife includes the black bear, porcupine, flying squirrel, snowshoe hare (PA at risk), and bobcat (PA at risk).

History. In the Lenni Lenape (Delaware Indian) language lacawac means fork, though nobody knows if the fork referred to the branching of a woodland path or of a stream. It may refer to a fork in the nearby Minisink Trail, which was an important path used by the Lenni Lenape and early settlers, linking the Delaware River Valley and the Wyoming Valley.

The Wallenpaupack basin became part of the holdings of the Penn family, which maintained amicable ties with the Lenape. Their successors, however, succumbed to the pressure to get more land for arriving settlers. In 1849, logging began in the virgin forest to support a sawmill and tannery erected at Ledgedale. Logging ceased when the tannery went up in flames in 1895.

In the early twentieth century, plans were laid for damming Wallenpaupack Creek and constructing a power plant. The Pennsylvania Power and Light Company later bought the site, and the power plant went into service in 1926.

In 1966, Lake Lacawac was donated to a nonprofit group for scientific research and education. The preserve was later transferred to the Pennsylvania Chapter of the Nature Conservancy and in 1985 to the Lacawac Sanctuary Foundation. In 1968, the U.S. Department of the Interior designated the pristine glacial lake a national natural landmark.

Pine Lake State Forest Natural Area

Though bordered by an open utility line and state forest logging tracts, Pine Lake, a glacial kettle lake rimmed with thickets, remains untainted.

Ownership. Pennsylvania Department of Environmental Protection, Bureau of Forestry.

Size and Designation. This 67-acre site is a state forest natural area.

Nearby Nature Attractions. Delaware State Forest (surrounding Pine Lake); Bruce Lake, Little Mud Pond Swamp, Pennel Run, Buckhorn, and Stillwater state forest natural areas; Promised Land State Park; Lake Wallenpaupack; Bushkill Falls, Delaware Water Gap National Recreation Area; and Lacawac Sanctuary.

Features. The only way to reach this remote preserve is on foot beneath a power line. On Beaver Dam Road, note the sign beside the road marking the boundary of Delaware State Forest.

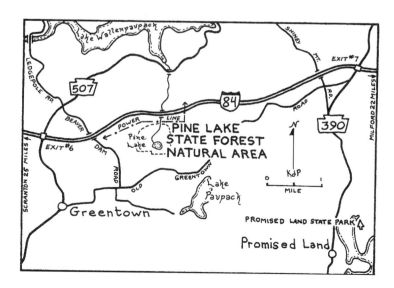

Ahead, the power line, heading northeast, is the trail to the preserve. Take your bearings from the utility poles. Look for the metal plates on each pole. When you reach a pole designated "BLGR-Jack" in yellow and numbered "67992-N43792," follow the jeep trail going to the right into swampy woods. This is a C-shaped path leading to Pine Lake. Eventually, the path curves back to the power line near pole "67827-943754."

There are no facilities in this nature preserve, and trails are not well developed. Rest rooms, picnic tables, phones, and camping, fishing and swimming areas can be found at nearby Promised Land State Park.

Maps of the area are available at the Promised Land State Park office, from the Pennsylvania Department of Environmental Resources, Bureau of Forestry, P.O. Box 1467, Harrisburg, PA 17120, or from the Department of Environmental Resources, District Forester, 474 Clearview Lane, P.O. Box 150, Stroudsburg, PA 18360, telephone (717) 424-3001. Also, you can contact the Department of Environmental Resources, Promised Land State Park, R. D. 1, Box 96, Greentown, PA 18426, telephone (717) 676-3428, or (800) 63-PARKS.

Geology. Pine Lake typifies many ponds on the Pocono Plateau. It started as a chunk of ice that broke off the retreating Wisconsinan glacier 12,000 years ago. When the climate warmed, the ice melted and formed a kettle hole lake.

Over many millennia, sediment from surrounding hills has been slowly filling Pine Lake. This, in combination with vegetation growing from the shore toward the open water, has reduced the lake's original surface area and depth. A tiny stream trickles from the northern edge of the lake and flows about a mile into Lake Wallenpaupack.

Wildlife. Between the power line and Pine Lake, you will see hemlock, yellow birch, American beech, and chestnut oak. At the lakeshore, the natural world changes. The shore is ringed with bog shrubs, such as great rhododendron *(Rhododendron maximum)*, swamp azalea *(Rhododendron viscosum)*, sheep laurel *(Kalmia angustifolia)*, leatherleaf *(Chamaedaphne calyculata)*, mountain holly *(Nemopanthus mucronata)*, swamp laurel *(Kalmia polifolia)*, winterberry *(Ilex verticillata)*, bog rosemary *(Andromeda polifolia,* PA rare), blueberry, and cranberry.

On the water are yellow water lily *(Nuphar variegatum)*, pickerelweed *(Pontederia cordata)*, pondweed *(Potamogeton epihydrus)*, and bladderwort *(Utricularia geminiscapa)*, a carnivorous plant that gets its nourishment from tiny crustaceans, insects, and algae.

Tamarack, black spruce, and red maple prevail in the swamp.

Dead trees still standing in the mire become homes for swamp creatures and perches for birds. Dwarf mistletoe *(Arceuthobium pusillum)*, a parasitic evergreen, clings to the spruces.

Orchids such as pink lady's slipper *(Cypripedium acaule)* and white-fringed orchid *(Habenaria blephariglottis)* favor this wet habitat. Other carnivorous plants, the pitcher plant *(Sarracenia purpurea)* and round-leaved sundew *(Drosera rotundifolia)*, grow on the sphagnum moss mats. Also look for swamp candle *(Lysimachia terrestris)*, arrowhead *(Sagittaria latifolia)*, water arum *(Calla palustris)*, blue flag *(Iris versicolor)*, and marsh St.-John's-wort *(Hypericum Triadenum virginicum)*. Several imperiled species of sedges grow here.

The open, meadowy area beneath the utility line is an ecotone, a transition zone between two or more natural communities. Other man-made ecotones are roadways and stone fence rows. Natural ones include the edges between forest and field, and the gradual grading between conifer and hardwood forests. Deer and bears might be observed crossing the clearing.

History. The Pennsylvania Department of Environmental Resources designated this parcel of Delaware State Forest a natural area in 1975.

Bruce Lake State Forest Natural Area

The quiet, pristine Bruce Lake lies in a basin at the edge of the Pocono Plateau. In spite of intense logging, farming, and tourists, this preserve has stayed wild and uncorrupted.

Ownership. Pennsylvania Department of Environmental Resources, Bureau of Forestry.

Size and Designation. Bruce Lake is a state-designated natural area protecting 2,845 acres.

Nearby Nature Attractions. Pine Lake, Pennel Run, Stillwater, and Buckhorn state forest natural areas; Promised Land State

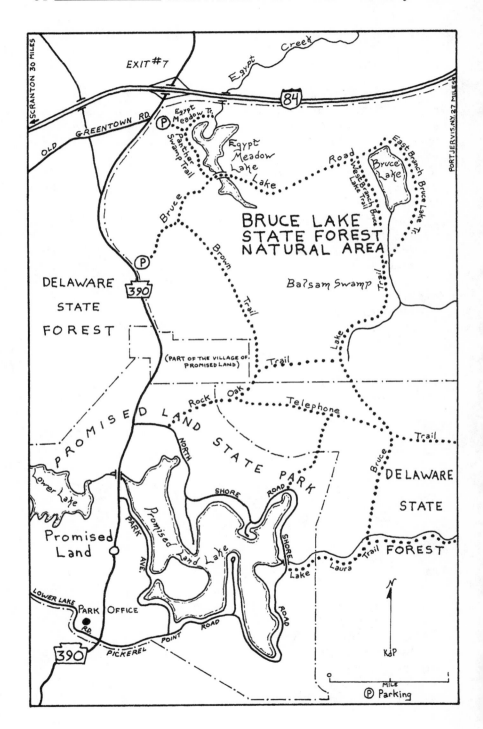

Park; Lake Wallenpaupack; Bushkill Falls; and Delaware Water Gap National Recreation Area. The Appalachian Trail passes through the county.

Features. Go to Promised Land State Park for conveniences—rest rooms, telephones—and recreational opportunities such as picnicking, fishing, camping, and swimming.

The brochure for Promised Land State Park has a good map of the Bruce Lake Natural Area. Pick one up at the park or contact Department of Environmental Resources, Promised Land State Park, P.O. Box 96, R.D. 1, Greentown, PA 18426, telephone (717) 676-3428, or 800-63-PARKS. Also obtain a map of Delaware State Forest from the Pennsylvania Department of Environmental Resources, Bureau of Forestry, P.O. Box 1467, Harrisburg, PA 17120, or Department of Environmental Resources, District Forester, P.O. Box 150, 474 Clearview Lane, Stroudsburg, PA 18360, telephone (717) 424-3001.

Primitive, walk-in camping (two-day maximum) is allowed at special sites on the north shore of the lake. You must obtain a camping permit at the Promised Land State Park office.

Geology. Bruce Lake has a rich geological history. About 385 million years ago, streams and rivers flowing off the western slope of the Acadian Mountains (predecessors of the Appalachians) carried eroded sediment into a sea that covered the western half of Pennsylvania. At that time, Pennsylvania was located south of the equator. Much of this sediment accumulated along riverbanks, forming the sandstone and conglomerate rock (a mixture of cemented pebbles and sand) seen at Bruce Lake. Crossbeds—arc-shaped curves in the rock layers—can be seen in outcrops along the Bruce Lake Trail and on the north shore of the Lake. These troughs were made by Acadian-era mountain streams. The crossbeds often overlap, indicating shifting channels on the alluvial plain. Fossils from this period have been found in rocks on the northeastern shore of Bruce Lake.

Twenty thousand years ago, a continental ice sheet known as the Wisconsinan glacier created Bruce Lake and nearby swamps. As the glacier moved, it broke off chunks of rock. These are the boulders you see scattered about in the preserve and adjacent state park. Many boulders, as well as gravel and sand, froze to the bottom of the glacier. As the glacier moved, they created scratches, or striations, in the underlying rock. Examples of striations are visible alongside the East Branch Trail, just east of the fork with the West Branch Trail.

Bruce Lake is a watery remnant of the ice age. When the glacier withdrew, it stranded huge icebergs across the landscape. Sediment transported by glacial meltwater wrapped around the icebergs. Slowly, some of the icebergs melted, creating basins by the force of their own weight and the surrounding banks of sediment.

Though larger in area (60 acres) Egypt Meadow Lake, built by the Civilian Conservation Corps in 1935, is shallower than Bruce Lake. Balsam Swamp drains into Egypt Meadow Lake, bringing with it naturally acidic, brown-stained water.

Wildlife. This forest has survived clear-cut logging, fires, gypsy moths, and acid rain. Chestnut, red, white, black, and scarlet oaks grow among the boulders. Red and sugar maples, shagbark hickory, black and gray birches, eastern hemlock, American yew, white and pitch pines, white ash, tulip tree, and aspen have established smaller colonies. Balsam fir, black spruce, and tamarack thrive in the acidic habitats of the swamps.

The understory includes mountain laurel (the state flower), sheep laurel, huckleberry, sweet fern, azalea, blueberry, shadbush (serviceberry), sassafras, great rhododendron, and hay-scented, royal and cinnamon ferns.

In spring, woodland flowers dot the forest floor. The most intriguing (and rare) blossoms flourish in the swampy spots, notably bog rosemary *(Andromeda polifolia,* PA rare) and grass pink *(Calopogon pulchellus).* Leatherleaf *(Chamaedaphne calyculata)* and cranberry *(Vaccinium macrocarpon)* occupy the edge of the bog. Two carnivorous plants—the pitcher plant *(Sarracenia purpurea)* and the round-leaved sundew *(Drosera rotundifolia)*— inhabit the sphagnum moss mat floating at the southern end of the lake. Another carnivore is the bladderwort *(Utricularia inflata),* an aquatic plant that preys on tiny crustaceans, water insects, and algae. When special sensory hairs are touched, the plant opens a tiny door for a fraction of a second and sucks the victim into a bladder, where digestive juices dissolve it. The plant's tiny yellow blossom sticks above the surface, but most of the bladderwort remains submerged.

Other rarities surviving in the preserve are an orchid called heart-leaved twayblade *(Listera cordata)* and slender mountain-ricegrass *(Oryzopsis pungens),* both endangered in Pennsylvania. Fragrant water lily *(Nymphaea odorata),* spatterdock *(Nuphar advena),* and golden club *(Orontium aquaticum)* may appear on the lakes.

Panther Swamp gets its name from the panthers, or mountain lions, that once roamed it. There are no panthers there today, but the bobcat (PA at risk) leaves tracks in the woods. Other animal inhabitants include the black bear, white-tailed deer, gray fox, and spotted blue darner, an imperiled invertebrate. Beaver lodges rise above the lake surface. The southern bog lemming, porcupine, and mink, known to live in Delaware State Forest, may also have found a home here.

Bald eagles, ospreys (both PA endangered), and belted kingfishers take fish from the lake—mostly sunfish, largemouth and smallmouth bass, yellow perch, pickerel, and whatever baitfish are tossed into the water by fishermen. In the woodlands, you might spot wild turkeys, ruffed grouse, (the state bird), black-capped chickadees, brown creepers, yellow-shafted flickers, and red-bellied, downy, and hairy woodpeckers.

Delaware State Forest, of which Bruce Lake is a part, is host to 22 kinds of warblers, four species of vireos, 17 frog and salamander varieties, and 21 turtles and snakes (including the snapping turtle and rare timber rattlesnake).

History. Members of the religious group known as Shakers thought they had reached the land of milk and honey when they settled here in 1878. What they got, instead, was land too rocky for their farming commune. They soon departed and ironically dubbed the place "the Promised Land."

Twenty years later, the commonwealth began buying this land in order to restore Penn's Woods after centuries of poor logging practices, erosion, and fires. Delaware State Forest started in 1898. Promised Land State Park opened in 1905. The state continued to buy land into the 1930s. During the 1930s, the Civilian Conservation Corps constructed roads and trails in the state forest and park. In 1935, the brook that flowed through Egypt Meadow was dammed to create Egypt Meadow Lake. The Bruce Lake section of the state forest was set aside on July 2, 1945, as a state forest monument, a preservation designation. It was reclassified a state forest natural area in April 1975.

14

Little Mud Pond Swamp State Forest Natural Area

L ittle Mud Pond Swamp, both a pond and a swamp, is the home of several rare plants and possibly a community of black bears.

Ownership. Pennsylvania Department of Environmental Resources, Bureau of State Forests.

Size and Designation. This state natural area totals 182 acres.

Nearby Nature Attractions. Buckhorn, Bruce Lake, Pine Lake, Pennel Run, and Stillwater state forest natural areas; Delaware State Forest; and Promised Land State Park.

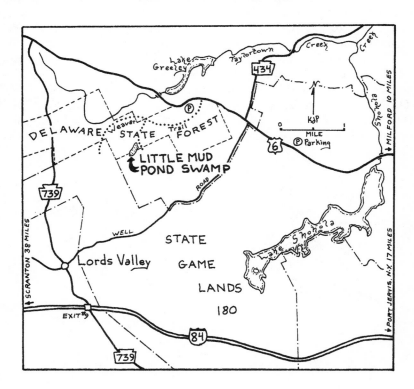

Features. The Weaver Trail, an old woods road, leads to the preserve. Bear left at the first fork in the trail. After 1.5 miles, the trail descends into a swampy area on the left. This is the northern edge of Little Mud Pond Swamp. The tall black spruces mark the location of the boreal conifer swamp, or northern evergreen wetland. From here, you can roam about and explore the preserve, but remember the location of the Weaver Trail.

Another approach is follow the trail to where it briefly leaves the state forest and enters private property. At this point, the natural area is to your left. Expect a tough and soggy walk after you leave the main trail.

Go to nearby Promised Land State Park for picnic tables, toilets, or drinking water. Hunting is permitted in the state forest.

Maps of the state forest are available from the Pennsylvania Department of Environmental Resources, Bureau of Forestry, P.O. Box 1467, Harrisburg, PA 17120; or Department of Environmental Resources, District Forester, 474 Clearview Lane, P.O. Box 150, Stroudsburg, PA 18360, telephone (717) 424-3001. Do not confuse the natural area with Little Mud Pond, also in Delaware State Forest, next to Stillwater Natural Area.

Geology. Little Mud Pond Swamp was formed in the same way as Lehigh Pond (see that chapter). As the Wisconsinan glacier retreated northward 12,000 years ago, massive chunks of ice broke off. Eventually, the chunks melted into lakes and ponds.

Little Mud Pond Swamp was once a bigger body of water. Over the centuries, sediment has washed off surrounding slopes and shrunk the pond. The shallow shoreline became swampy, and vegetation common in cooler northern climates moved in. There is a deposit of peat, formed by the accumulation of plant material, in the southern section of the swamp.

Today, Little Mud Pond Swamp is considered a glacial bog, an acidic body of water replenished by runoff. Left alone for many more centuries, it may become part of the chestnut oak forest, though many natural forces, as well as human manipulation, could maintain the wetland.

Wildlife. The trail to the preserve passes through a boulder-strewn chestnut oak forest typical of the region. Red and white oaks, white pine, and eastern hemlock also grow here, as well as mountain laurel and a shrub called sweet fern.

Dense growths of black spruce dominate the boreal conifer swamp that surrounds the bog. In some places, the thick canopy blocks sunlight from reaching the ground. Tamarack, white pine, and red maple are also found here. Highbush blueberry, great rhododendron, and mountain holly *(Nemopanthus macronata)* grow in thickets between the trees. Also thriving here are the swamp-loving cinnamon and Virginia chain ferns, the latter spreading roots beneath the water surface, and several kinds of sedges, notably mud sedge *(Carex limosa)*, whose numbers may be declining.

Mats of various kinds of sphagnum moss, spread out on muddy flats at the south end of the bog, make the ground spongy. Insect-eating plants, such as the northern pitcher plant *(Sarracenia purpurea)* and round-leaved sundew *(Drosera rotundifolia)*, live on the mats.

Closer to the center of the bog, now just a few acres of open water, live dwarf mistletoe *(Arceuthobium pusillum,* PA threatened), capitate spikerush *(Eleocharis olivacea,* PA rare), and bog rosemary *(Andromeda polifolia,* PA rare). Leatherleaf shrubs *(Chamaedaphne calyculata)* grow like islands in the open water. Other bog plants include two kinds of cranberry, sheep laurel *(Kalmia angustifolia),* rose pogonia *(Pogonia ophioglossoides),* arrowhead *(Sagittaria latifolia),* fragrant water lily *(Nymphaea odorata),* tawny cotton grass *(Eriophorum virginicum),* swamp loosestrife *(Decodon verticillatus),* and swamp candles *(Lysimachia terrestris),* which have showy, yellow flowers in the summer.

The bog berries attract black bears, and white-tailed deer have made trails around the edge of the bog. Ruffed grouse, coyote, and red fox also roam in the area. The swamp is a good place to look for wood ducks, flycatchers, and other wetland birds.

History. Little Mud Pond Swamp became a state forest natural area in May 1993.

15

Buckhorn State Forest Natural Area

I n many of the state's preserves, some reminder of humanity always seems to encroach—the distant roar of traffic on an interstate highway, a factory whistle, a farmer's tractor, or simply the expectation that sooner or later another human will appear beside you.

But at Buckhorn you can find deep solitude—the feeling of being completely away from civilization, and total alertness to your natural surroundings.

Ownership. Pennsylvania Department of Environmental Resources, Bureau of Forestry.

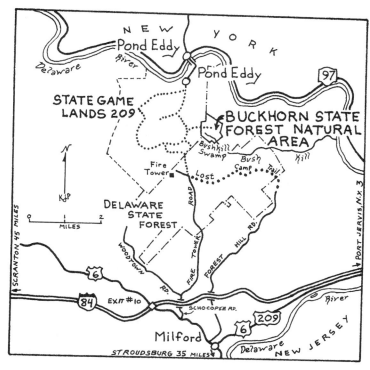

Size and Designation. This state natural area, also a state-designated amphibian and reptile protection area, encompasses 535 acres.

Nearby Nature Attractions. Delaware Water Gap National Recreation Area, Bushkill Falls, Lake Wallenpaupack, Promised Land State Park, and Bruce Lake, Pennel Run, Pine Lake, Stillwater, and Little Mud Pond Swamp state forest natural areas.

Features. A jeep road through State Game Lands 209 will take you to Bushkill Swamp and to a vista at Stairway Lake.

Obtain a map of Delaware State Forest from the District Forester, 474 Clearview Lane, Stroudsburg, PA 18360, or from the Pennsylvania Department of Environmental Resources, Bureau of Forestry, Division of Forest Advisory Services, 400 Market Street, 3rd Floor, P.O. Box 8552, Harrisburg, PA 17105-8552, telephone (717) 787-3444.

Geology. Buckhorn State Natural Area lies behind the escarpment that marks the gorge of the Delaware River to the north. The gritty bedrock exposed on the ledges—sandstone and shale of the Catskill Formation—developed during the Devonian Period, roughly 380 million years ago.

Bushkill Swamp and the other smaller wetlands in the preserve started as a mammoth block of ice that broke off the Wisconsinan glacier about 12,000 years ago. The ice melted into a pond, which over time has grown into a swamp. Bushkill (kill is Dutch for "stream") trickles out of the swamp and flows to the Delaware River, opposite Sparrow Bush, New York. (Don't confuse Bushkill with Little Bushkill and its famous waterfalls.)

Wildlife. The rocky ridges hold chestnut and white oaks, hemlock in shady areas, white and black birches, lowbush blueberry, and sweet fern. Here and there, individual white pine and spruce grow into the canopy. Mountain laurel thrives in dense clusters. Ferns of many kinds are abundant.

In swampy areas are red maple, tamarisk, spruce, hemlock, leatherleaf *(Chamaedaphne calyculata),* labrador tea *(Ledum groenlandicum,* PA rare), cinnamon fern, and sedges. Buckhorn is part of a solid wilderness tract that includes some of Delaware State Forest and State Game Lands 209. Creatures that need a lot of unbroken wild space—black bear, coyote, bobcat (PA at risk), and warblers—have discovered this place. From time to time, hunters and hikers report seeing a mountain lion in these woods, possibly a former pet or zoo animal. Alert hikers may find evidence of large mammals—the rubbings of buck deer on saplings, deer trails, bear scat near outcrops, bear dens—and hear coyote yelps at night.

Birds that frequent the area include warblers, indigo buntings, scarlet tanagers, northern orioles, rufous-sided towhees, wild turkeys, ruffed grouse, vireos, and wrens.

This is timber rattlesnake country. Your chances of encountering one are slim—you are more likely to see a ribbon, black rat, or green snake. Nevertheless, be on guard. Rattlers are unpredictable. They could be anywhere. When you approach, they may strike, lie still, bluff, or retreat. Rattlers usually shake their rear rattles when provoked, but they also can be silent attackers.

History. Unregulated logging and forest fires had ruined the forests in northeastern Pennsylvania by the end of the 19th century. That prompted the commonwealth to purchase 53,000 acres of land between 1898 and 1904 to create Delaware State Forest, named after the Delaware, or Lenni Lenape, Indians who settled here. By 1948, the state forest had grown to 73,000 acres. Today it comprises more than 80,000 acres in four counties. Buckhorn, part of Delaware State Forest, became a state forest natural area in April 1975.

16

Delaware Water Gap National Recreation Area

Dingman's Falls
George W. Childs Recreation Site
Pocono Environmental Education Center
Mount Minsi and Lake Lenape

The Delaware Water Gap is a narrow opening in a mountain ridge through which the Delaware River, refreshed by the cool water that flows off the Pocono and Catskill plateaus, begins its slow glide across the Piedmont and into the Atlantic Ocean. North of the gap, dozens of waterfalls plunge down the tall escarpment of the Allegheny Plateau. Great rhododendrons and hemlocks shade the steep gorges; on top of the plateau, oaks dominate the forest.

In the 1960s, the U.S. Army Corps of Engineers wanted to tame the Delaware by building a dam across the gap. Fortunately, con-

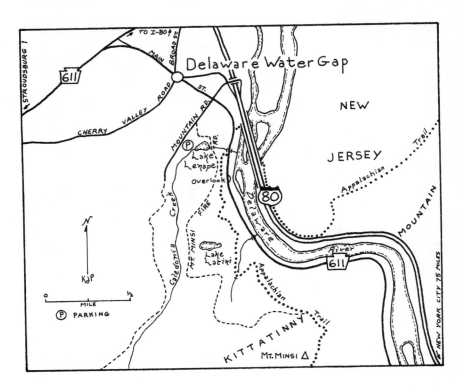

servationists defeated the project and kept the Delaware the only major free-flowing river east of the Mississippi.

Ownership. U.S. Department of the Interior, National Park Service. The Pocono Environmental Education Center is a private, nonprofit education center within the national recreation area.

Size and Designation. 7,000 acres. This 38-mile stretch of the Delaware River has been designated a national scenic and recreation river.

Nearby Nature Attractions. Bushkill Falls; Buckhorn, Bruce Lake, Pennel Run, Pine Lake, Little Mud Pond Swamp, and Stillwater state forest natural areas; Delaware State Forest; Tannersville Cranberry Bog; Long Pond, Lost Lakes, and Thomas Darling Jr. preserves; Devil's Hole; Monroe County and Jacobsburg environmental education centers; Promised Land, Big Pocono, Gouldsboro, and Tobyhanna state parks. The Appalachian Trail follows the Monroe-Northampton county line.

Delaware Water Gap National Recreation Area lines the New Jersey shore of the Delaware, too. Stop at the Kittatinny Visitors Center (first exit off I-80 in New Jersey) for more information on attractions in that state.

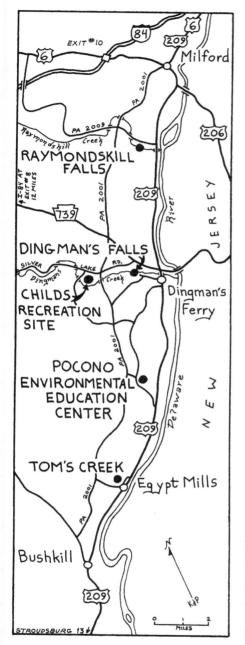

Features. Sixty trails wind through the recreation area, including twenty-five miles of the Appalachian Trail (only five miles on the Pennsylvania side). You can enjoy canoeing, rafting, angling, and tube floating on the Delaware River. Motorists can sightsee on 200 miles of roads, and visit historic sites.

Dingman's Falls. The easy, half-mile loop trail at Dingman's Falls follows the hemlock-lined gorge of Dingman's Creek. The path, open year-round, begins at the visitors center, leads first to slender Silver Thread Falls, then to 130-foot Dingman's Falls, the second highest cataract in Pennsylvania. You can climb to a deck at the brim of the cascade via a steep path and stairway.

The trails abound with great rhododendron, which is covered with pink-white blossoms sometime between May and July. This plant is poisonous to humans if eaten, so identify the plant before hiking, and keep an eye on small children.

The visitors center at Dingman's Falls has trail guides for the entire Delaware Water Gap recreation area, exhibits, books, gifts, rest rooms, drinking water, and a picnic area.

Naturalist-led hikes are offered on weekends. The visitors center, telephone (717) 828-7802, is open daily from 9 A.M. to 5 P.M., May through October. The nearby Dingman's Campground is the only full-service campground in the recreation area.

Childs Recreation Site. The nearly two-mile loop trail at the Childs Recreation Site circles a trio of cascades in Dingman's

Creek, upstream from Dingman's Falls. Wooden bridges, board-walks, and stairs assist hikers. You can also visit an old cemetery and an abandoned mill. Hemlocks shade the picnic tables scattered along the trail. Rest rooms are located in the parking lot on the southwest side of the stream.

Pocono Environmental Education Center (PEEC). At the PEEC, which encompasses 20,000 acres of public land, you'll find a variety of trails, ranging from the quarter-mile Sensory Trail, for visually impaired strollers, to the challenging and rugged five-mile Sunrise Trail. The three-mile Tumbling Waters Trail leads to a pair of cas-cades in a shady glen; the two-mile Scenic Gorge Trail follows the course of a stream; the one-and-a-half-mile Fossil Trail descends a steep escarpment to rock walls in which you can see fossils of ancient sea creatures; and the two-mile Two Ponds Trail loops around two ponds.

The PEEC offers courses, workshops, nature trips, and educa-tional programs for all ages. It operates family vacation camps year-round, with 45 modern cabins that accommodate up to 350 people, an indoor pool, a dining hall, a bookstore, an arts and craft center, a darkroom, and even personal computers. The PEEC has won national honors by being chosen a National Environmental Study Area and Center for Excellence in Education.

For more information, contact the Pocono Environmental Edu-cation Center, R.D. 2, Box 1010, Dingman's Ferry, PA 18328, tele-phone (717) 828-2319.

Mount Minsi and Lake Lenape. Scenic views of the gap are the main attractions in the hilly Mount Minsi area, and there are sev-eral routes to choose from. From the Resort Point Overlook, south of the village of Delaware Water Gap on PA 611, cross the road and take the blue-blazed trail to several destinations. The right fork leads to Mount Minsi Fire Road and Lake Lenape; the left fork joins the Appalachian Trail near the first of three panoramic over-looks. Turn left onto the white-blazed Appalachian Trail and head downstream to two more overlooks, the last one on 1,463-foot Mount Minsi.

From the Lake Lenape parking area, on Mountain Road off PA 611, you can hike the Appalachian Trail to Mount Minsi, stroll on smooth Mount Minsi Fire Road to Table Rock Spur Overlook and Mount Minsi, or take the short loop trail around the lake. A path branches from Mount Minsi Fire Road and the Appalachian Trail and circles Lake Latini.

Shallow riffles and calm pools make this section of the Delaware River popular with canoeists. Choose among five access points, spaced eight to ten miles apart. Eighty-eight primitive campsites are available to boaters on longer trips. Local outfitters rent, launch, and pick up canoes, rafts, and tubes. Get the park's river guide before paddling.

Other Sites. Other recommended sites within the recreation area are Raymondskill Falls, on SR 2009 three miles south of Milford, and the easy walk along Tom's Creek, a good place for birdwatching. The trail begins at Tom's Creek picnic area, off the west side of U.S. 209 three and a half miles north of Bushkill.

For more information, contact Superintendent, National Park Service, Delaware Water Gap National Recreation Area, Bushkill, PA 18324, telephone (717) 588-2435.

Geology. This stretch of the Kittatinny Ridge, a massive ridge of erosion-resistant quartzite and shale, has zones of weakness—faults, fissures, and warps. Normally, rivers and streams will follow the direction of ridges. But here, the river found the soft spot and created the gap. Its erosive work was hastened by an uplift that increased water velocity and by the meltwater of at least three continental glaciers.

The gap is 300 yards wide at river level. Mount Tammany, on the New Jersey flank, rises to 1,527 feet; Mount Minsi, 1,463 feet. Both are peaks on the long Kittatinny Ridge. Notice that Mount Tammany is 200 yards northwest of Mount Minsi and more steeply angled. That is the zone of weakness.

The striations on rock outcrops along the Mount Minsi trails were made by rocks embedded in the bottom of the Wisconsinan ice sheet. They show the path of the glacier when it passed over Kittatinny Ridge. Boulders of foreign rock embedded in the ice, known as erratics, settled on the ground during the meltdown.

Lake Sciota was a glacial meltwater impoundment eight miles long and 200 feet deep located north of the gap. While ice covered the gap, Lake Sciota drained toward Saylorsburg. When the glacier retreated farther north, the lake emptied through the reopened gap.

Lake Lenape started as a chunk of ice that split from the retreating glacier during the ice age. Sediment washing off the glacier piled around the stranded ice chunk forming a basin for the water as the ice melted.

The gap exposes three rock formations. Erosion-resistant quartzite caps Mount Minsi. This metamorphic rock dates back 435 million years. Beneath the quartzite lies an older bed of dark gray shale. Red sandstone, a few million years more recent than the quartzite, occurs northwest and below the angled peak of Mount Minsi.

Kittatinny Ridge marks the physiographic boundary between the Appalachian Mountains and the Allegheny Plateau. The steep escarpment that faces the Delaware River north of the gap is the Allegheny Front. The area's many waterfalls spill off the edge of the plateau.

The escarpment and waterfalls reveal sandstone, siltstone, and shale that developed on sea floors 365 to 405 million years ago. These strata were since uplifted, but the layers stayed horizontal. Downcutting by streams created the gorges and ravines characteristic of the region.

The rock pile beneath an imposing cliff off US 209, between Milford and the Raymondskill Creek turnoff, contains Devonian fossils—crinoids, brachiopods, bryozoans, coral, and pelecypods. Examining fossils is encouraged, but collecting is prohibited. A peat bog in nearby Marshalls Creek yielded a mastodon skeleton.

The floodplain along this section of the river is known as the Minisink, named after the Munsee-speaking people of that name who settled in the upper Delaware Valley.

Wildlife. The towering hemlocks in the cool ravines are almost as impressive as the waterfalls—some have been around as long as 600 years. These giants avoided the ax because they grew in steep ravines. Today, an insect predator called the woolly adelgid ravages these hemlocks.

Black and yellow birches, American beech, basswood, tulip tree, and red maple also grow here. Great rhododendron dominates the understory.

Chestnut, white, and red oaks prevail on the drier ridges above the waterfalls, along with clusters of sugar maple and shagbark hickory. Before the blight, chestnut trees also grew abundantly here. At the PEEC, you'll find an evergreen plantation (pine and spruce), scrub oak, mountain laurel, blueberry, deerberry, and Virginia creeper.

Wildflowers common in the gap include purple loosestrife *(Lythrum salicaria)*, whorled loosestrife *(Lysimachia quadrifolia)*, butter-and-eggs *(Linaria vulgaris)*, spotted knapweed *(Centaurea maculosa)*, oxeye daisy *(Chrysanthemum leucanthemum)*, bloodroot *(Sanguinaria canadensis)*, false spikenard *(Aralia racemosa)*, chickweed *(Stellaria media)*, Queen Anne's lace *(Daucus carota)*, spring beauty *(Claytonia virginica)*, pokeweed *(Phytolacca americana)*, spiderwort *(Tradescantia virginiana)*, common cinquefoil *(Potentilla simplex)*, black-eyed Susan *(Rudbeckia hirta)*, marsh marigold *(Caltha palustris)*, cardinal flower *(Lobelia cardinalis)*, pink lady's slipper *(Cypripedium acaule)*, miterwort *(Mitella diphylla)*, purple trillium *(Trillium erectum)*, Joe-Pye weed *(Eupatorium maculatum)*, wild blue phlox *(Phlox divaricata)*, bull thistle *(Cirsium vulgare)*, wild bergamot *(Monarda fistulosa)*, periwinkle

(Vinca minor), chicory *(Cichorium intybus),* Canada mayflower *(Maianthemum canadense),* trout lily *(Erythronium americanum),* moss pink *(Phlox subulata,* PA endangered), columbine *(Aquilegia canadensis),* wild ginger *(Asarum canadense),* lyre-leaved rock cress *(Arabis lyrata),* jack-in-the-pulpit *(Arisaema triphyllum),* wild geranium *(Geranium maculatum),* and hellebore *(Veratrum viride),* whose roots and foliage are poisonous. A community of prickly pear *(Opuntia humifusa),* a desert cactus, survives on the sunbaked cliffs near Milford.

The grounds at the PEEC also support jewelweeds *(Impatiens* spp.), spotted wintergreen *(Chimaphila maculata),* coltsfoot *(Tussilago farfara),* partridgeberry *(Mitchella repens),* and butter-and-eggs.

Many ferns grow in the gap, including the delicate maidenhair, Christmas (an evergreen fern that grows throughout the state), sensitive, cinnamon, hay-scented, common polypody, upland lady (attractive, burgundy stalks), fragile, maidenhair spleenwort, long beech, liverwort (whose leaves look like reptile skin), and several wood ferns, notably, evergreen marginal and spinulose. The long beech fern, whose bottom pair of leaves droops downward, likes to be bathed in waterfall mist.

Birders watch the fall migration of hawks from the Mount Minsi overlooks. Birds of prey have long taken advantage of the favorable wind currents and thermals along the Kittatinny Ridge (see Hawk Mountain Sanctuary listing). Red-tailed, red-shouldered, broadwinged, and sharp-shinned hawks are common during fall migration, which is also the best time to see the bald eagle (PA endangered), northern harrier (PA at risk), American kestrel, and osprey (PA endangered). Ospreys build stick nests in March and lay their eggs in April. They migrate to the tropics in September and October.

The gap's endless forest once supported hordes of the now-extinct passenger pigeons. Their flocks flowed for hours in wide rivers, their dense swarms darkening the daytime sky. Pioneers wrote that their nesting colonies stretched for five or six miles. People killed them by the hundreds as they flew by, sometimes simply by holding a stick or net in the air from rooftops.

Today you might see the red-winged blackbird, red-eyed vireo, northern oriole, eastern meadowlark (a year-round resident), rose-breasted grosbeak, pine siskin, rufous-sided towhee, indigo bunting, hermit thrush, catbird, cedar waxwing, eastern bluebird, purple martin, Henslow's sparrow (PA at risk), common nighthawk, great horned owl, eastern phoebe (nests near Dingman's Falls), great crested flycatcher, American redstart, and black-and-white, Tennessee, cerulean, prairie, black-throated green, black-throated blue, Blackburnian, chestnut-sided, and common yellowthroat warblers.

Waterbirds include the pied-billed grebe (PA rare), great blue heron, mute swan, mallard, black duck, goldeneye, bufflehead, wood duck, and common merganser. Lesser yellowlegs appear at Lake Lenape.

Lake Lenape supports aquatic plants and animals. Water lilies cover two-thirds of the surface. In late July, the white blossoms of a submerged plant called fanwort sparkle on the surface. Red maple, alder, buttonbush, and bur reed encircle the lake, which hosts green frogs and bullfrogs, painted turtles, northern water and eastern garter snakes, damselflies, and dragonflies.

In the recreation area, you also may find the red eft, the terrestrial stage of a newt species, as well as snapping turtles, wood and pickerel frogs, and hognose, eastern ribbon, and black rat snakes. Look under creek rocks and logs for northern dusky, northern red, and two-lined salamanders. Be alert for the venomous northern copperhead and timber rattlesnake, which, though rare, have been reported.

Fifty-five kinds of fish inhabit this section of the Delaware River. The chilly streams are home to brook, brown, and rainbow trouts, sunfish, dace, and bluegill. Shad, American eel, sturgeon, and striped bass are indigenous. The various trout species, black bass, carp, and muskellunge have been introduced. Other species include white sucker, and smallmouth bass.

Resident mammals include the black bear; white-tailed deer; fox; river otter (PA at risk); porcupine; southern flying squirrel; long-tailed weasel; star-nosed moles; woodland jumping mouse; little brown, big brown, and red bats; and masked, smoky, and short-tailed shrews.

The area attracts monarch, eastern tailed blue, great spangled fritillary, red-spotted purple, and eastern tiger swallowtail butterflies; and cecropia, luna, and Isabella moths.

History. The area's first human inhabitants wandered into the Delaware Valley soon after the departure of the Wisconsinan glacier, 10,000 to 12,000 years ago. The cold climate resembled that of northern Canada today. They roamed the countryside hunting mastodon, mammoth, and musk ox (all extinct) with spears. Several of their fluted spearheads have been uncovered here.

As they became better established in the region, they gathered first in larger campsites and then in villages with wigwams as homes. These so-called Woodland Indians (3,000 years ago) fished with nets and cultivated corn, squash, pumpkin, and tobacco.

The Munsees, which means "the people of the stony country," built villages in the Minisink. The Europeans lumped them and the

Unami who lived downstream together with the Lenni Lenape (Delaware Indians), though each tribe had its own language.

The Dutch were the first Europeans to arrive, traveling from the Hudson River Valley to mine copper and other valuables in the mountains. English Quakers from Philadelphia and Germans from New Jersey arrived next and built farms, mills, and industries. These developments put great stress on the native people, who were also being harassed by the Iroquois Confederacy to the north.

In the 1730s James Logan, representing the interests of the Penn family, and John Shickellamy, negotiator for the Iroquois, hoodwinked the Lenni Lenape and the Munsees. To avoid long negotiations with individual tribes and warfare with the powerful Six Nations, Logan and Shickellamy agreed that the Penns would strike land deals only with the Iroquois.

Logan then activated a 1686 pact with the Lenape, which said the western border of a land purchase would be a line marked by the distance one man could walk from the Delaware River in one day. The Lenape thought that no white man could walk more than 30 miles across such tough terrain. Logan solicited swift runners and trained them for the grueling cross-county race. The fastest among them traveled 55 miles, almost twice the distance the Lenape expected.

Logan's trick, known as the Walking Purchase, even though the participants sprinted most of the way, amounted to a gain for the colonists of 1,200 square miles. The swindle sent the Lenape packing.

Since then, farming, fishing, ice making, logging, and tourism have been the principal industries along this section of the Delaware River Valley. Severe flooding in 1955 prompted Congress to authorize funds (the Flood Control Act of 1962) for the construction of the Tocks Island Dam a few miles north of the gap. The dam would have created a 70,000-acre national recreation area and a 37-mile lake, which developers boasted would attract ten million people annually; however, the project also would have flooded 12,300 acres of land (most of it forest, some prime habitat for bears and bald eagles).

The plan energized a number of environmental groups, which formed the Save the Delaware Coalition and challenged the dam. Because of environmental concerns, huge cost overruns, and some clumsy actions by dam planners, the project was finally scrapped in 1975 (though officially it lingered until 1992). Instead, the 7,000-acre Delaware Water Gap National Recreation Area was created. Four million people visit the area each year. In 1978, this 37-mile segment of the Delaware was designated a national scenic and recreational river.

17

Grey Towers National Historic Landmark

T he French chateau that overlooks the Delaware River from the heights above Milford obscures the real legacy of Gifford Pinchot, the father of modern forestry. You will find Pinchot's spirit at Sawkill Falls among the boughs of the hemlocks and white pines that shade the gorge.

Owner. U.S. Department of Agriculture, Forest Service.

Size and Designation. Grey Towers, which sits on 102 acres, is a national historic landmark.

Nearby Nature Attractions. Delaware Water Gap National

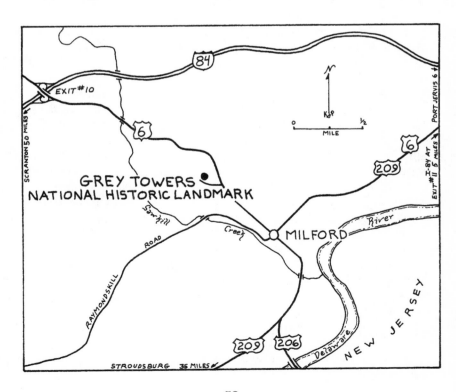

Recreation Area; Buckhorn, Stillwater, Pennel Run, Little Mud Pond Swamp, Bruce Lake, and Pine Lake state forest natural areas; Delaware State Forest; Bushkill Falls; Promised Land State Park; and the Delaware River, a national scenic river.

Features. To reach Sawkill, or Pinchot, Falls, walk down the driveway, past the mansion, to a field on the right. A half-mile trail begins in the far left corner. The delightful cascade is well worth the hike.

Sawkill Falls and the surrounding woods still begong to the Pinchot family. Respect the family's privacy and generosity by staying on the trail and removing litter. The trail is open daily from 8 A.M. to 5 P.M.

Sixty-five species of trees have been planted on the grounds. Pick up a tree guide at the park office.

In Grey Towers, the Pinchot family mansion, 45-minute tours are given daily between 10 A.M. and 4 P.M. from Memorial Day weekend to Labor Day. Tour guides recount Pinchot's remarkable achievements as Pennsylvania's governor and the nation's first chief forester. Groups of 20 or more must call in advance, and individuals who want to visit during the off season should also make a reservation. A small donation is requested to see the estate.

For more information, contact Grey Towers National Historic Landmark, Forest Service, P.O. Box 188, Milford, PA 18337, telephone (717) 296-6401.

Geology. Near Grey Towers, Sawkill Creek tumbles down the Allegheny Front, an escarpment that rises steeply above the Delaware River to elevations higher than 1,000 feet. This long, massive cliff marks the boundary of the Allegheny Plateau.

Downcutting by rivers and streams sculpted the gorges, cataracts, and ravines characteristic of the region. At Sawhill Falls, the creekbed is 380-million-year-old sandstone.

The source of the creek is a few miles away at Sawkill Pond, a tiny glacial lake atop the Allegheny Front. Two small tributaries, Sloat Brook and Vantine Brook, feed the stream at Grey Towers, and Sawkill Creek flows into the Delaware River at Milford.

Wildlife. The gorge is the wildest setting on the grounds. Tall hemlocks and white pines reign, though a few yellow birches grow along the edge of the ravine.

The tree guide helps you identify 65 species of trees including sugar maple, white birch, swamp white oak, cucumber magnolia, black walnut, tulip tree, shadbush, pitch pine, quaking aspen, European linden, black locust, and black tupelo.

History. Gifford Pinchot came from a wealthy, energetic, and well-traveled family. His father, James Pinchot, grew up in Milford but made his fortune in New York City manufacturing wallpaper. He helped found the American Museum of Natural History and Yale University Forest School, served on the committee for the Statue of Liberty, and was a mainstay in the American Forestry Association.

James Pinchot and his wife, Mary, shared an interest in natural history, social reform, and public service—gifts they passed to their three children. The rape of America's forests outraged the Pinchots. With his father's encouragement, Gifford Pinchot pursued forestry studies at Yale University and in France. In 1890, he became the forest manager at the Biltmore Estate, the North Carolina mansion of George Vanderbilt. The nation's chief forester from 1898 to 1910, mostly under President Theodore Roosevelt, Pinchot increased the number of national forests from 32 to 149 during his watch. From 1920 to 1922, Pinchot served as Pennsylvania Commissioner of Forestry. He was elected governor in 1922 and again in 1931. He died at age 81 in 1946.

Renowned architect Richard Morris Hunt designed Grey Towers in the style of a French summer chateau in 1885. Hunt used local materials: Pennsylvania bluestone and fieldstone for the exterior walls, and New Jersey slate for the roof. The original estate totaled 3,600 acres.

In 1963, the family deeded the mansion and 102 acres to the Forest Service, and Pinchot Institute for Conservation Studies opened that fall, with President John Kennedy as the speaker.

18

Stillwater State Forest Natural Area

Civil War draft dodgers and deserters hid in the swamps of this preserve. They built shacks and lived off the land far from the rage on the battlefield. Today this peaceful, remote place is a refuge for the fisher and the black bear.

Ownership. Pennsylvania Department of Environmental Resources, Bureau of Forestry.

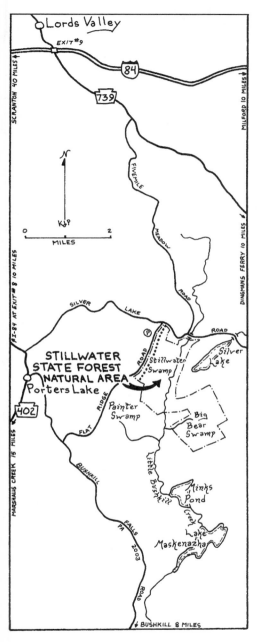

Size and Designation. This 1,931-acre woodland and swamp forest is a state forest natural area.

Nearby Nature Attractions. Buckhorn, Bruce Lake, Pine Lake, Little Mud Pond Swamp, and Pennel Run state forest natural areas; Delaware Water Gap National Recreation Area; Delaware State Forest; Promised Land State Park; and Lake Wallenpaupack.

Features. About a mile of Little Bushkill Creek meanders through the natural area. Its calm water makes for good canoeing. The creek passes under Silver Lake Road beside the state forest office. Foot travelers can hike on the Flat Ridge Trail or simply roam in the woods. A map and compass are recommended. The preserve is open daily from sunrise to sunset.

To get a map of the state forest, contact the Pennsylvania Department of Environmental Resources, Bureau of Forestry, P.O. Box 1467, Harrisburg, PA 17120; or Department of Environmental Resources, District Forester, P.O. Box 150, 474 Clearview Lane, Stroudsburg, PA 18360, telephone (717) 424-3001.

Rest rooms, drinking water, and phones can be found at the nearby Delaware Water Gap National Recreation Area visitors center at Dingman's Falls (open May through October). Picnic at George Childs Park (part of the national recreation area) or Peck's Pond.

Geology. Although the surrounding countryside has steep mountains and deep gorges, the terrain around the Stillwater preserve is relatively flat and poorly drained. The last ice age glacier, the Wisconsinan, worked over the landscape clean to its bedrock of sandstone and shale. As the glacier retreated 12,000 years ago, it deposited gravel, rocks, and sand in small ridges and mounds over the landscape. Blocks of ice that split from the front of the glacier melted into shallow basins, creating small ponds. Eight swamps still soak this poorly drained tract.

As Little Bushkill Creek enters a narrow, flat valley in the preserve, its water spreads out to form Stillwater Swamp. To the southeast, water from the 400-acre Big Bear Swamp trickles into Little Bushkill Creek. Coon Swamp lies in a pocket in the southwestern part of the preserve.

Wildlife. Half the preserve is second-growth forest, meaning that it has been logged at least once. Foresters recently rated the woods "poor quality" for commercial logging, but that assessment does not apply to wildlife.

Chestnut, white, red, black, scarlet, and bear oaks rise from the ridge along the Flat Ridge Trail. Red maple, white pine, sassafras, and pitch pine also live on the ridge. Huckleberry grows densely in the understory, along with sweet fern (a shrub), bracken fern, and mountain laurel *(Kalmia latifolia)*.

Nearing the soggy wetland that flanks Little Bushkill Creek, the hardwood forest is replaced by thickets of alder, highbush blueberry, winterberry holly, meadowsweet *(Spiraea latifolia),* bog azalea, sheep laurel *(Kalmia angustifolia),* and various viburnums. Beyond, in the marshy area, rushes and sedges reign, along with cattails, cinnamon and sensitive ferns, knotweed *(Polygonum pensylvanicum),* skunk cabbage *(Symplocarpus foetidus),* and jewelweed *(Impatiens capensis).* There are clumps of swamp hardwoods—black gum, red maple, and yellow birch—and conifers—eastern hemlock, white pine, and black spruce.

Big Bear Swamp, a boreal (northern) bog with deep muck beds, has some open water, as well as a carpet of sphagnum moss that supports carnivorous plants like the round-leaved sundew *(Drosera rotundifolia)* and pitcher plant *(Sarracenia purpurea).* Cranberry bushes make the edge of the marsh impenetrable.

Black spruce grow here, along with white pine, hemlock, red maple, and yellow birch. Trees usually grow slowly in nutrient-poor bogs, and the spruces in Big Bear Swamp have not reached their natural mature size.

As the name suggests, black bears visit the swamp. Deer trails crisscross the heath, and ruffed grouse take cover in the berry thickets. Beavers have built lodges in Big Bear Swamp, and their dams on the Little Bushkill Creek flood the swamp. Yellow-bellied flycatcher (at the southern extreme of its range), Nashville warbler, and red-winged blackbird perch on the treetops.

Two unusual residents are the porcupine and the fisher. Porcupines gnaw on the upper branches of tall spruces, pines, and hemlocks, especially in winter. The white or yellow of exposed wood indicates their presence. A full-grown porcupine has 30,000 quills. The reclusive fisher, rare in this area, has been seen in the preserve. This weasel-like mammal has dark brown to black fur with white tips, giving it a frosted appearance. This clever animal beds down in hollow trees and is one of only a few mammals bold enough to prey on porcupines.

History. At the turn of the century, this part of Pike County was desolate from logging and forest fires. Many fires were set so that huckleberry, a local cash crop at the time, would take over the land.

Between 1898 and 1904, the state purchased 53,000 acres to establish Delaware State Forest, and by 1948, an additional 20,000 acres had been acquired. The Stillwater tract became a state forest monument in 1949 and a state forest natural area in 1975.

19

Pennel Run State Forest Natural Area

The first mile of the trail to Pennel Run is a challenging hike across a boulder field. Then the blue blazes of the path all but disappear in a swampy hemlock grove. The rewards, though, outweigh the obstacles. Stop and listen to the forest sounds—the wind tossing leaves, oaks dropping acorns, birds flapping wings, chipmunks burrowing in leaves, crows crying overhead.

Ownership. Pennsylvania Department of Environmental Resources, Bureau of Forestry.

Size and Designation. Pennel Run State Forest Natural Area is a state-designated reptile and amphibian refuge comprising 936 acres.

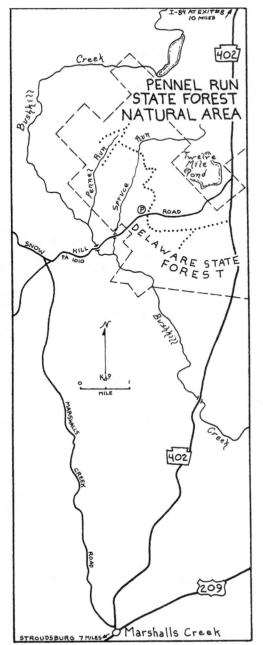

Nearby Nature Attractions. Delaware Water Gap National Recreation Area, Grey Towers National Historic Landmark, Promised Land State Park, Delaware State Forest, and Bruce Lake, Pine Lake, Stillwater, Little Mud Pond Swamp, and Buckhorn state forest natural areas.

Features. The trailhead is a few paces west of the parking lot; look for signs. Follow the rocky, blue-blazed trail about 1.5 miles, then take the red-blazed trail into the preserve. The first mile of the hike goes slowly across boulder-strewn terrain and through woodland swamp. The route thins out in a hemlock swamp, and you must look carefully for the blue blazes.

Hikers seeking solitude and natural sounds will enjoy this remote preserve, open daily from dawn to dusk. There are no rest rooms or drinking water. Obtain a map of Delaware State Forest before hiking.

For more information, contact Delaware State Forest, District Forester, 474 Clearview Lane, Stroudsburg, PA 18360, telephone (717) 424-3001.

Geology. About 385 million years ago, streams and rivers flowing off the western slope of the Arcadian Mountains (predecessors of the Appalachians) washed sand and sediment into an ocean. These sediments later became sandstone and conglomerate (a mixture of cemented pebbles and some sand).

Crossbeds, or arching curves in the rock layers, are visible along the trail. These were troughs made by Arcadian-era mountain streams. The crossbeds overlap, indicating shifting channels on the alluvial plain.

Twenty thousand years ago, the Wisconsinan glacier, the last continental ice sheet of the ice age, buried this landscape beneath 2,000 to 3,000 feet of ice. Water at the bottom of the glacier seeped into rock seams, or partings. When the water refroze, it expanded, loosening the bedrock along the partings. As the glacier moved, it broke off chunks of rock and transported them, hence the loose rocks that are scattered about in the preserve and adjacent state forest.

Two small creeks—Pennel and Utt's runs—flow south out of the preserve into Big Bushkill Creek, a tributary of the Delaware River. Utt's Run briefly widens into a swamp in the northwestern part of the preserve.

Wildlife. The forest is made up of chestnut, white, and scrub oaks; pitch and white pines; hemlock; yellow birch; shadbush; witch hazel; and ironwood. Blueberry shrubs and barberry *(Berberis vulgaris)* also grow here.

The presence of pitch pine means that the land has suffered from fire. The cones of this fire-resistant evergreen are heavily coated with resin, or pitch, and require an extremely high temperature such as that produced by fire to release their seeds. The nutrients in the ash resulting from the fire fertilize the seeds. Fire also promotes the resilient scrub oak, which bounces back quickly and resprouts rapidly from charred stumps. Other oaks need a decade or more to make acorns, but scrub oak produces acorns in just three years. Blueberries also move into burned areas quickly.

The preserve's vernal (springtime) ponds, streams, and swampy areas provide ideal habitats for reptiles and amphibians, which are protected here. Be wary of the poisonous timber rattlesnake, though you are unlikely to encounter one.

Black bear, deer, and ruffed grouse are common here. Inventories of birds and wildflowers have not been conducted.

History. By the end of the nineteenth century, uncontrolled logging and repeated forest fires had devastated the forests in northeastern Pennsylvania. This prompted the state to purchase 53,000 acres of land between 1898 and 1904 for Delaware State Forest, named after the Delaware Indians (Lenni Lenape) who once resided here. Today the state forest encompasses more than 80,000 acres in four counties. The state forest also protects watersheds and wildlife habitats, and offers recreational opportunities.

Pennel Run became a state forest natural area in 1975 and a reptile and amphibian sanctuary in 1979.

Bushkill Falls

I t has the trappings of a tourist spot, and you have to pay an admission. Nevertheless, it is a beguiling place with eight striking waterfalls.

Ownership. Privately owned.

Size and Designation. 300 acres.

Nearby Nature Attractions. Delaware State Forest, Lake Wallenpaupack, Promised Land State Park, and Buckhorn, Bruce Lake, Pennel Run, Pine Lake, Stillwater, and Little Mud Pond Swamp state forest natural areas. To see more waterfalls, drive

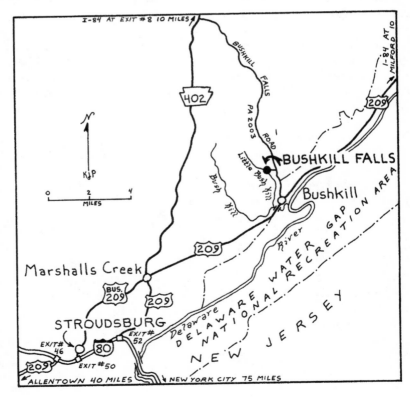

north to Dingman's Falls and the adjacent Childs Picnic Area, in Delaware Water Gap National Recreation Area.

Features. Four well-developed and clearly marked trails of various lengths and difficulties lead to a series of waterfalls. Pick up a trail map at the entrance. Wooden bridges, stairways, and boardwalks make hiking easier and keep people from trampling the foliage and climbing the cascades.

The admission fee also entitles you to view a mounted wildlife exhibit. Also on the grounds are a miniature golf course, picnic tables and grills, a fishing pond, gift shops, food, and rest rooms.

For more information, contact Bushkill Falls, P.O. Box 151, Bushkill, PA 18324, telephone (717) 588-6682.

Geology. The falls tumble over the Allegheny Front, a massive escarpment of 365-million-year-old (Devonian Period) red shale and sandstone. The Front marks the boundary of a physiographic province known at the Appalachian Plateau.

At one time the region was a high plateau, but it was carved over the millennia by the action of watercourses. Two streams continue to sculpt the waterfalls. The larger, Little Bushkill, produces the most dramatic cascades; the other, Pond Run Creek, descends in a series of smaller waterfalls. Downstream from the lower gorge, the two streams converge to form Big Bushkill Creek.

The waterfalls eroded the less resistant (softer) rock layers faster than the resistant (harder) ones on top, creating steps.

The amber color of the water comes from tannin, a natural brown dye contained in hemlock bark and other forest debris.

Wildlife. Mosses and ferns thrive on the slopes of the moist ravines, flanked by hemlocks, birches, and stands of great rhododendron. Notice the J-shaped trunks of the trees that grow from the ledges.

En route to the Main Falls, you will pass a white pine that stands 150 feet and is about 150 years old. The trails to Bridal Veil Falls and Pennel Falls pass through a forest of white and chestnut oaks. Here you may spot deer, squirrels, and chipmunks.

History. Charles E. Peters opened Bushkill Falls as a public attraction in 1904 and charged adults 10 cents to see the "Niagara of Pennsylvania." In the early years, a single trail led to a swinging bridge (now gone) over the Main Falls. Trails were lengthened and improved as the attraction became more popular. The site is now visited by more than 200,000 people a year.

21

Nuangola Bog Nature Preserve

Nuangola Lake was born from a chunk of a glacier 12,000 years ago. Today thick mats of floating sphagnum moss have transformed the southern tip of the lake into a bog harboring plants that have adapted to a harsh acidic habitat.

Ownership. Wilkes University. The Pennsylvania Chapter of the Nature Conservancy possesses a deed assuring the natural integrity of the site.

Size and Designation. Nine acres.

Nearby Nature Attractions. Seven Tubs Natural Area; Susquehanna Riverlands; Frances Slocum, Ricketts Glen, Lehigh Gorge, and Nescopeck state parks; the Lehigh River, a state-designated scenic river.

Features. The grassy trail from the parking spot leads to a boardwalk through the bog. Bog plants and their habitats are especially fragile, so stay on the boardwalk. The preserve is open daily from dawn to dusk. Wilkes University conducts classes and research labs at the wetland. Toilets and drinking water are not available. The remaining lakeshore is privately owned and used for recreation activities. Stay off private property.

For more information, contact the Department of Biology, Wilkes University, Wilkes-Barre, PA 18701, telephone (717) 831-4758.

Geology. Nuangola Lake started as a block of ice that broke off the retreating Wisconsinan glacier thousands of years ago. Sediment called till (gravel, sand, and silt) that washed off the melting glacier accumulated around the base of the ice block. That, along with the weight of the ice, created a basin. The ice eventually melted into the basin and formed Nuangola Lake. Gay Avenue sits atop a glacial till ridge. Scientists believe the water volume was once at least four times greater than it is today.

Nuangola Creek drains the lake in the northeast corner and flows into the Little Wapwallopen drainage area.

Wildlife. There are five distinct vegetation zones in the bog. Thirteen species of sphagnum moss are found here, and at least one flourishes in each zone.

Sphagnum moss absorbs certain metal ions from water and gives off hydrogen protons, a process that increases the acidity of the water. Bacteria does not fare well in acidic environments, so decay of dead plant material by bacteria occurs slowly in a bog.

Swamp loosestrife, *(Decodon verticillatus)*, smooth alder *(Alnus serrulata)*, and various sedges occupy the edge zone. Though it resembles a willow, swamp loosestrife is not related to the willows. Its stem grows spongy, buoyant tissue at the water level, which helps it stay upright and spread roots.

Floating mats of leatherleaf *(Chamaedaphne calyculata)* are characteristic of the open mat zone. Mats of this heath shrub can spread out from shore at a rate of one foot per decade. Two carnivorous plants that sustain themselves by trapping insects, the northern pitcher plant *(Sarracenia purpurea)* and round-leaved sundew *(Drosera rotundifolia)*, as well as sedges and cranberry *(Vaccinium macrocarpon)*, take root on the mossy mat.

The coniferous zone is composed of black spruce and American larch, or tamarack. Little vegetation grows beneath tamaracks, one of only two conifers that lose their needles in autumn, because the needles accumulate in mats and choke out other plants.

River birch, white pine, red maple, great rhododendron, mountain laurel, and cinnamon and royal ferns, occupy another zone. The drier original shore zone consists of mixed oaks and maple, with skunk cabbage *(Symplocarpus foetidus)* and mountain laurel in the moister spots.

Open water blossoms such as water lily *(Nymphaea tetragona)* and spatterdock *(Nuphar advena)* dangle their roots from the surface of the lake to the bottom. Cattails *(Typha latifolia)*, alder thickets, and clusters of meadowsweet *(Spiraea latifolia)* ring the bog. Animals observed here include the black bear, snapping turtle and eastern hognose, black rat, and the poisonous northern copperhead snakes.

History. Nuangola Bog has been studied for decades. In 1984, a nine-acre parcel of the bog was donated to Wilkes University.

22

Susquehanna Riverlands

The 860-foot bluff looming above the North Branch of the Susquehanna River offers a sweeping view of the valley, a scene rich in natural and human history. The view is blemished, however, by its benefactor's nuclear power plant.

Ownership. Pennsylvania Power and Light Company and Allegheny Electric Cooperative.

Size and Designation. Susquehanna Riverlands encompasses 1,200 acres. Roughly 800 acres lie on the east side of the river, 400 on the west. The utilities have designated two locations as natural areas.

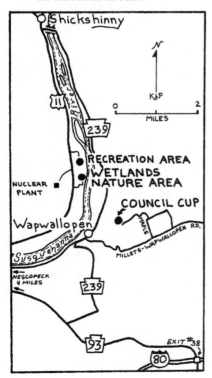

Features. The Energy Information Center at the entrance to the recreation area on the west side also houses the Riverlands Nature Center. It offers wildlife exhibits and activities, maps, rest rooms, and drinking water. Nature programs led by a resident naturalist usually begin here. From April through October, the center is open Monday through Saturday from 8 A.M. to 5 P.M., Sunday noon to 5 P.M. From November through March, it is open only on Saturday from 11 A.M. to 3 P.M.

Farther down the entrance road, you will find picnic areas, a ballfield, a boat launch (motors prohibited), and three hiking trails. The 1.5-mile Riverside Trail follows the shore of the North Branch of the Susquehanna River. Biking and cross-country skiing are allowed on the Towpath Trail, which follows the former North Branch Canal. Licensed anglers can fish Lake Took-A-While for panfish, bass, and catfish. (Ice fishing is prohibited.)

The Wetlands Nature Area is south of the recreation area. Here you will find two hiking trails. The section of the two-thirds-mile Wood Duck Trail along the river was once the main route used by Iroquois and other overland travelers and is known as the Great Warriors Path. The half-mile Beaver Trail visits a pond inhabited by beavers and waterfowl. The western stretches of the Wood Duck and Beaver trails also trace the old North Branch Canal. Look for the ruins of eel traps (V-shaped stone walls) and coal-dredging operations along the shore of the Susquehanna, near the cottage. Pets are not permitted in the nature area.

At the Council Cup Natural Area, a mile-long trail begins in the parking lot and leads to a vista overlooking the river and nuclear power plant. Birders find the spot worth visiting during the autumn and spring raptor migrations. A checklist is available at the information center. The three-quarter-mile east loop travels through an upland forest sprinkled with mountain laurel.

Hunting is permitted in the Riverlands except in the recreation area and Wetlands Nature Area. State laws apply.

Trails open at 8 A.M. and close at dusk every day. For more information, contact Susquehanna Riverlands, R.R. 1, Box 1797, Berwick, PA 18603, telephone (717) 542-2131.

Geology. Susquehanna Riverlands straddles the North Branch of the Susquehanna River. Upstream from Wilkes-Barre, the North Branch enters the Wyoming Valley, famous for its veins of anthracite coal. The valley ends near Nanticoke, where the river has cut through Penobscot Mountain. Riverlands is located downstream, in a wide valley of gravel terraces. These terraces are glacial depositions. Look for them at the Council Cup lookout, atop a summit called Hess, or Lee's, Mountain.

Between 65 and 135 million years ago, this part of Pennsylvania was underwater. Sediment similar to that found along the coast buried an existing valley. At that time, the North Branch flowed southeasterly and emptied into the Delaware River near Trenton. When the area gently heaved, streams began washing away this uplifted coastal plan. The fastest downcutting stream was the main stem of the Susquehanna, then making its way northeast. In an act of stream piracy, it captured the North Branch and diverted the water from Delaware Bay to the Chesapeake Bay.

A lobe of the Illinoisan glacier moved into the valley as far as the confluence of the branches at Northumberland 350,000 to 550,000 years ago. This ice mass and the next, the Wisconsinan glacier (12,500 to 22,000 years ago), left sediment piled in terraces above the river level. It also dumped more loose sediment on top of the ancient hidden valley.

Coal miners know the risks of sinking shafts beneath this section of the river. Usually there is a sturdy, safe layer of rock above the coal beds, enabling rivers, roads, and towns to remain above the mines. That is not always the case here. Around Nanticoke, north of Riverlands, the coal seams sometimes lie below the rubble of the ancient valley. Miners have died when mines dug beneath the buried valley collapsed.

Wildlife. Mouse-eared chickweed (*Cerastium arvense* var. *villosissimum*, PA endangered) occupies a patch of wetland habitat here. Other dwellers in damp places include ground ivy *(Glechoma hederacea),* lady's-thumb *(Polygonum persicara),* cuckoo flower *(Cardamine pratensis),* Pennsylvania bittercress *(Cardamine pensylvanica),* and cut-leaved toothwort *(Dentaria laciniata).*

At Council Cup, look for fringed polygala *(Polygala paucifolia),* a pinkish, orchid-like blossom. Virginia bluebells *(Mertensia virginica)* and golden alexanders *(Zizia aurea)* emerge along the Riverside Trail in the spring. A white cluster of shepherd's purse *(Capsella bursa-pastoris)* flourishes in the picnic area. Virginia waterleaf *(Hydrophyllum virginianum),* Venus' looking-glass *(Specularia perfoliata),* and Deptford pink *(Dianthus armeria)* grow in the fields.

Also look for bouncing bet *(Saponaria officinalis),* hairy beard-tongue *(Penstemon hirsutus),* butter-and-eggs *(Linaria vulgaris),* lance-leaved goldenrod *(Solidago graminifolia),* blue vervain *(Verbena hastata),* and Asiatic dayflower *(Commelina communis).*

Over the last two decades, 234 species of birds have been spotted at the Riverlands. The nesters include the American black and wood ducks, hooded merganser, great blue heron, Cooper's and broad-winged hawks, American kestrel, spotted sandpiper, yellow-billed cuckoo, common nighthawk, pileated woodpecker, five kinds of flycatchers, blue-gray gnatcatcher, purple martin, barn owl, bobolink, scarlet tanager, pine siskin, and twenty-five kinds of warblers, including Brewster's, Lawrence's, hooded, mourning, yellow-rumped, prairie, black-throated green, and chestnut-sided.

There is licensed hunting for wild turkey, ring-necked pheasant (stocked), and ruffed grouse, and fishing for catfish, bass, panfish, and eel.

Mammals include the bobcat (PA at risk), river otter (PA at risk), black bear, striped skunk, masked shrew, starnose mole, and big and little brown bats. Beaver and muskrats build lodges in the wetlands. Other residents include snapping and painted turtles, black rat and northern water snakes, gray tree and pickerel frogs, and red-spotted newt.

History. Council Cup was originally called Kansal Kopf, meaning "pulpit rock" by German settlers. Kansal Kopf sounds like Council Cup in English, hence the name. According to pioneer stories, Indian tribes held peace talks, or councils, on the promontory. The overlook is also known as Hess Mountain, after an early settler, and Lee's Mountain, honoring Col. Washington Lee.

The Great Warriors Path was the main trail used by the tribes of the Six Nations, or Iroquois Confederacy, for conquest and commerce in Pennsylvania. The Susquehannocks and Lenape also took this path, and many other well-trodden trails connected with it. The nearby communities of Shickshinny, Berwick, and Bloomsburg grew alongside this route, which continued to the confluence of the West and North branches of the Susquehanna River and north to Tioga.

Though Indian Canoes could easily ply long stretches of the Susquehanna, the first Europeans found it impassable. The river, in fact, is regarded as the longest unnavigable river in North America. The Susquehanna succumbed to the innovations of nineteenth-century engineers, however, who dug the North Branch Canal and filled it with river water. From 1830 to 1900 mule-drawn wooden boats transported cargo the 72 miles between Pittston and Northumberland. Sections of the canal pass through the Wetlands Nature Area and the recreation area.

The Susquehanna River passes through anthracite coal country. East of the parking lot in the Wetlands Nature Area, you can see abandoned coal-dredging equipment. One coal-mining facility was stationed at Mocanaqua, a few miles upstream. Coal dust flowing downstream from Mocanaqua polluted the river and settled on the bottom at this location. The dredging gear scraped the coal particles from the riverbed. The coal was then dried and used as heating fuel.

In the late nineteenth century, Hick's Ferry carried travelers and cargo across the Susquehanna at Wapwallopen. A hotel served passengers using the ferry and canal. For a good number of years, the ferry was the only dry way to cross the river between Berwick and Nescopeck.

The Lake Took-A-While section of Riverlands opened in 1980, followed by Council Cup in 1981. The nuclear plant began generating power in 1983.

23

Lehigh Gorge State Park

For 30 miles, the serpentine Lehigh River—a stream that hosts 800-pound black bears and eight-pound trout—scours a precipitous gorge with plunging waterfalls, swift rapids, thick thatch, and refreshing air. Most people see the sights by boat, but scenic wonders can also be enjoyed by bike, skis, snowmobile, or on foot.

Ownership. Pennsylvania Department of Environmental Resources, Bureau of State Parks.

Size and Designation. The skinny state park totals 4,548 acres. It straddles a 32-mile portion of the Lehigh River designated a state scenic river.

Nearby Nature Attractions. State Game Lands 141, 149, and 40, Hickory Run State Park; Carbon County Environmental Education Center; Hickory Run, Beltzville, Ricketts Glen, Frances Slocum, and Nescopeck state parks; Weiser State Forest; Nuangola Bog Preserve; Seven Tubs Natural Area; and Susquehanna Riverlands. The Appalachian Trail passes nearby.

Features. Thousands of boaters run the rapids in the gorge each year. Spring is the most exciting time because the current is swift. A trip from White Haven to Jim Thorpe covers 24 miles—a day-long outing for most paddlers. Shorter trips include White Haven to Rockport (just under nine miles) and Rockport to Jim Thorpe (15.4 miles).

Inexperienced boaters should take a guided tour. Canoeists, kayakers, and rafters must enter the river at designated locations. Get a park brochure and read the precautions and check the maps. To obtain one, contact the Pennsylvania Department of Environmental Resources, Lehigh Gorge State Park, R.D. 2, Box 56, Weatherly, PA 18255, telephone (717) 427-5000, or (800) 63-PARKS.

Also find out the river's flow rate before boating. A flow rate below 250 cubic feet per second (cfs) means the river is probably too low for enjoyable boating. When the rate becomes 1,000 cfs, you can expect a safe and thrilling trip. When the flow rate tops 5,000 cfs, only experts should be on the river. Call the park office of the U.S. Army Corps of Engineers at (215) 597-5091 for a flow report.

More than 30 miles of abandoned railroad grade lets hikers,

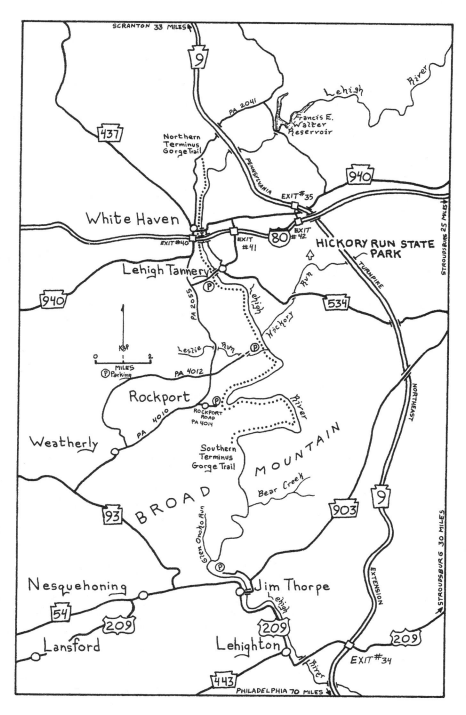

bicyclists, skiers, and snowmobilers enjoy the gorge. The wide, smooth, and flat trail runs along the west bank of the river from White Haven to Penn Haven. Hikers, bicyclists,and skiers can also use the two mile section from White Haven to Port Jenkins. During the winter, frozen gorge walls and waterfalls are breathtaking. Climbing the rock walls is hazardous and is prohibited. Access areas offer toilets, but not drinking water. The trail is open daily during the daylight hours.

Geology. The Lehigh River begins its 100-mile journey on the pristine Pocono Plateau. Below Stoddartsville, the Great Falls of the Lehigh marks the river's descent from the plateau. It empties into the Delaware River after passing through the Allentown-Bethlehem-Easton industrial area. The scenic gorge is the middle third of the route.

The oldest rocks in the gorge are the sandstone, siltstone, and claystone of the Devonian and Mississippian periods (365 to 320 million years ago). Thin layers of younger light gray sandstone and of limestone and grayish red shales also appear. The youngest formation is composed of gray, red, and purplish sandstone.

These formations do not erode easily, as evidenced by the steepness of the gorge. Nearly vertical walls topping 1,000 feet rise above the river at Jim Thorpe.

Several stunning waterfalls spill over the layers of sandstone and siltstone. A small stream in Glen Onoko tumbles 860 feet in one mile, creating a series of cascades. Chameleon Falls is the largest (150 feet), but some prefer the charm of Onoko Falls (90 feet). Other waterfalls are located a quarter mile upstream from the Rockport access.

At Palmerton, downstream from the park, the river squeezes through the Lehigh Gap, an opening in Blue Mountain, or the Kittatinny Ridge. The run through the gorge roughly ends there.

Wildlife. Eastern hemlock, great rhododendron, mountain laurel, and yellow birch grow profusely on the slopes. Higher elevations are topped with oak and hickory. Red maple, staghorn sumac, wild grapes, and spinulose wood fern grow along the trail.

Hunters bag deer, wild turkey, black bear, and small game in the park and surrounding state game lands. The northern third of the park is the most productive for fishermen, because the river is stocked with trout between the Francis E. Walter Dam and Sandy Run. Park officials discourage whitewater boating between the dam and White Haven—a plus for anglers.

History. For two decades in the nineteenth century, engineers tamed the frothy wildness of the Lehigh River. The discovery of anthracite coal at nearby Summit Hill in 1791 sparked rapid development in the valley. From 1835 to 1838, the Lehigh Coal and Navigation Company built 20 dams, 29 locks, and five miles of canals over the 26-mile stretch between White Haven and Jim Thorpe (then known as Mauch Chunk). Boats hauled coal along the canals. The ruins of the canal system, destroyed by severe floods in the mid-1800s, still stand in the park.

Railroads also transported anthracite to markets on both sides of the river. The Pennsylvania Department of Environmental Resources converted the abandoned line on the west bank into a hiking trail.

24

Hickory Run State Park

The boulders here could not have been arranged with more precision. They spread out to form a level plain a quarter mile long, 400 feet wide, and a dozen feet deep. Except for lichens and microscopic organisms, nothing grows in the middle of this harsh habitat, not even a weed. There is no movement of mouse, no fluttering wing of bird, no buzz of mosquito. Just acres of scattered stones.

Ownership. Pennsylvania Department of Environmental Resources, Bureau of State Parks.

Size and Designation. The state park measures 15,500 acres. The 60-acre boulder field has been designated a national natural landmark. Hickory Run is a state scenic river.

Nearby Nature Attractions. Lehigh Gorge and Beltzville state parks; and the Lehigh River, a state-designated scenic river for most of its course through the county.

Features. Besides the boulder field, the park offers many recreational opportunities including 37 miles of hiking trails. Pick up a park brochure, available at park offices, campgrounds, and ranger stations.

The rugged gravel road to the boulder field may be impassable in winter.

Hawk Falls is worth visiting. Take the hiking trail leading south (to the right) from the boulder field parking lot (a round trip

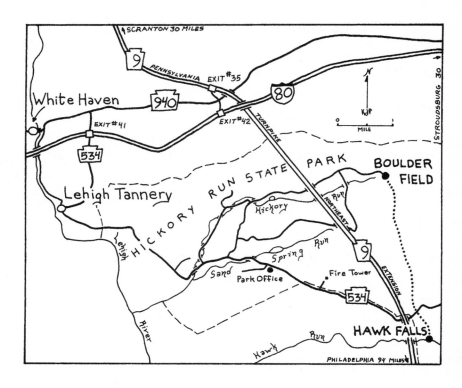

of 5.5 miles), or continue east on PA 534 (past the fire tower) to a parking lot on the south side of the road just beyond the overpass for the Northeast Extension of the Pennsylvania Turnpike. The walk to the falls, along Hawk Run, measures 3/4 of a mile. You can also hike north to the boulder field from here.

For more information, contact Hickory Run State Park, Department of Environmental Resources, P.O. Box 81, R.D. 1, White Haven, PA 18661, telephone (717) 443-9991 or (800) 63-PARKS. A free geological guide of the boulder field is available from the Department of Environmental Resources, Bureau of Topographic and Geologic Survey, P.O. Box 8453, Harrisburg, PA 17105-8453. Ask for Park Guide 2.

Geology. About 18,000 to 20,000 years ago, a finger of the Wisconsinan glacier stopped north and a little east of a rocky ridge here. The glacier idled here for a long time, perhaps for several millennia, and sediments in the form of loose rock, gravel, sand, and silt piled up at the front end, forming a long ridge called an end moraine. The moraine marks the southernmost boundary of the glacier's range. A mile south and west of the moraine stood bedrock outcrops composed of red conglomerates (sandstone with large, white quartz pebbles) and red sandstone, both formed 375 million years ago. These Devonian Period rocks are the ones you will find in the boulder field—red sandstone in the northern half of the field, red conglomerate in the southern half.

The winter climate at the edge of the glacier was similar to the arctic conditions of northern Canada. During the summer, however, glacial ice melted and water seeped into the cracks and seams of the nearby bedrock. The water froze again at night. This went on for centuries. Since water expands when it freezes, the ice that seeped into the rock fractures slowly broke the rocks apart into large chunks, first the top layer, then the lower beds. The boulders rolled to the bottom of the rock ridge.

Meanwhile, glacial meltwater carrying sand, clay, and bits of ice mixed with the boulders. During a summer thaw, this soupy blend of boulders and debris gradually slid down the slope of the ridge. The underlying ground remained frozen. As the mixture migrated, the boulders jostled each other, smoothing their rough edges. The boulders near the parking lot are rounder than the blocks at the northern end of the field because they traveled farther and were subjected to more bumping and grinding.

Later, when warmer temperatures speeded up the glacier's retreat, streams of meltwater whisked away sand, clay, and other detritus down Hickory Run and left the boulders exposed to the elements. Today the boulder field marks the headwaters of Hickory Run, and after a rain you can hear its flow trickling through the boulders.

Scattered boulders litter both sides of the gravel road and dot the periphery of the field. They derive from the same natural forces and were part of the boulder field long ago. Their location on the perimeter of the original field made them more susceptible to erosion and drifting, and they spread out from the pack. That allowed sediments to collect, which in turn let vegetation flourish. Slowly, very slowly, vegetation is creeping into the tightly packed field.

The boulders range from immovable monsters 25 feet long to others that can be lifted by a child. The small depressions in the field were excavated by curious humans searching for the bottom of the rock pile.

Wildlife. The boulder field is relatively young, dating back less than 20,000 years. Over the millennia, the forces of erosion will eventually pulverize these rocks into powder, and the boulder field will gradually become a forest.

The rubble looks lifeless because a luxuriant woodland surrounds it. Nevertheless, life is present on the rocks. Crustose lichens have established colonies on the dry, bare rocks and have begun their job of preparing the way for other plants. They appear as multicolored stains, growing outward in circles. As they enlarge, they accumulate bits of organic materials, such as spores, dust, and seeds, and collect soil. They may be able to provide a base for foliose lichen, which resemble small, spreading spongy patches, or rock tripe, a cup-shaped lichen. Beard lichen, a foliose lichen, may sprout from a twig embedded in a rock, or pixie cups, tiny goblet-shaped fructiose lichens, may grow in dents or chips in the boulders.

Mosses, which require more soil and moisture, have become established on shaded rocks along the edge of the field. Many of the boulders scattered on the periphery are covered by a moss mat, tufts of grass, and herbaceous plants.

Shrubs and trees—birch, pine, and hemlock—have moved in from the edge. A few small clusters of trees have become rooted in the southeast corner of the field. This is not a huge invasion, but it becomes more significant over time. The leaves from these trees, along with those from the surrounding woods, provide a mat for more seedlings. Excrement from the birds that perch on their branches contains nutrients and seeds that may rise and flourish in this forbidding habitat.

Logging was a major industry here in the nineteenth century, but the lumberjacks seem to have overlooked a splendid spruce forest encircling the boulder patch. According to a mid-1970s inventory, it may be one of only a few surviving virgin forests of its kind in Pennsylvania.

The surrounding parkland is filled with the plants and animals typical of the Pocono Mountain region. A stroll around man-made Hickory Run Lake, where a cushion of sphagnum moss lies atop the surface at the east end, leads you to mountain laurel, sheep laurel, teaberry, various ferns (notably common polypody), and boulders covered with a collection of plants.

The path between the boulder field and Hawk Falls wanders through a second-growth forest (meaning it has been logged at least once) of eastern hemlock, tulip tree, black and gray birches, American beech, white pine, maples, and red, white, and black oaks. In the understory are rhododedron and mountain laurel. Wildflowers are abundant, and there are three varieties of club moss. Quiet, keen observers may see a black bear or a turkey.

History. Europeans acquired this land in a treaty with the Lenni Lenape (Delaware) Indians during the eighteenth century. From 1790 to 1835, the commonwealth sold 400-acre tracts. One buyer in the Hickory Run area was Robert Morris, a signer of the Declaration of Independence and the Constitution and one of the financial underwriters of the American Revolution. Another was

Stephen Decatur, a naval hero of the Barbary Coast War and War of 1812.

In the early nineteenth century, the area was known as the Shades of Death because it was a dark, thick forest of white pine, hemlock, oak, and maple. Today the Shades of Death Trail winds along Hickory Run.

Lumber camps and hamlets arose after the Civil War. Hemlock bark was used for tanning, white pine for lumber. The sawmills relied on water power generated at dams constructed across creeks. Once such dam still plugs Hickory Run Lake, visible from the hiking trail of the same name. A village called Hickory Run grew near the confluence of Hickory and Sand Spring runs. The park office and chapel are surviving buildings of the village.

The Saylorsville Dam, located near the park campgrounds, is all that remains of Saylorsville, once a thriving lumber town on the stagecoach route between Bethlehem and Wilkes-Barre. The Stage Trail traces that old stagecoach road.

By the late nineteenth century, the lumber companies had plundered all the hemlocks and white pines, and the towns went into fast decline. An Allentown businessman named Col. Harry C. Trexler bought several large parcels. When he died, the trustees of his estate offered 12,908 acres to the National Park Service, which developed the parkland in the 1930s. In 1945, the park service gave the site to the commonwealth of Pennsylvania, which turned it into Hickory Run State Park.

25

Thomas Darling Jr. Preserve

This preserve is one of Pennsylvania's biggest and least disturbed peat lands. It supports one of the largest and healthiest natural spruce forests in the state. The claw marks high on trees indicate that resident black bears must be huge.

Ownership. The Pennsylvania Chapter of the Nature Conservancy.

Size and Designation. About 400 acres.

Nearby Nature Attractions. Delaware Water Gap National Recreation Area; Monroe County Environmental Education Center; Tannersville Cranberry Bog; Long Pond Preserve; Devil's Hole; Delaware State Forest; Tobyhanna, Big Pocono, and Gouldsboro state parks; and the Delaware River, a national scenic river. The Appalachian Trail follows the Monroe-Northampton county line.

Features. The trails made by deer and other animals are the only paths through this trackless preserve. A compass and topographic map may come in handy, especially in summer. Impenetrable thickets also make hiking challenging. In this wetland, the ground stays spongy and soggy year-round, so wear appropriate shoes and watch your footing.

Geology. This wetland originated during the ice age, which last buried the area under ice 12,000 years ago. When the glacier retreated, an enormous chunk of ice split off and melted here, creating the wetland. The wetland serves as the headwater of Twomile Run, a small tributary of Tobyhanna Creek.

There is an abundance of peat at the preserve, which is classified as peat land. Peat is formed when grasses, sedges, reeds, mosses, trees, and other vegetation accumulate underwater and decompose.

Wildlife. The preserve includes a variety of wetland habitats—a boreal (northern) conifer swamp, an acidic shrub fen, a mixed hardwood and conifer swamp, a beaver meadow, small ponds, and a stream.

In the conifer swamp are great black spruce, some rare balsam fir, and tamarack. Azalea, rhododendron, blueberry, honeysuckle, and sheep, bog, and mountain laurels, grow in the shrub fen. The wet mixed hardwood forest includes red maple, spruce, black cherry, yellow birch, and American beech, as well as bunchberry and goldthread. Steeplebush *(Spiraea tomentosa),* bog rush, bulrushes and sedges grow in the beaver meadow, along with two rarities, thread rush *(Juncus filiformus,* PA rare) and bog sedge *(Carex paupercula,* PA threatened).

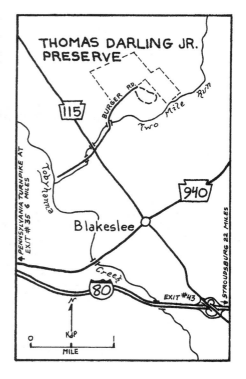

In late September, the forest bordering Berger Road is carpeted with club mosses, including shining club moss, ground cedar, and ground pine. Cinnamon, marginal, and hay-scented ferns also grow there.

This remote preserve abounds with black bear, several of them quite husky. According to the Pennsylvania Game Commission, black bears rely on wetlands for dens and feeding grounds and as a place to escape from hunters. The snowshoe hare (PA at risk), river otter (PA at risk), and coyote also find refuge in the preserve.

Fieldwork in this preserve remains incomplete, and scientists believe they will discover other rare plants and animals living in the wetland.

History. The site at Twomile Run owes its preservation to Grace Hydrusko of Spotwood, New Jersey, who bought up the valuable wildlife habitat in order to protect it. Hydrusko's 280-acre acquisition and a 61-acre tract owned by Albert Hanna made up the original preserve in the early 1990s. The site was dedicated a preserve in October 1993 by the Nature Conservancy, which today seeks to protect 2,600 to 3,000 acres here. The preserve is named after Thomas Darling, Jr., a naturalist and botanist who has spent several decades exploring and researching in the Poconos. He has discovered many plants and a half century ago donated his fern and wildflower collection to the Smithsonian Institution.

26

Lost Lakes Preserve

Halfmoon Lake Preserve

Impenetrable thickets girdling all but one of the pools keep out human intruders. Half a dozen imperiled species survive here, but scientists suspect there are many more.

Two of the Lost Lakes are glacial remnants, the other the handiwork of beavers. Halfmoon Lake, another glacial offspring, is the source of Tunkhannock Creek and Long Pond Preserve.

Ownership. Pennsylvania Chapter of the Nature Conservancy owns the Lost Lakes Preserve. Halfmoon Lake belongs to the Bethlehem Water Authority.

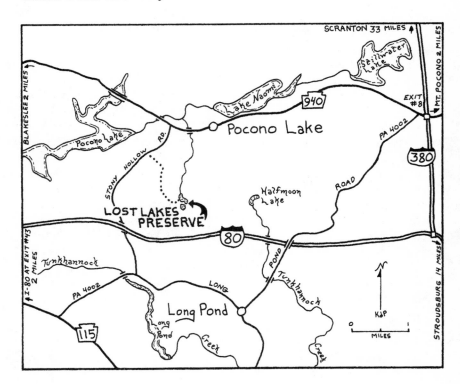

Size and Designation. Lost Lakes Preserve measures 852 acres; Halfmoon Lake Preserve, 76 acres. Both preserves are part of the Long Pond ecosystem.

Nearby Nature Attractions. Tannersville Cranberry Bog; Long Pond and Thomas Darling Jr. preserves; Devil's Hole; Delaware Water Gap National Recreation Area; Monroe County Environmental Education Center; Delaware State Forest; and Tobyhanna, Big Pocono, and Gouldsboro state parks. The Appalachian Trail traces the Monroe-Northampton county line. The portion of the Delaware River that forms the eastern boundary at Monroe County is a national scenic river.

Features. A mile walk on an old woods road will take you to the shore of one of the lakes. Paths to the other lakes—zigzag courses through thickets of rhododendron and laurel—are known to just a handful of guides. You could get lost trying to find them on your own. Join one of the conservancy-led hikes to the lakes. (A fee may be charged.) For more information, contact the Nature Conservancy, Pocono Mountains Office, P.O. Box 211, Blakeslee, PA 18610-0211, telephone (717) 643-7922.

Geology. The Lost Lakes and Halfmoon Lake are kettle lakes created by the Wisconsinan glacier at the end of the ice age 12,000 years ago, when enormous blocks of ice broke off the withdrawing glacier and then melted in the depressions created by their own weight. Over the years, the lakes have shrunk because they have filled in with sediment and vegetation. There are several small bogs and swamps, all derived from the glacier, in the preserves.

The lakes rest on the last undisturbed terminal moraine in the state. The moraine, a ridge of glacial sediment (gravel, boulders, and sand), runs east-west across the preserves and marks the farthest advance of the ice sheet. It is a mile wide and 300 to 400 feet higher than the land north and south of it. The ridge was formed as sediment carried by meltwater accumulated in front of the glacier.

The tracts are located on the Pocono Plateau. Tunkhannock Creek drains from Halfmoon Lake and flows into Tobyhanna Creek, a tributary of the Lehigh River.

Wildlife. The plants thriving in the various wetlands make these preserves special. Some of the rarities are labrador tea (*Ledum groenlandicum,* PA rare), few-seeded sedge (*Carex oligossperma,* PA threatened), bog sedge (*Carex paupercula,* PA threatened), thread rush (*Juncus filiformis,* PA rare), southern bog club moss (*Lycopodium appressum,* PA threatened), and yellow cowlily (*Nuphar lutea* ssp. *pumula,* declining in population). The northeastern bulrush (*Scirpus ancistrochaetus,* PA endangered), considered close to extinction, is protected at Halfmoon Lake.

Pitcher plants *(Sarracenia purpurea)* and round-leaved sundew *(Drosera rotundifolia)* flourish on floating sphagnum moss mats.

Several forest types grow in these sanctuaries. The tracts may have the state's best stand of red spruce, an evergreen common in northeastern U.S. forest but found only in scattered communities in Pennsylvania. It grows in swamps with acidic soil and can endure cold weather. Tamarack, red maple and white pine also form the canopy in this moist habitat.

Northern hardwoods dominate the drier uplands. These include some mature American beech, black cherry, yellow birch, red maple, and scarlet oak. Some of these specimens must be a century old. Other oaks line the trail to the first lake. Hemlocks grow here too.

Ancient, tangled growths of rhododendron ring the lakes and prevent the sunlight from reaching the ground. Highbush blueberry, alder, witherod *(Vibrunum cassinoides),* and wild cranberry also form thickets. Bears, ruffed grouse, wild turkeys, pheasants, and two dozen other species of birds favor the berries of the black gum, which also grows here.

Several kinds of club moss carpet the forest floor. Keen observers find goldthread *(Coptis groenlandica),* and mushrooms such as dead man's fingers *(Xylaria polymorpha).*

Animals at Lost Lakes Preserve include beaver, the coyote, deer, fox, and a large population of black bear. Look for the black bear's signature claw marks on trees. These scratches designate territorial boundaries and perhaps serve as messages to prospective mates.

Scientists expect to find more rare and unusual plants and animals here. Several rare dragonflies, damselflies, and moths may be present.

History. The Nature Conservancy acquired its first Lost Lakes tract in 1989. In 1994, the conservancy purchased the remaining parcels. This acquisition blocked any prospective development of the property, enlarged the Long Pond preservation site, and created a vast, unfragmented natural tract composed of state game commission lands, conservancy holdings, Bethlehem Water Authority property, and several private areas.

The conservancy acquired 76 acres along the edge of Halfmoon Lake, near the village of Pocono Pines, in 1992. It traded the parcel with the Bethlehem Water Authority for a parcel at the Long Pond barrens.

27

Long Pond Nature Preserve

Adams Swamp Preserve

Long Pond Nature Preserve is a vast mosaic of habitats—swamps, oak and pine groves, heaths, moors, and barrens—all linked by the Tunkhannock Creek.

The ecosystem may protect Pennsylvania's largest concentrations of imperiled plants and animals—32 species altogether, seven of which are globally endangered. The Pocono glacial till barrens may be the only natural community of their kind.

Ownership. Pennsylvania Chapter of the Nature Conservancy.

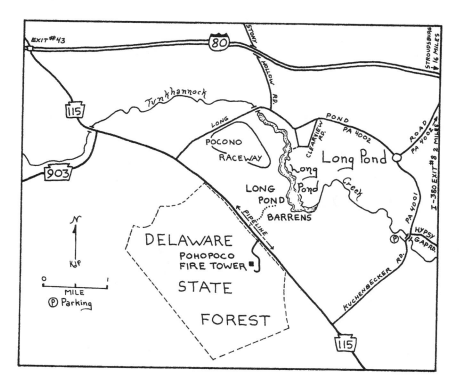

Size and Designation. Long Pond Preserve encompasses 367 acres, and informal agreements protect another 1,100 acres of this 31-square-mile ecosystem. Adams Swamp Preserve measures 1,158 acres.

Nearby Nature Attractions. Tannersville Cranberry Bog; Thomas Darling Jr. and Lost Lakes preserves; Big Pocono, Tobyhanna, and Gouldsboro state parks; Delaware State Forest; Delaware Water Gap National Recreation Area; and Monroe County Environmental Education Center. The Appalachian Trail follows the Monroe-Northampton county line. The portion of the Delaware River that forms the eastern boundary of Monroe County is a national scenic river.

Features. The main trail into the barrens begins as a smooth gravel lane, but it becomes a narrow, boulder-strewn creekbed as it enters rhododendron thickets and tall woods. The path vanishes in a hemlock grove at the edge of the wetland. From this point you can backtrack or follow one of the paths that branch from the main stem.

From the Clearview Road access, the pond is just a short walk down a farm lane. From the canoe access on Kuchenbecker Road, another path follows a creek.

The best way to experience Long Pond is by canoe when the water is high. Begin at the bridge across Tunkhannock Creek on Kuchenbecker Road, which runs between Long Pond Road and PA 115.

Special permission is required from the Nature Conservancy (Pocono office) to visit Adams Swamp Preserve. For more information, contact the Nature Conservancy, Pocono Mountains Office, P.O. Box 211, Bakeslee, PA 18610-0211, telephone (717) 643-7922.

Geology. Both preserves are situated on the Pocono Plateau at an elevation between 1,800 and 2,000 feet. Winters here are longer and colder than in neighboring regions, and summers cooler.

At least three continental glaciers passed over the plateau during the ice age. Adams Swamp originated at the end of the ice age, roughly 12,000 years ago, as the Wisconsinan continental glacier slowly retreated northward. Huge blocks of ice broke off from the retreating glacier and melted into kettle-hole lakes and ponds. Over centuries, sediment and vegetation filled many ponds, turning them into swamps.

Long Pond technically is not a pond but a wide, slow-moving section of Tunkhannock Creek that stretches for several miles and spreads out to create wetlands. The vegetation on the Long Pond barrens grows on the largest remaining deposit of glacial till from the Illinoisan glacier, which covered the spot 140,000 years ago. At Adams Swamp barrens, however, plants have migrated to soils derived from the Wisconsinan glacier, whose terminal moraine (an accumulation of earth and stones marking the glacier's farthest advance) covers the northwestern third of the barrens tract. Soil from an earlier glaciation has been discovered here too.

Wildlife. The Nature Conservancy calls the Long Pond area one of the richest and most important ecosystems in eastern North America. Its variety of habitats enables it to support a growing list of imperiled plants and animals.

The expansive scrub oak-pitch pine barrens found in the Long Pond and Adams Swamp preserves may appear stark. The scrub oak rarely exceeds eight feet in height, and the pitch pine is scraggly. But these trees survive well on harsh, low-nutrient, thin-soiled land. Both are fire resistant, an important characteristic because the barrens have been subjected to many fires. Scrub oaks produce acorns in just three years, compared with ten or more years for other oaks, and pitch pines regenerate soon after burnings. These adaptations enable them to recover quickly.

Scarlet oak, bigtooth aspen, sassafras, and a few white birch are scattered across the barrens. Tamarack, a water-loving tree associated with bogs, red spruce, and balsam fir sink their roots in small pools. The trail across the Long Pond barrens ends at a hemlock and white pine grove marking the boundary between the barrens and wetland. The ground here is spongy and dotted with hummocks. Great rhododendron and gray birch are also found here.

In May, the purple-pink blossoms of rhodora azalea *(Rhododendron canadense),* a waist-high shrub, can be seen all across the barrens and along Tunkhannock Creek. Sheep laurel *(Kalmia angustifolia)* and sweet fern *(Comptonia peregrina)* also live here.

The world's largest community of variable sedge *(Carex polymorpha,* PA endangered) finds refuge in the barrens. This globally threatened plant lives in only a dozen other known locations. Collin's sedge *(Carex collinsii,* PA endangered), few-seeded sedge *(Carex oligosperma,* PA threatened), and bog sedge *(Carex paupercula,* PA threatened) also grow here.

Other rarities include fall dropseed muhly *(Muhlenbergia uniflora),* blunt manna-grass *(Glyceria obtusa),* small-floating manna-grass *(Glyceria borealis),* oblong-fruited shadbush *(Amelanchier bartramiana),* and Farwell's water-milfoil *(Myriophyllum farwellii),* all endangered in Pennsylvania, as well as thread rush *(Juncus filiformis,* PA threatened), Hartford fern *(Lygodium palmatum,* PA rare), Tuckerman's pondweed *(Potamogeton confer-*

voides, PA threatened), creeping snowberry (*Gaultheria hispidula,* PA rare), purple bladderwort (*Utricularia purpurea,* PA rare), sweet bayberry (*Myrica gale,* PA threatened), and labrador tea (*Ledum groenlandicum,* PA rare).

Other common plants are blueberry, bracken fern, trailing arbutus, loosestrife (*Lysimachia quadrifolia*), and fly poison lily (*Amianthium muscaetoxicum*), whose poisonous alkaloid (which will kill livestock if consumed) is blended with sugar, then used to kill flies. It is also the host plant of the rare amianthium (fly poison) borer moth, which is endemic to Pennsylvania.

Adams Swamp is the largest undisturbed boreal conifer swamp in the state, according to the conservancy. It grows on peat soils, an oxygen-deficient muck largely derived from sphagnum moss and other plant matter. Found here are red and black spruces, tamarack, balsam fir, hemlock, yellow birch, black gum, red maple, leatherleaf (*Chamaedaphne calyculata*), cranberry (*Vaccinium macrocarpon*), labrador tea, and snowberry. The pitcher plant (*Sarracenia purpurea*), round-leaved sundew (*Drosera rotundifolia*), wild calla (*Calla palustris*), small purple-fringed orchid (*Habenaria psycodes*), and small woodland orchid (*Habenaria clavellata*) also may be spotted.

The southern part of the swamp is more open. White pine is present here, but oddly its needles are shorter than elsewhere.

The unique habitats attract butterflies and moths considered rare and imperiled, such as the barren buckmoth, sundew moth, barrens itame, twilight moth, blueberry gray, pink sallow, pointed sallow, November moth, and six noctuid moths. Two threatened dragonflies—the elegant skimmer and spotted blue darner—have also been observed here. Other butterflies and moths include European cabbage butterfly, European skipper, clouded sulphur, banded hairstreak, great spangled fritillary, long dash, alfalfa (orange), tiger and black swallowtails, sulphur, monarch, northern broken dash, and cross line skipper.

Animal inhabitants include the black bear, coyote, short-tailed weasel, deer, cottontail rabbit, river otter (PA at risk), mink, and beaver. Waterfowl arrive in flocks during their autumn migrations. The northern harrier (PA at risk), osprey (PA endangered), great blue heron, and wood duck have been observed. In spring, listen for prairie and Nashville warblers and catbirds.

History. Although this land is not fertile enough for farming, it has been used for recreation, pipelines, quarries, and blueberry harvests. Slowly the area's precious habitats were disappearing. In the late 1980s, the Nature Conservancy sought to preserve what remained of this imperiled area, purchasing a 367-acre tract and obtaining agreements to protect an additional 1,100 acres.

In 1992, the conservancy and the University of Pennsylvania obtained a grant to study the Pocono till barrens, as well as serpentine barrens in Chester County. The study will identify key properties for preservation.

28

Devil's Hole

Stand above this canyon on a windy day. Close your eyes and listen. A gust whisking across the gorge at just the right angle produces hellish sounds—moans, groans, howls, and hoots. Some people swear they hear the grim chants and barks of Satan on deathly, still nights. The gorge, they say, conceals the hole that leads to his earthen dungeon. Others say the haunting sounds are the restless groans of nineteenth century stonecutters who struggled in nearby quarries. You can decide for yourself the origin of the Devil's Hole.

Ownership. Pennsylvania Game Commission.

Size and Designation. State Game Lands 221 totals 4,618 acres.

Nearby Nature Attractions. Delaware Water Gap National Recreation Area; Tannersville Cranberry Bog; Long Pond, Lost Lakes, and Thomas Darling Jr. preserves; Big Pocono, Gouldsboro, and Tobyhanna state parks; and Delaware State Forest. The Appalachian Trail passes through the county and so does the Delaware River, a national scenic river.

Features. A two-mile trail from the parking lot leads to Devil's Hole. The trail follows Devil's Hole Creek. Upstream, the creek has carved a deep gorge, which is shrouded in mist on late-summer mornings. Seven Pines Mountain, from which Devil's Hole Creek begins its swift descent, rises to the northeast. Some of the old stones mined from quarries on Seven Pines Mountain still pave the start of the trail. Cross the creek and follow the trail upstream. The

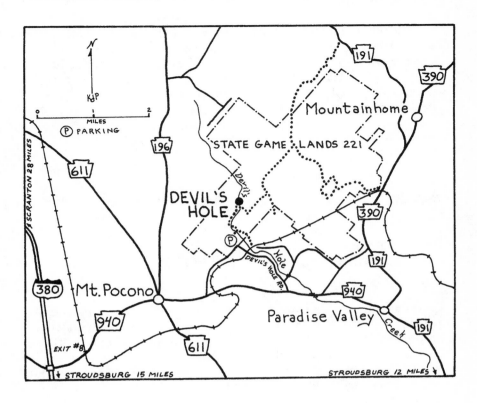

trail branches and braids, crosses and recrosses the creek. Just keep heading upstream.

A small grove of pines about 1.25 miles down the trail is faint evidence of an old estate at this location. Continuing upstream, the gorge narrows, deepens, darkens, and cools (refreshing on a hot summer day). The trail thins here, but you can make your way by boulder hopping. Expect to get wet feet. Your hike ends in another half-mile or so, when you reach a 25-foot cascade plunging into a pothole known as Devil's Hole.

Don't hike to Devil's Hole during the high-water period in early spring or after heavy rain. The creek becomes impassable, and stepping-stones disappear underwater. Instead, come here in midsummer, autumn, or midwinter, when the water level is low.

Licensed hunting and fishing are permitted. Campers and picnickers must go to Tobyhanna State Park (PA 611 north, then right on PA 423). Swimming and climbing at the pothole are dangerous and destructive to the fragile wildlife growing on the rocks; stay off the steep cliffs.

Geology. The pothole known as Devil's Hole lies near the foot of the Pocono Plateau escarpment, or Pocono Front, a steep-sided, east-facing wall stretching across northeastern Monroe County and into Pike County. Devil's Hole Creek starts in a swamp atop Seven Pines Mountain, a ridge on the Pocono Front, and drops 500 feet in less than two miles. Its water flows into Paradise Creek, then Analomink Creek, Brodhead Creek, and finally the Delaware River.

The Pocono Plateau is a jutting height one step higher than the larger Allegheny Plateau, which is part of a land mass called the Appalachian Uplands, essentially the highlands on the western side of the Appalachians running from New York to Alabama.

The Pocono region is actually an elevated plain created hundreds of millions of years ago when colliding continental plates formed the Appalachian ridges to the south and southeast. The land to the west and northwest of the ridges also uplifted but did not compress like an accordion. Since then, erosion has been carving the plateau, creating what look more like mountains than flat tablelands.

At Devil's Hole, 10,000 to 15,000 years ago, as the Wisconsinan glacier retreated northward, wild torrents of meltwater formed a stream strong enough to carry rocks, pebbles, and gravel, which plunged over the escarpment and swirled in the whirlpool beneath the waterfall. The abrasive power produced by the spinning water and pebbles gouged the pothole known as the Devil's Hole. The gorge downstream was also formed by the meltwater stream.

Wildlife. As you hike, note the changes in vegetation, most pronounced in the tree communities. The predominately oak forest on the high ground above the gorge gives way to beech, red and sugar maples, and black birch, which thrive better in cooler, damper habitats. Here and there are black cherry, aspen, white ash, white pine, and hemlock. Mountain laurel and rhododendron spread out in the understory.

Closer to the falls, in the dark ravine, mountain and striped maples dominate the understory, along with red-berried elder, red baneberry, and purple-flowering raspberry. The rare three-toothed cinquefoil, found in higher elevations on acidic rock cliffs, has been found here. These plants are more typical in colder, northern climates. They probably moved in during the period of glaciation, and continue to survive in scattered microhabitats.

Around the spot of the former estate grow some oddities like cypress, fir, and some unknowns imported by the former owner. The claw marks of black bears, which mark territorial boundaries, may appear on some of the cedars here.

Black bears are generally nocturnal and shy, and it's rare to see one in the wild during the day. Occasionally, bears venture to Devil's Hole Creek for brown or brook trout. Also present in the woods are wild turkey, ruffed grouse, deer, snowshoe hare (PA at risk), and bobcat (PA at risk).

29

Tannersville Cranberry Bog

In this unusual habitat, 300-year-old trees are only 40 feet tall. Here, some plants eat bugs because the water holds little nourishment. Here, the imperiled bog turtle, river otter, bobcat, and bog copper butterfly find refuge.

Ownership. The Pennsylvania Chapter of the Nature Conservancy.

Size and Designation. More than 1,000 acres. The bog has been designated a national natural landmark.

Nearby Nature Attractions. Long Pond, Lost Lakes, and Thomas Darling Jr. preserves; Delaware Water Gap National Recreation Area; Delaware State Forest; Monroe County Environmental Education Center; Big Pocono, Gouldsboro, and Tobyhanna state parks; and the Delaware River, a national scenic river. The Appalachian Trail runs along the Monroe-Northampton county line.

Features. Because of endangered wildlife and the sensitive bog habitat, you must sign up for a guided tour or get permission to see the cranberry bog. A 1,600-foot floating boardwalk takes you into that strange world.

The North Woods Trail is a 4,000-foot self-guiding loop. The Fernridge Trail, actually a chain of paths, offers a longer and more rugged hike. Both are open daily during daylight hours. Special permission is not required for these two trails.

For information on guided tours, contact the Monroe County Conservation District, 8050 Running Valley Road, Stroudsburg, PA 18360, telephone (717) 629-3061; or the Pennsylvania Chapter of the Nature Conservancy, 1211 Chestnut Street, 12th Floor, Phila-

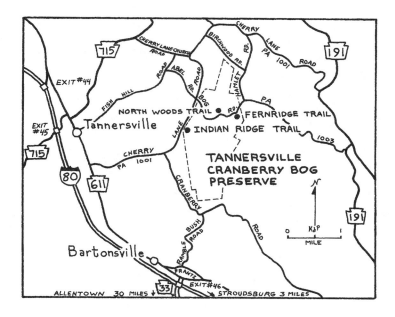

delphia, PA 19107, telephone (215) 963-1400. Special tours can be arranged for classes and other groups.

Geology. Tannersville Bog is the southernmost glacial conifer swamp in the eastern United States, and the lowest in altitude, at 900 feet. This type of ecosystem is more common to the north, in the Adirondack Mountains and Canada.

Around 12,000 to 16,000 years ago, the Wisconsinan glacier covered the Poconos region. When the ice mass retreated northward, blocks of ice broke off and were left behind. Sediment washing off the glacier created ridges around the stranded ice chunks. The ice melted into these depressions, forming kettle hole lakes, bogs, and other wetlands. Tannersville bog started as a 715-acre glacial lake. Indian Ridge rings the wetland and is formed of till, a glacial sediment composed of rocks, gravel, sand, or silt.

Technically, this wetland is an acid fen, not a bog. A fen is refreshed and flushed by flowing water from a stream or spring. Here, groundwater seeps into the fen, and Cranberry Creek flows through it. A bog, on the other hand, is fed by precipitation from surrounding higher ground and usually has no year-round outlet. Fens and bogs often contain the same kinds of vegetation.

Wildlife. The sluggish water in this wetland contains little oxygen and is acidic from the accumulation of sphagnum, or peat, moss. Consequently, specialized plants that thrive in an acidic environment grow here. Sphagnum moss releases hydrogen ions that combine with other chemicals to form acids. Dead moss settles to the bottom of the bog and makes peat. It releases tannic acid, which stains the water dark brown. The plants that can live in an acidic environment retain their nutrients. Even bacteria, the agents of decomposition, have trouble surviving in this oxygen-starved habitat, and thus decay proceeds slowly.

Sphagnum moss absorbs 18 times its own weight, and then slowly releases water in summer, cooling the fen. The moss extends into the fen as a floating mat, which acts as insulation in the spring, blocking sunlight that would melt ice beneath the surface. Ice has been found in bogs as late as June.

Bogs are repositories of natural history because they preserve pollen and plant debris that settles on the bottom. The plant and climate history of an area can be learned by studying a core sample from a bog.

Peat accumulates at a rate of one foot every 120 years. In the center of this fen, peat is more than 50 feet deep, making it more than 6,000 years old.

In the bog are zones of plant life. On Indian Ridge, the outermost ring, red maple, alder, blueberry, black gum, and other small hardwoods prevail. Next comes a zone of conifers and hardwoods, including white pine, great rhododendron, hemlock, yellow birch, poison sumac, and red maple. The ground is deep and soggy here, as the peat is two to fifteen feet deep. If you were to step off the trail, you would sink to your knees. Near the center of the bog, black spruce, and American tamarack (larch) struggle in the mire. These impoverished-looking conifers are rooted in hummocks of sphagnum moss. The tamarack is the only North American conifer that sheds its needles in the fall.

Sheep and bog laurels, swamp azalea, and highbush blueberry grow here beside rarities such as bog rosemary (*Andromeda polifolia,* PA rare), leatherleaf (an evergreen shrub, *Chamaedaphne calyculata*), and labrador tea (*Ledum groenlandicum,* PA rare). The mat supports cranberry, wild calla *(Calla palustris),* and the northern pitcher plant *(Sarracenia purpurea)* and round-leaved sundew *(Drosera rotundifolia),* both of which are carnivorous. Orchids brighten the mat, notably grass pink *(Calopogon pulchellus),* white-fringed *(Habenaria blephariglottis),* large purple-fringed *(Habenaria fimbriata),* yellow lady's slipper *(Cypripedium calceolus),* rose pogonia *(Pogonia ophioglossoides),* and the rare heart-leaved twayblade (*Listera cordata,* PA endangered). Another rarity is cotton grass (*Eriophorum* spp.). In Pennsylvania, two species—slender and rough —are endangered, and the thin-leaved is threatened.

The Nature Conservancy lists the bog copper butterfly as imperiled. This diminutive butterfly resides only in cranberry marshes. It dines on cranberries and deposits eggs on the plant's leaves. The population in each community numbers about 100.

The North Woods and Fernridge trails wander through an oak forest. White, red, and chestnut oaks predominate. Shagbark hickory, tulip tree, and witch hazel grow here too. A large specimen of shadbush grows along the North Woods Trail.

The preserve hosts the marginal wood, marsh, royal, cinnamon, sensitive, and common polypody ferns. Wildflowers include the twinflower *(Linnaea borealis)*, downy rattlesnake plantain *(Goodyera pubescens)*, whorled loosetrife *(Lysimachia quadrifolia)*, and goldthread *(Coptis groenlandica)*.

Yellow-eyed grass (*Xyris montana,* decreasing in population) and other sedges stand in fertile patches. Dwarf mistletoe (*Arceuthobium pusillum,* PA threatened) is a nickel-sized parasite that grows on black spruce and causes growths on its host called witches'-brooms.

Muhlenberg's (bog) turtle (PA endangered) is the smallest turtle, with a shell measuring just three to four inches. Look for orange marks on its neck. This reptile wallows in the shallows and stays out of sight.

Approach the open water slowly to spot a river otter. Sometimes it will leave the remains of fish on the boardwalk. Black bear, deer, coyote, snowshoe hare (PA at risk), bobcat (PA at risk), and gray fox also roam in the preserve.

Birds observed here include the wild turkey, barred owl, hermit thrush, gray catbird, red-eyed vireo, veery, and Nashville, common yellowthroat, Canada, magnolia, Blackburnian, golden-winged, chestnut-sided, yellow, and black-throated green warblers.

History. The bog has long been a laboratory for scientists, but it was not until after 1955 floods that it was decided that the bog was worth preserving. The floods destroyed bridges in the Poconos, except the ones below the bog, indicating that the bog helped prevent flooding by absorbing water.

In 1956, a local committee and the Nature Conservancy purchased 62.5 acres of the swamp. More tracts were acquired between 1957 and 1963. The preserve has grown to more than 1,000 acres. The boardwalk into the bog opened in May 1992.

30

Monroe County Environmental Education Center

This recovering farmland offers various habitats for wildlife—woodlots, meadows, pond, shrubs, and fields. The best of this preserve may be yet to come.

Ownership. County owned; managed by the Monroe County Conservation District.

Size and Designation. The center is situated on the 120-acre, county-designated Kettle Creek Wildlife Sanctuary.

Nearby Nature Attractions. Big Pocono, Gouldsboro, and Tobyhanna state parks; Delaware Water Gap National Recreation

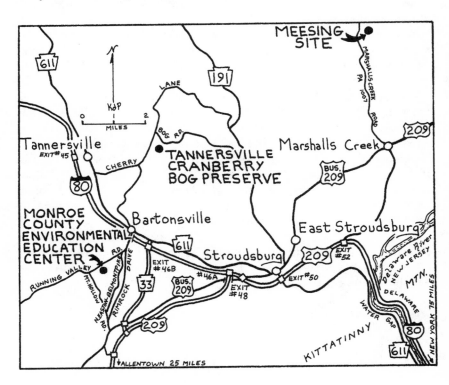

Area; Delaware State Forest; Devil's Hole; Tannersville Cranberry Bog; Long Pond, Lost Lakes, and Thomas Darling Jr. preserves. The Appalachian Trail follows the Monroe-Northampton county line. The Delaware River along the border of Monroe County is a national scenic river.

Features. At the Monroe County Environmental Education Center, staff naturalists lead numerous education programs, as well as trips to satellite sites such as Tannersville Cranberry Bog and the Meesing woods, the sanctuary's former nature center. In the center are classrooms, exhibits, a library, a gift store, rest rooms, and drinking water. Outside are an observation deck and bird-feeding area. The center is open from 8:30 A.M. to 4:30 P.M. Monday through Friday, 9 A.M. to 4 P.M. Saturday.

Trails into Kettle Creek Wildlife Sanctuary begin at the center and the parking lots. Pick up a trail map at the center. Visitors in wheelchairs can take the paved Black Bear Trail from the lower parking lot to Swink Pond. The Deer and Songbird trails depart from the center and explore various open, forested, and wetland habitats. Grey Fox Loop begins at the overflow parking lot on the north side of Running Valley Road and circles through a mature hardwood forest. The trails—for hiking and cross-country skiing only—stay open daily from dawn to dusk. At the nearby Meesing site, a 100-acre tract north of Marshalls Creek, four miles of trails are open daily from dawn to dusk.

For more information, contact the Monroe County Environmental Education Center, 8050 Running Valley Road, Stroudsburg, PA 18360, telephone (717) 629-3061.

Geology. The sanctuary gets its name from nearby Kettle Creek, which flows south into Appenzell Creek. The sanctuary lies within the Appalachian Mountain range. The landscape took shape 290 million years ago during a mountain-building period referred to as the Alleghenian Orogeny.

The nearby Meesing center is located on the Pocono Plateau, a part of the larger Appalachian Plateau. The bedrock on this table-land consists of shale and sandstone. Downcutting by streams accounts for the mountainous terrain in this region.

Wildlife. Chestnut oak dominates the highest and driest spots. Elsewhere, spruce, wild cherry, pitch and white pines, flowering dogwood, white birch, and witch hazel grow. In the late spring, tent caterpillars weave cottony webs in the crotches of these trees. Hundreds of these inch-long worms mass in the web. Kettle Creek Sanctuary is a refuge for the black bear, deer, coyote, river otter (PA at risk), red fox, skunk, and white-footed mouse. Birds observed here include the hooded merganser, wild turkey, crow, blue-winged and pine warblers, gray catbird, ruffed grouse, eastern bluebird, screech owl, and red-winged blackbird. At dusk, the elegant luna moth may be observed.

Other residents include the bullfrog, spring peeper, green and wood frogs; and garter, ringneck, and eastern hognose snakes. When disturbed, the chubby hognose seems ferocious. It hisses, inflates its head, and strikes. But it is all an act; it never bites. After this show of force, it plays dead.

At the Meesing site, a young forest rises from the ruins of a clear-cut. In March, sap is collected from sugar maples and processed in a sugar shack. The site also has a pine grove, pond, brook, and swamp.

History. Rusting farm equipment and neglected stone walls remind the visitor of this land's agriculture legacy. Kettle Creek Wildlife Sanctuary was established in 1984, when the land for the preserve was given to Monroe County. Hiking trails opened in 1988. The new center opened in June 1991, replacing the Meesing Nature Center.

31

Carbon County Environmental Education Center

Mauch Chunk Lake Park

Slowly, nature restores this clearcut and cultivated land. Black bears have returned to the valley the Lenni Lenape called *Mauch Chunk,* or "sleeping bear." The nearby coalfields are reminders of the lush tropical fields of 300 million years ago.

Ownership. Carbon County Parks and Recreation Commission.

Size and Designation. Carbon County Environmental Education Center is part of the 2,300-acre Mauch Chunk Lake Park, owned by the Carbon County Parks and Recreation Commission and the Pennsylvania Fish and Boat Commission.

Nearby Nature Attractions. Beltzville, Lehigh Gorge, and

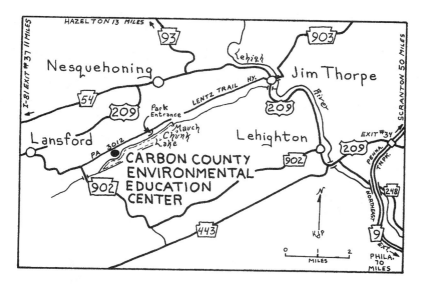

Hickory Run state parks. Portions of the Lehigh River, and a tributary called Mud Run, are state scenic waterways. The Appalachian Trail follows the Carbon-Lehigh county line.

Features. The main attractions are the environmental education center and 18 miles of hiking trails through woods, fields, and wetlands and over rocky slopes.

Children especially enjoy the center's exhibits and live animal collection, which includes snakes, spiders, bats, turtles, and furry creatures. The centers also serves as a hospital for injured and abandoned birds and animals. Red-tailed hawks, a great horned owl, and a caracara (a South American bird of prey) were housed in the rehab center when I visited. Birds that fully recover are released, but those that remain disabled are used in nature programs. The center also holds hunting, fishing, and trapping programs.

Also on the grounds are a butterfly and hummingbird garden and a 200-year-old gristmill, in which lives a colony of some 200 brown bats. At the lakeshore is a bird observatory, with a double-deck platform and a bird blind.

Neighboring Mauch Chunk Lake Park offers swimming, picnicking, fishing, boat rentals, volleyball, horseshoes, tent camping, a refreshment stand, and in the winter, cross-county skiing. The park is open daily from 10 A.M. to 8 P.M. There is an admission fee for the park; the nature center is free.

For more information, contact the Carbon County Environmental Education Center, 626 Lentz Trail, Jim Thorpe, PA 18229, telephone (717) 645-8597.

Geology. This area of the state is rich in anthracite coal, which is 95 percent carbon, hence the name Carbon County. One of the richest lodes of anthracite was discovered at nearby Summit Hill in 1791.

Coal is a fossil fuel, derived from plant life that flourished 280 to 345 million years ago. As the plants died, they accumulated in thick, carbon-rich beds on the forest floor. Over time, the organic litter became buried and was compressed and hardened into coal. Coal is graded according to the content of moisture and other material.

Mauch Chunk Lake was created when a dam was built on Mauch Chunk Creek at what is now the east end of the park.

The creek continues east and meets the Lehigh River in Jim Thorpe.

Wildlife. Near the center are red maple, spruce, cattails, and berries. Showy lady's slipper (*Cypripedium reginae,* PA threatened), a May-October orchid, grows near the center. Look for jack-in-the-pulpit *(Arisaema triphyllum),* skunk cabbage *(Symplocarpus foetidus),* and painted trillium *(Trillium undulatum)* in the wet forest at the west end of the lake. Skunk cabbage, named for its fetid odor, grows as early as February. Its speedy growth from cellular respiration produces heat that melts snow.

At the bird observatory, look for waterfowl, including old-squaws, wood ducks, and egrets, as well as swallows, ruby-throated hummingbirds, ospreys, bald eagles, great horned and saw-whet owls, red-tailed hawks, eastern bluebirds, American woodcocks, and red-winged blackbirds.

A colony of brown bats inhabits the gristmill. The area around the mill supports beavers, screech owls, and copperhead, water, garter, hognose, and ringneck snakes. Look for carp, minnows, suckers, crayfish, stone nymphs, and mayflies in Mauch Chunk Creek.

Deer, rabbit, turkey, and black bear can be hunted in the park, but not around the nature center. Check park restrictions before hunting or fishing.

History. Carbon County still has a sizable population of black bears, some of which reside in the park.

The Switchback Trail, which begins across the road from the main park entrance, follows the tracks of a gravity railroad that hauled coal from Summit Hill to the Lehigh Canal in Jim Thorpe. Gravity pushed the loaded coal cars nine miles down the track to the canal, then mules pulled the empty cars back to the mine. It was only the second "working" railroad (meaning it carried cargo instead of people) when it opened in May 1827.

In 1844, a second track was built, creating a figure-eight design so that cars could run continuously. By 1872, steam locomotives replaced the gravity railroad, which was converted into a tourist attraction a few years later. For a while it was one of the most popular tourist destinations in the East. The Great Depression of the 1930s ruined business, and the Switchback Railroad stopped running in 1933.

In 1954 community activists considered restoring the railroad. Efforts finally got under way in 1986, and plans are to bring back the 18-mile round-trip ride from Summit Hill to Jim Thorpe, with a stop at the county park.

Mauch Chunk merged with East Mauch Chunk in 1954; the new town was called Jim Thorpe, after the American Indian athlete who won the pentathlon and decathlon gold medals for the United States in the 1912 Olympics. He was stripped of the titles in 1913, but the International Olympic Committee restored them in 1982. Sportswriters acclaimed Thorpe as the nation's greatest male athlete and football player for the first half of the twentieth century.

The dam across Mauch Chunk Creek was finished in 1972, and two years later Mauch Chunk Lake Park opened. Environmental education programs were started in 1976.

Jacobsburg Environmental Education Center

The factories of iron and armaments that once made Jacobsburg famous have disappeared beneath a canopy of green, and the sounds of the forge and furnace have been replaced by birdsong and the rush of Bushkill Creek.

Ownership. Pennsylvania Department of Environmental Resources, Bureau of State Parks.

Size and Designation. The park measures 1,166 acres. The historic district in the park is listed on the National Register of Historic Places.

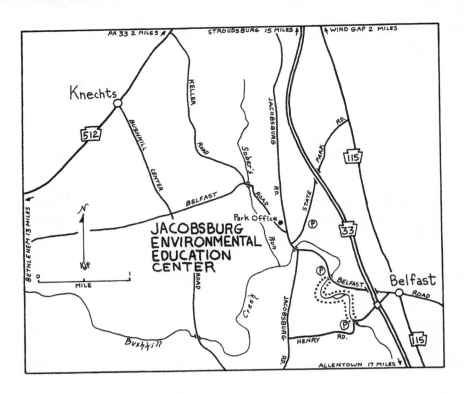

Nearby Nature Attractions. Delaware Water Gap National Recreation Area and Lost River Cavern. The Appalachian Trail follows the Northampton-Monroe county line.

Features. The Jacobsburg Environmental Education Center offers year-round outdoor nature programs for students (and teachers) ranging from preschool to graduate levels. Programs are held at an amphitheater at Henry's Woods Picnic Area, and throughout the park. Though the facility caters to groups, individuals also can visit the site.

Hikers can explore 12.5 miles of trails through grassy meadows, young forests, and mature woodlands and historic sites. The most popular path is Henry's Woods Nature Trail, which wanders through a 100-acre tract of white oak and hemlock along Bushkill Creek and climbs a steep ridge above the south bank of the stream. The Jacobsburg Trail leads to the ruins of Jacobsburg, and the Homestead Trail features a bird blind.

The Henry and Boulton gun factories are located within the park on Henry Road, west of PA 33. The Henry Homestead and John Joseph Henry House are open the fourth Sunday of the month from April through October, 1 to 5 P.M.

There are two picnic areas—one at the trailhead for Henry's Woods, the other beside the ruins of the village of Jacobsburg. Both have rest rooms, but only Henry's Woods offers drinking water.

Horseback riding, biking, and cross-country skiing are permitted in designated areas. Bike riding is no longer allowed in Henry's Woods.

Bushkill Creek boasts great trout fishing in April and May, thanks to an annual stocking by the Pennsylvania Fish Commission. If Bushkill Creek gets too crowded, try a swifter and cooler tributary called Sober's Run (unstocked) for brown trout. Hunting and trapping are allowed in designated areas; state and park regulations apply.

Geology. Jacobsburg lies in the Lehigh Valley, part of the Great Valley. The terrain here is rolling and a bit hilly, and it lacks the abrupt steepness of the ridges in the Appalachian Mountains that rise a few miles to the north.

The Great Valley extends from New York to Georgia. In Maryland it is known as the Hagerstown Valley; Virginians call it the Shenandoah Valley. Pennsylvania's portion of the valley divides into three regions—the Cumberland Valley (southern section), the Lebanon Valley (middle), and the Lehigh Valley (northern) where Jacobsburg is located.

Shale, slate, and sandstone underlay the center. The slate, a more compressed shale, is low-grade because it contains less silica than hard slate. Still, it was valuable enough for mining.

Here, Bushkill Creek washes over bedrock, gravel, pebbles, boulders, sand, and finer sediments. In the shallows, the rubble base makes riffles, which aerate the water. In deeper, calmer pools, sand and silt filter to the bottom and debris accumulates on shore. The changing flow of the creek provides different habitats and increases the diversity of aquatic life. The creek is refreshed by Sober's Run and smaller tributaries, precipitation, runoff, and a few springs.

Wildlife. Two hundred and fifty-five years ago, the area was a dense forest of oak and chestnut. The trees were cut, however, to meet the demands of agriculture and industry. Today, a forest of second-growth hardwoods covers about 770 acres of the center. Some tracts, like Henry's Woods, boast mature trees, a 100-acre stand of white oak and hemlock alongside Bushkill Creek. The rest of the land consists of meadows in various stages of succession, from open grassy fields to young hardwood thickets.

Fifty-four kinds of trees grow at the center, including several varieties of oaks, birches, maples, and sumacs. White and red oaks, white ash, shagbark hickory, red maple, walnut, tulip tree, dogwood, spicebush, and ironwood predominate.

More than 200 species of wildflowers cover the ground, including white monkshood (*Aconitum reclinatum,* PA endangered), wild hyacinth (*Camassia scilloides,* PA threatened), mugwort (*Artemisia vulgaris)*, annual wormwood *(Artemisia annua)*, dame's rocket *(Hesperis matronalis)*, bouncing bet *(Saponaria officinalis)*, yellow goat's beard *(Tragopogon pratensis)*, square-stemmed monkey flower *(Mimulus ringens)*, bugleweed *(Lycopus virginicus)*, butter-and-eggs *(Linaria vulgaris)*, homewort *(Cryptotaenia canadensis)*, and pale smartweed *(Polygonum lapathifolium)*.

Mushroom and fungus number 46 species here, notably orange peel *(Aleuria aurantia)*, destroying angel *(Amanita phalloides)*, scrambled egg slime mold *(Fuligo septica)*, dead man's fingers *(Xylaria polymorpha)*, and witches' butter *(Tremella mesenterica)*.

Eight varieties of ferns are represented, including northern maidenhair, hay-scented, cinnamon, common polypody, and bracken ferns.

Twenty-five kinds of fish inhabit the waterways, including three trout species, bass, stonecat, creek chub, Johnny darter, white sucker, and American eel. Bushkill Creek is stocked with trout for anglers; and Sober's Run supports a year-round population of brown trout.

Fifteen types of frogs and salamanders and 12 kinds of snakes and turtles have been identified here including the spring peeper, two-lined salamander, black racer snake, and wood turtle. Twenty-three species of mammals include the white-tailed deer, mink, opossum, meadow vole, red and gray foxes, and little brown bat.

One hundred forty-seven kinds of birds have been sighted here, including the barn owl (PA at risk), long-eared owl, northern goshawk (PA rare), northern harrier (PA at risk), Swainson's thrush (PA rare), northern bobwhite, eastern bluebird, indigo bunting, orchard oriole, cedar waxwing, ruby-crowned kinglet, and Brewster's, Lawrence's, Wilson's, and Cape May warblers. Some, like the endangered osprey, only occasionally drop in during their migrations.

History. Jacob Hubler came to these forested hills from Bern, Switzerland, in 1740. He established Jacobsburg on his 400-acre tract. Jacobsburg's fame, however, derives from the Henry family, whose arms were carried by pioneers and soldiers from the Colonial period through the Civil War.

William Henry, the first Henry gunsmith, set up shop in Lancaster, Pennsylvania, in 1750. He was the local gun manufacturer for the British army during the French and Indian War. In 1778, Henry's son, William, Jr., built a gun factory near Nazareth. He expanded his operations to Jacobsburg in 1792. Having secured a government contract after the outbreak of the War of 1812, he constructed a bigger factory in nearby Boulton, beginning the golden years for the Jacobsburg area. His son, Matthew, started the Ann

Catherine Furnace in Jacobsburg in 1824. The furnace produced high-quality iron for the Boulton works and for cooking utensils, until it was sold in 1833. The business passed through the family until mass-produced firearms drove handcrafted-gun factories out of business. Granville Henry, the last of the gun-makers, closed the forge in 1904.

The Henry Homestead, the family home from 1813 to 1904, was restored in 1980. Other historic sites are the Benade House (the iron master's house, circa 1808, across the road from Henry's Woods Picnic Area), the Henry Homestead (1812), and the John Joseph Henry House (1832), located on Henry Road near the site of the Boulton Works.

The original tract for what became Jacobsburg State Park was purchased by the state in 1959, and additional land was purchased in 1969. The Jacobsburg Historic District was added to the National Register of Historic Places on October 17, 1977. In 1985, Jacobsburg State Park became Jacobsburg Environmental Education Center.

Hawk Mountain Sanctuary

On an ideal autumn day, with a northwest tailwind, thousands of southbound hawks soar above a long, rocky ridge called Hawk Mountain. Several lookouts offer breathtaking panoramas of mountains and valleys, as well as views of soaring raptors.

Ownership. Hawk Mountain Sanctuary Association.

Size and Designation. The sanctuary encompasses 2,226 acres. Hawk Mountain is on the National Register of Natural Landmarks. A Revolutionary-era cottage on the property is listed on the National Register of Historic Places.

Nearby Nature Attractions. Nolde Forest Environmental Education Center, Blue Marsh Lake Project, Ruth Zimmerman State Forest Natural Area, French Creek State Park, and the Schuylkill River and Tulpehocken Creek, both state scenic waterways. The Appalachian Trail runs through Hawk Mountain Sanc-

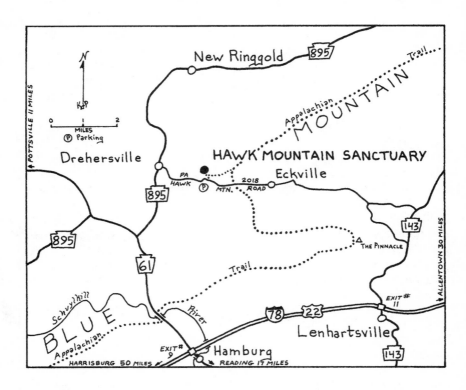

tuary, down the spine of Kittatinny Ridge, through Weiser State Forest, and along the Berks-Schuylkill county line.

Features. The major attraction at Hawk Mountain is observing birds of prey. There are two lookouts from which to view the raptors as they soar over the ridge on their seasonal migrations.

The South Lookout is just 300 yards from the visitors center and is easy to reach. The lookout marks the trailhead of a demanding 3.5-mile loop path that descends to the River of Rocks, a boulder field at the bottom of the valley.

A challenging, rocky, 3/4-mile trail to the left (north) leads to the North Lookout, which rises 1,000 feet above the Little Schuylkill River to the north and offers the best view. Here you have a sweeping 200-degree panorama and can look down the spine of Kittatinny Ridge. On clear days, you can see for 70 miles. A 1.5-mile spur from this lookout leads to the Appalachian Trail.

From the North Lookout, you can make your way to the west-facing Sunset Lookout or hike two miles down the Skyline Trail to East Rocks, another viewing outpost.

The lookouts are open every day during daylight hours. There is a small admission fee. The visitors center has a museum, bookstore, art gallery and rest rooms. It is open daily from 9 A.M. to

5 P.M. December through August, and 8 A.M. to 5 P.M. September through November.

The sanctuary also has an outdoor amphitheater, a habitat garden, and a classroom for the many nature programs, lectures, and workshops offered. For more information, contact Hawk Mountain Sanctuary Association, P.O. Box 191, Kempton, PA 19529-9449, telephone (610) 756-6961.

Geology. The lay of the land explains why raptors stream over Hawk Mountain. Kittatinny Ridge, which the Indians called the Endless Mountain, runs southwest-northeast across northern New Jersey and Eastern Pennsylvania.

To the southeast, the mountains cease and the topography descends quickly into the Great Valley. Migrating birds of prey are diurnal (active in the daytime), and the Kittatinny Ridge, also called Blue Mountain, is an easy landmark for them to spot and follow. The birds zero in on the heights and get their bearings. (Other features, such as the Atlantic coastline and major rivers, serve as raptor routes too.)

Tuscarora sandstone caps Kittatinny Ridge for many miles in both directions. Four hundred million years ago, the sandstone formed the floor of an ancient sea or low, exposed ground. When the continents collided, the sandstone buckled and collapsed, and areas were uplifted. Erosion and weathering have since sculpted the shapes and contours you see at the summit. Some of the rocks reveal the fossils of ancient creatures, like the tunnels of a sea worm called arthophycus.

From the lookouts, you can sometimes see the River of Rocks, 500 to 700 feet below to the east. It looks like an abandoned riverbed filled with truckloads of boulders, but this boulder field was actually created indirectly by the last continental glacier 12,000 years ago.

Though the mile-high ice sheet itself only edged as far south as the Pocono Mountains, the climatic conditions of the ice age produced extreme freezing and thawing in the region. Water that froze in the tiny cracks of rock acted like wedges. During thaws, melting water dissolved a chemical that cemented the rock, and carried away bits of sand. This loosened the boulders, then gravity sent them tumbling down to accumulate at the base of the ridge. A brook called Upside Down River, is said to flow beneath the rocks.

Wildlife. As many as 20,000 to 30,000 raptors, representing 14 or more species, pass over the sanctuary each year. On clear autumn days, hundreds of people flock to the ridge to watch the annual exodus. Birders, volunteers, interns, and staffers have been keeping track of raptor sightings for more than 60 years now. Few places have kept better records of migratory birds of prey.

Plan your visit during the peak of migration. Here is a migration timetable for 15 birds of prey seen at Hawk Mountain Sanctuary.

Bird	Peak Migration
Broad-winged hawk	August, *September,* October
Bald eagle (PA endangered)	August, *September,* October, November
Golden eagle	September, October, *November,* December
Osprey (PA endangered)	August, *September,* October, November
Northern goshawk (PA rare)	September, October, *November,* December
Sharp-shinned hawk	August, September *October,* November
Northern harrier (PA threatened)	August, September, *October,* November, December
Red-tailed hawk	September, *October,* November
Red-shouldered hawk	September, *October,* November
Cooper's hawk	September, *October,* November
Rough-legged hawk	October, *November*
Peregrine falcon (PA endangered)	August, *September,* October, November
American kestrel	August, *September,* October, November
Merlin	September, *October,* November
Turkey vulture	August, September, *October,* November

An ideal day improves your chances of observing the birds. What are the perfect conditions? A clear sky is best, but a "white" overcast sky is okay. The birds don't fly on foggy or rainy days. Check weather reports for a low-pressure system with cold Canadian air pushing across New York and New England and wind flowing from the north or northwest. A cold front up north encourages the birds to head south, especially if the wind in moving in that direction too.

Under these prized conditions, broad-winged hawks may appear in the thousands in mid-September. The record sighting was 21,448 broad-wings on September 14, 1978.

The ridge helps keep the birds aloft, especially if the wind is blowing from the north or northwest. Wind striking the ridge is deflected upward, creating brisk updrafts. The raptors tilt and angle their wings to catch the wind just right, then ride the current as fast and as far as they can. Soaring on air currents is easier than flapping all day, and it conserves energy. It also makes for a faster migration because the birds stop fewer times to refuel and rest. Some raptors have been clocked going 80 miles an hour when pushed by strong wind. On a day with perfect weather, they might travel at 40 miles an hour and stay airborne six hours. On gentler days, they will climb thermal currents, swirling drafts that rise from the valley. Thermal currents lift the birds far above the ridge top, where they leave the thermal and glide on the migration route. At a certain altitude they rise on another thermal and repeat the procedure.

Identification may be easiest on days with gentle breezes, because the birds spread their wings and tails to maximum length to take full advantage of the current. Moderate wind requires them to retract their wings slightly and close their tails. Those that can navigate in strong wind will draw in their wings even more. Bring along a field guide to help you identify the raptors. Veteran hawk-watchers will often help with identification.

After wintering south, the raptors fly to their northern nesting grounds in the spring. The spring migration is less intense than the fall migration. The birds' pace appears less hurried, and they return by different and scattered routes. In the spring, Hawk Mountain does not offer the favorable flying conditions that it does in the fall.

Other migrants pass by Hawk Mountain. Warblers and water-birds move across the ridge on their spring and fall migrations. Some stay to nest here; others move on. Look for cerulean, northern parula, myrtle, hooded, bay-breasted, blackpoll, pine, and pro-thonotary (PA at risk) warblers.

Waterbirds migrate through here on a flight path that drives right through prevailing winds and at a right angle to the route followed by raptors. They rarely stop here to rest. The common loon, American egret, brant, pintail, canvasback, and bufflehead ducks, ibis, yellow-crowned night heron (PA threatened), and other herons, swans, snow and blue geese, have been observed.

A total of 246 bird species have been observed, which also includes the northern oriole, goldfinch, wild turkey, and scarlet tanager. Sharp-eyed observers might detect migrating ruby-throated hummingbirds, which winter in Mexico and Central America and may nest as far north as central Ontario.

About 70 percent of the sanctuary's property is dedicated for research. Hawk Mountain provides a sanctuary for white-tailed deer, black bears, and long-tailed weasels. The sanctuary also protects streams, vernal pools, and bogs, which provide shelter and food for the migratory birds.

Hawk Mountain proves that research and habitat preservation are vital to wildlife preservation. Studies conducted at Hawk Mountain helped provide evidence that led to the banning of DDT, an insecticide that greatly diminished the reproductive capabilities of birds of prey.

In spring, wildflowers dot the wooded slopes below the lookouts. Mountain laurel and rhododendron blossom in June and July.

History. A well-trodden Indian trail, principally used by the Lenni Lenape (Delaware), traversed Kittatinny Ridge. By 1793, when Jacob Gebhardt occupied a stone cottage atop Hawk Mountain, the Lenape had been permanently displaced. The cottage was built alongside the old Indian trail, probably during the American Revolution. By mid-nineteenth century, the trail had widened into a wagon route that carried supplies from the settlements in the Great Valley to the logging camps and coal mines in the mountains.

Gebhardt's cottage was later used as a tavern called "Schaumbochs," which attracted rowdies and suspicious-looking itinerants. Today, the building is a historic landmark.

By the late 1800s, the ridges had been logged clean of chestnut and oak trees. The timbers were used in mine shafts up north or to construct barns in the valley. From time to time, local residents torched the summit to improve the yield of mountain blueberries.

Logging, mining, and berry picking did not stop the hawks from flying along the Kittatinny. They kept to their ancient flight path and their predictable schedule. And that was almost their downfall.

Nobody knows when the first hawk gunner appeared on the ridge, but it did not take long for hordes of hunters to begin deliberately slaughtering the raptors. It became a local pastime, and the hunters declared that they were performing a civic service by ridding the state of these "wanton killers." They would kill hundreds of them at a time, line the carcasses in rows according to species, and take pictures.

One such picture was taken by Dr. Richard Pugh, an ornithologist at the Massachusetts Institute of Technology and the first conservationist to recognize the importance of the Hawk Mountain flyway. He had been informed of the massacres and sped to the Kittatinny one autumn in the early 1930s.

He showed the picture to environmental activist Rosalie Edge, who, with her New York City-based Emergency Conservation Committee, established the world's first sanctuary for birds of prey in 1934 at Hawk Mountain. To keep gunners off the sanctuary, Mrs. Edge hired ornithologist Maurice Broun, who spent the next 32 years on the mountain as the sanctuary's first curator. He wrote about the sanctuary's early years in his book, *Hawks Aloft.*

Over the years, Hawk Mountain Sanctuary has continued to draw bird-watchers and to serve as a center for avian research. About 80,000 people visit the site every year, and many research projects are currently being conducted.

34

Swatara State Park

At the narrowest point of a gap through Blue Mountain, where Swatara Creek squeezes between hard, gray walls of shale and siltstone, you can see what life looked like in a shallow, tropical sea 440 million years ago. Upstream, at a higher elevation, are fossilized creatures of another era. Bring a pick (geologist's) hammer, a cold chisel, a magnifying glass, a field guide, and a bag for fossils.

Ownership. Pennsylvania Department of Environmental Resources, Bureau of State Parks. The fossil site beneath I-81 is owned by the Pennsylvania Department of Transportation.

Size and Designation. The state park comprises 3,330 acres.

Nearby Nature Attractions. Memorial Lake State Park, Middle Creek Wildlife Area, Weiser State Forest, Hawk Mountain

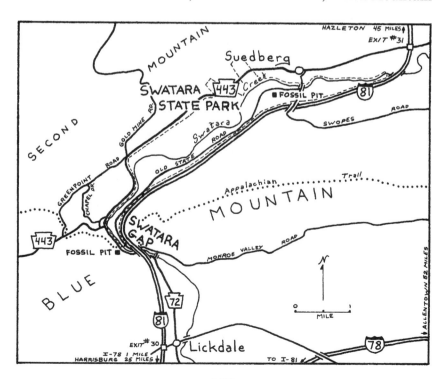

Sanctuary, Blue Marsh Lake Project, and Tulpehocken and Stony creeks, both state-designated rivers. The Appalachian Trail goes through Swatara State Park.

Features. Swatara State Park is one of the few places that allow fossil collecting. Two sites have been designated for this pastime: the Swatara Gap site, an abandoned quarry beneath the northbound lane of I-81 on PA 72; and the Suedberg site, a pit off Swopes Valley Road, south of Suedberg.

About 1.5 miles of the Appalachian Trail traverse the state park near the gap. This is the only developed trail in the park. It crosses the creek just upstream from the Swatara Gap fossil site. An abandoned railroad bed extends along the northwest bank of Swatara Creek. It is overgrown and impassable in places, especially during the summer. If you hike it, look for the old station stops along the route.

Spring is a good time to canoe Swatara Creek, eight miles of which flow through the park.

The park is underdeveloped and lacks facilities such as rest rooms, marked hiking trails, or picnic areas, but these improvements plus an artificial lake are on the drawing board.

Hunting and fishing are permitted in designated areas. Pullovers along PA 443 give hunters and anglers access to the grounds. Trout Run, which flows into Swatara Creek north of the gap, is the only trout-stocked stream in the park. Swatara Creek offers smallmouth bass, pickerel, trout (from stocked streams), and suckers. Wagner's Pond (off Swopes Valley Road) and Irving's Pond (off PA 443) have bluegill, and pumpkinseed. Regulations for hunting and fishing are given in the park guide, available at the park office on PA 443 between Suedberg and Greenpoint.

For more information, contact the Pennsylvania Department of Environmental Resources, Swatara State Park, c/o Memorial Lake State Park, R.R. 1, P.O. Box 7045, Grantville, PA 17028-9682, telephone (717) 865-6470.

Geology. The origin of Pennsylvania's water gaps remains open to debate, though nobody disputes that water did most of the work.

The Appalachian Mountains were formed 290 million years ago, and horizontal strata of bedrock were folded and wrinkled into long, steep, wavy ridges. The impact metamorphosed sedimentary formations into harder rock.

The most southeasterly Appalachian ridge in Pennsylvania is Blue Mountain, or Kittatinny Ridge. The next ridge is Second Mountain. Blue Mountain is capped by a heavy, white to gray quartzite that also contains conglomerates, mostly white quartz pebbles.

Another dense and durable sandstone and conglomerate tops Second Mountain. Both formations resist weathering and erosion.

Swatara Creek may have created the gap in this rock by cutting down through hairline fractures, or cracks. Another theory holds that Swatara Creek had already established a valley before the mountains were uplifted and somehow managed to hold its position and carve the gap. At its widest spot, the gap is a mile across, and at one point it is 800 feet deep.

On the south side of the road cut where I-81 goes through the gap are vertical bands of rock—dark, thin sheets of shale and siltstone and light gray layers of Tuscarora quartzite and conglomerate. Originally these layers were laid horizontally, with the younger rock (then sandstone) on top. What is unusual is that 20 million years of rock layers are missing between these two formations. Geologists call an odd gap like this an unconformity. It often signals the presence of oil, gold, platinum, or other valuable minerals.

The theory to explain this phenomenon is as follows: Over the millennia, there was a cycle of seas flooding land (depositing sediment) and receding (allowing erosion). Sediments eventually buried the older shale and siltstone, and hardened into rock. Later, erosion washed away these topmost layers and exposed the older formation. That was followed by the deposition of sand and quartz pebbles that became the Tuscarora quartzite and conglomerate seen today.

The fossil bed at Swatara Water Gap is a 100-foot wall of finely grained, charcoal-colored shale and coarser brown or gray siltstone. The fossils date back about 440 million years, when a calm, shallow, sunlit sea covered this area. Food was plentiful, and marine life teemed in the undisturbed water. When the sea creatures died, their remains sank to the seafloor, where they were buried by fine clay and silt. Water propelled by gentle waves circulated through the sediment and slowly dissolved the skeletons and shells. After the sea receded, the soupy sediment hardened into rock, and impressions, or molds, of the animals remained in the rock. Sometimes sediment filled the mold to form a cast fossil. The most common fossil found here, however, is a mold.

The Swatara Gap site is especially rich in trilobites, which are found both as whole specimens and in fragments. Lucky diggers may unearth a rare and highly prized starfish, called Hellaster. You can also find various species of brachiopods (fan-shaped shells), gastropods (snails), crinoids (stacks of discs), pelecypods (clam-shaped shells), cephalopods (tubes or nautiluslike curls), and graptolites (delicate spears).

The environment at Suedberg proved ideal for fossils too. The organisms at this site, however, thrived in a different ocean 65 million years later and appear in olive-gray siltstone and claystone dating back 375 million years.

The west end of the pit is the best spot. Here, in lens-shaped formations, you are likely to find molds of brachiopods, bryozoans (coral), and crinoids. Pelecypods appear as white, powdery casts in the claystone (try the east side of the dig). This quarry is more abundant that the one at the gap; every palm-sized rock contained a fossil or two. The impressions are easy to recognize and better preserved. Also, claystone crumbles in your hand, so you won't need tools, but handle the rock carefully.

This fossil site also shows an example of exfoliation, a weathering process in which rock sheds layers. Exfoliation begins when water seeps down joints (a pattern of fractures) in rock strata, in this case shale and siltstone. The water mixes with clay-forming agents, causing stress in the rock block. The clay-bearing shell breaks off, or exfoliates, from the rock core. Advanced exfoliation produces an oval or circular rock.

Trilobites were among the earliest forms of visible life. They lived in warm, shallow seas with other marine life. These extinct arthropods ranged from thumbnail size to about a foot long. Their armored bodies were made up of three lobes, or segments, with jointed legs. Like modern arthropods (lobsters, crabs, and so on), trilobites usually wallowed on the seafloor, though some species floated or propelled themselves.

Crinoids, or sea lilies, had stems made of many disc-shaped segments, tentacles that gripped the seafloor, and flowerlike cups. Thousands of species of crinoids once covered the ocean bottom. A couple hundred varieties still live in tropical seas today. The fan-shaped brachiopods, which live in tepid seas, may be the most abundant type of fossil. Their number has dwindled from 30,000 species 570 million years ago to 250 today. Most were an inch in size, but some grew to nine inches.

Pelecypods are similar to brachiopods, but the shells of pelecypods are mirror images, whereas brachiopods are symmetrical. Pelecypods usually have a slight curve in their shell. Some pelecypods reached lengths of eight to ten inches.

Bryozoans grew in colonies like coral. As fossils, they look like ferns, twigs, and moss mats. The animal's crusty exterior protected vital organs. They are fragile fossils, so be gentle if you find one.

Graptolites look like primitive bryozoans. Some resemble etchings or petroglyphs of plants, one to four inches in length, stamped in rock. These now-extinct animals also grew in colonies.

Cephalopods were the ancestors of octopuses, squids, and nautiluses. The oldest cephalod fossils are straight with suture lines; others have nautiluslike curves. Some grew as long as 15 feet.

Gastropods, snail-like creatures, have held up the best of all early sea animals. Of the 50,000 species that once existed, 35,000 still survive. Fossilized gastropods can be hard to identify, because their shells appear in various shapes and patterns—spiral tubes, coils, cones, and so forth. Certain shell designs match specific geological periods.

Fossilized land plants include the huge lycopods and ferns. Many of these plants later were transformed into coal, a fossil fuel. Pennsylvania's anthracite coal beds begin just a few miles north of Suedberg.

Wildlife. The state park has several habitats—woodland, meadows in various stages of succession, and riparian. These environments host a wide variety of trees, wildflowers, and birds, especially warblers and bluebirds.

In the fall, hawks and other migratory birds follow the crest of Blue Mountain to their wintering grounds. You can observe this phenomenon in the state park, but your best view is on Blue Mountain itself, which you can reach via the Appalachian Trail.

Swatara State Park is home to the black bear, deer, wild turkey, ruffed grouse, pheasant, rabbit, squirrel, muskrat, beaver, weasel, raccoon, opossum, and fox.

History. American Indians used Swatara Creek as a canoe route. One of their trails passed through the gap. The Susquehannocks reigned here when Europeans arrived in the seventeenth century.

By the 1750s, white men had moved into the valley. In the late 1820s, when the demand for nearby coal increased, a branch canal and reservoir connecting the Susquehanna and Schuylkill rivers were constructed along Swatara Creek (in present state park land). The 800-acre lake behind the dam was destroyed by a flood in 1862 and was never rebuilt. The ruins of five canal locks and the dam can still be seen along Old State Road.

A railroad line replaced the canal, but this mode of transportation faded too, supplanted by the interstate highway. The land and creek above the gap are again places for canoes and hiking.

35

Pool Wildlife Sanctuary

This quiet green oasis in the noisy industrial Lehigh Valley serves as the education headquarters for the Wildlands Conservancy, which over 20 years has preserved 16,000 acres of land.

Ownership. The Wildlands Conservancy, an independent, nonprofit land preservation, conservation, and education organization.

Size and Designation. The sanctuary encompasses 72 acres and includes the Trexler Environmental Education Center and conservancy offices.

Nearby Nature Attractions. South Mountain Preserve; Lost River Caverns; and the Lehigh River, a state scenic river. The Appalachian Trail follows the Lehigh-Carbon county line.

Features. More than four miles of hiking trails wind through the sanctuary's woodlands, wetlands, and meadows. Each trail at the sanctuary is a learning experience, from the Backyard Conservation Trail, which shows how to attract wildlife to a backyard, to the Urban Forest Trail, which demonstrates what trees can best survive city conditions, to the Pennsylvania Tree Identification Trail, which will help you learn to recognize Pennsylvania's native trees. Pick up a map at the information kiosk in the parking lot, at the nature center, or at the Harry C. Trexler Environmental Education Center. Other features include an arboretum, a bird blind, a butterfly garden, a wildlife rehabilitation center for injured or abandoned animals, and nature education programs for schoolchildren. The Trexler Center (open Sunday afternoons and other special times) has wildlife exhibits, a children's hands-on discovery room, and a library.

Trails are open daily from dawn to dusk. Office hours are 8 A.M. to 4 P.M., Monday through Friday. For more information, contact Pool Wildlife Sanctuary, The Wildlands Conservancy, 601 Orchid Place, Emmaus, PA 18049, telephone (215) 965-4397.

Geology. The conservancy seeks to protect seven tributaries in the watershed of the Lehigh River, a state scenic river between the Francis E. Walter Reservoir (north of White Haven) and Jim Thorpe. These tributaries are the Little Lehigh Creek, which snakes through the sanctuary, as well as the Jordan, Bushkill, Ontelaunee, Cedar, Monocacy, and Nescopeck creeks.

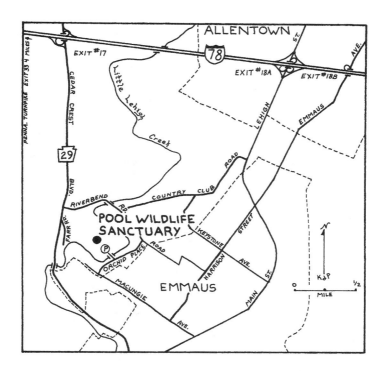

Wildlife. In the sanctuary's woods, you'll find the tulip tree, shagbark hickory, and other hardwoods. In spring, look for the mayapple *(Podophyllum peltatum)* on the forest floor. Hemlock, aspen, red maple, sycamore, black walnut, spruce, American elm, white and red oaks, red cedar, and birch also grow on the grounds. Multiflora rose, honeysuckle, and wild grape are abundant.

The sanctuary protects two imperiled plants: the broad-leaved water plantain *(Alisma plantago-aquatica* var. *americana,* PA endangered), and horned pondweed *(Zannichellia palustris,* PA possible decline).

A bird checklist is available. Birds in residence year-round include the red-bellied and hairy woodpeckers, cedar waxwing, northern mockingbird, black-capped chickadee, belted kingfisher, ring-necked pheasant, cardinal, and song sparrow. Also look for the American woodcock and sharp-shinned hawk.

The refuge is home to the red fox, groundhog, muskrat, and squirrel. Brown and rainbow trouts live in Little Lehigh Creek.

History. The sanctuary land was farmed beginning in the late eighteenth century. When Leonard Parker Pool became the owner, he established 42 plantations of trees and shrubs so that wildlife would have adequate food, shelter, and nesting areas.

The Trexler Center was named for Harry C. Trexler, who established reserves for elk and bison, donated 12,000 acres to the state for Hickory Run State Park, and helped create parks in Allentown.

36

South Mountain Preserve

Though surrounded by urban development, this trackless refuge attracts 143 kinds of birds, 34 species of reptiles and amphibians, and several mammals.

Ownership. The Wildlands Conservancy, a nonprofit land preservation and education organization.

Size and Designation. This nature preserve totals 250 acres.

Nearby Nature Attractions. Pool Wildlife Sanctuary (headquarters of the Wildlands Conservancy) and Lost River Caverns. The Appalachian Trail follows Lehigh County's northern border.

Features. Unmarked trails begin at the end of Alpine Street. These paths meander through the preserve. Remember your route

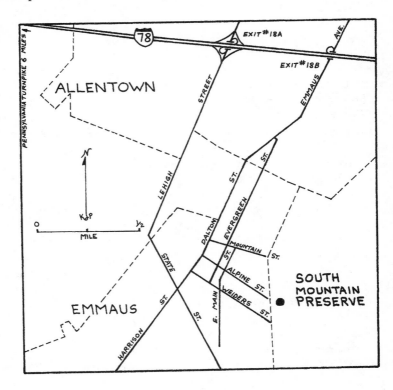

because there are no maps, signs, or blazes to help you. The Wildlands Conservancy holds its spring peeper and owl programs here. You will find rest rooms and picnic tables at a nearby municipal park. For more information, contact the Wildlands Conservancy, Pool Wildlife Sanctuary, 601 Orchid Place, Emmaus, PA 18049, telephone (610) 965-4397.

Geology. South Mountain Preserve rises in a geological region known as the Reading Prong, the southern terminus of a ridge that extends across New Jersey and into New York. During the creation of the Appalachian Mountains, a thin slab of granite slid off a tilted mountain to the southeast and formed this ridge. This rock is among the oldest in Pennsylvania dating back more than 570 million years, and it resists erosion. Iron ore was extracted from the mountain in the nineteenth century. The ridge emits radioactive radon gas, resulting from the decay of uranium in the rock.

Wildlife. Tulip tree, sweet birch, red, chestnut, and black oaks, and red maple stand in the forest. Spicebush and poison ivy are abundant.

Spring rains replenish permanent ponds and create vernal, or seasonal, ponds. These attract spotted salamanders, spring peepers, and wood and green frogs. When it rains in March, Jefferson salamanders emerge from their burrows and head for the vernal pools. They spend about three weeks breeding, then they return to their burrows and resume reclusive lives.

Other amphibians are the dusky, two-lined, spring, red-backed, red, and slimy salamanders; red-spotted newt; American toad; and gray tree, pickerel, and leopard frogs.

Reptiles include the bog turtle (PA endangered), and the snapping, wood, spotted, painted, red-eared pond slider, and musk turtles; and ringneck, black rat, black racer, eastern milk, northern water, northern brown, and eastern garter snakes.

The bog turtle, the smallest turtle in the world, and once a popular pet store species, has bright splashes of orange on its neck. The wood turtle (declining in population) has orange-red skin and a heavy, keeled top shell, or carapace. Each section on the carapace rises to a peak encircled with concentric grooves.

One-hundred-forty-three species of birds have been observed here, including 15 kinds of warblers, the common loon, and golden eagle. Also seen here are swallowtail butterflies and walkingsticks.

Mammals include deer, red fox, and skunk.

History. South Mountain Preserve was given to the Wildlands Conservancy as a gift by Robert Rodale, then owner of Rodale Press in Allentown. Acquisitions from other landowners have increased the size of the preserve to 250 acres.

37

Lost River Caverns

W ater is a powerful erosive agent below Earth's surface as well as on it. About 150 feet beneath the streets of Hellertown, an underground waterway carves intricate formations known as straws, drip stones, drapes, popcorn, and flowstones. Clusters of star-shaped anthodite crystals grow in the darkness.

Ownership. Privately owned.

Size and Designation. About 1,000 feet of the caverns are open to the public. Spelunkers have explored 1,969 feet of passageways.

Nearby Nature Attractions. Jacobsburg Environmental Education Center and Delaware Water Gap National Recreation Area. The Appalachian Trail follows the Northampton-Monroe county line.

Features. Guided tours take you along well-trodden, well-lit underground trails. Steps descend about 150 feet into the passages. There are a couple of narrow tunnels and several open chambers.

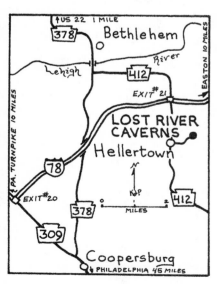

Dress appropriately: The temperature in the caverns is a constant 52 degrees, even in the summer. Eating, smoking, and rock collecting are not permitted.

While you wait for the tour to begin, enjoy the tropical garden and the Gilman Museum, which includes mounted animals and antique guns. Souvenir and rock shops await you at the end of the tour. Rest rooms and drinking water are available, as are picnic tables and trailer camping. The caverns are open daily from 9 A.M. to 6 P.M. Memorial Day to Labor Day, and 9 A.M. to 5 P.M. the rest of the year. There is an admission fee. For more information, contact Lost River Caverns, Box M, Hellertown, PA 18055, telephone (610) 838-8767.

Geology. The story of Lost River Caverns begins about 570 million years ago. For long periods of time, the region had been covered by seas teeming with marine life. When the sea creatures died, their calcium-rich remains accumulated in thick beds on the ocean floor. These sediments hardened into limestone and dolomite, later buried by layers of sandstone and shale.

When the continental plates crashed into each other and formed the Appalachian Mountains, the sedimentary rock layers became jostled, tilted, fractured, and uplifted. During this time, the limestone and dolomite were raised above the water table. Over millions of years, erosion removed the overlaying sedimentary rocks and allowed surface water and groundwater to seep through the cracks in the limestone and dolomite. Because the percolating water was often slightly acidic, it dissolved the rock en route to the water table, widening cracks and creating passageways and chambers underground.

The water that drips and trickles in the cave carries calcium carbonate in solution. As it travels, it releases carbon dioxide molecule by molecule and deposits calcite, the mineral that makes the cave formations. Over the centuries, the calcite crystals accumulated into stalactites (hanging from the ceiling of the cave), stalagmites (growing from the floor), columns, drapes (leaf-shaped formations), and other creations.

Stalactites start when calcite forms a ring around a drop hanging from the ceiling. As the process continues, a hollow soda straw develops, with water dripping outside and inside the tube. Eventually the inside tube clogs, but the stalactite continues to grow outward. Stalagmites develop in tiny puddles on the cave floor, sometimes directly below dripping stalactites. Stalactites sometimes merge with stalagmites to form columns.

Lost Caverns boasts coil-shaped stalactites called helicitites as well as uncommon anthodite stars. The crystals in the stars are huge, indicating that they grew slowly under special conditions. Gypsum or aragonite (calcium minerals) may be present in anthodite crystals. The reddish brown color on some formations is rusted iron oxide from the water. Zinc creates gray smears.

When caverns become flooded, which happens from time to time, silt, sand, and clay settle on the formations and occasionally fill rooms. Calcite that flows out on top of the sediment is known as flowstone. Another period of high water usually removes the sediment, leaving flowstone shelves and terraces.

Wildlife. Few creatures live in the caverns—a few insects, spiders, worms, and possibly salamanders. Colonies of algae thrive in illuminated areas. Algal spores were carried into the caverns on visitors' clothing. Nutrient-bearing cave water and the glow of electric lights keep the algae alive.

History. The caverns have been an attraction since they were discovered by limestone miners in the 1880s. Bootleggers reportedly hid their contraband in the passages during Prohibition.

During a drought in 1981-82, the water table fell and passages opened, but they became flooded again the following year. Scientists have been unable to find a surface outlet for the water inside the caverns.

38

Monroe Border Fault

Don't come a long way to see the Monroe Border Fault, but it's worth a peek if you are in the neighborhood. Here, a gash opened in Earth 200 to 250 million years ago reveals the oldest rocks in Pennsylvania overlaying the youngest.

Ownership. Multiple private owners.

Size and Designation. The U.S. Department of the Interior designated the fault a national natural landmark in 1980.

Nearby Nature Attractions. Bowman's Hill Wildflower Preserve; Bristol Marsh Preserve; Honey Hollow Environmental Education Center; David R. Johnson State Forest Natural Area; Silver Lake, Churchville, and Peace Valley nature centers; Ringing Rocks County Park; Tyler, Delaware Canal, Nockamixon, Ralph Stover, and Neshaminy state parks.

Features. The site is located on private property. Get owners' permission if you want to park and explore it. There is a small parking lot half a mile north, at the intersection of PA 611 and Durham Road (PA 212).

Geology. Sometime during the Triassic Period, 220 million years ago, rumblings deep within Earth began to break apart the

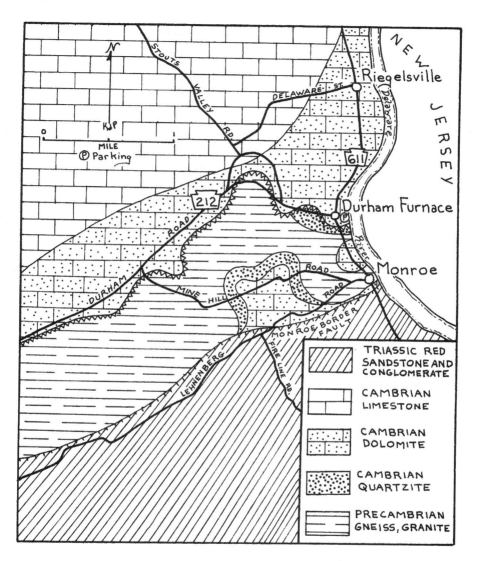

supercontinent of Pangaea. As the continents drifted apart and
forces pushed upward from deep inside Earth, the crust snapped
along faults, or break lines, in the bedrock. Rifts occurred along
these faults. Most of these rifts are buried beneath the continental
shelf of the Atlantic Ocean. The Monroe Border Fault is one of only
a few exposed rifts in the eastern United States. Here the fault
runs east-west. The southern block dropped and created an escarpment, or cliff, on the north side that reveals Earth's earlier history.

On this north face are igneous rocks (gneiss and granite) dating back perhaps a billion years. These ancient rocks have sustained repeated shocks from continents colliding, retracting, and eroding.

Oddly, these rocks overlay younger quartzite, dolomite, and limestone dating from 500 to 570 million years ago. Geologist calculate that during a mountain-building period 290 million years ago, a plate of the older granite rock slid off a tall ridge to the southeast, then became twisted and folded like the younger formations.

South of the fault, there is different and much younger bedrock that originated shortly after the fault developed. The rift created a deep valley south of the fault. Lakes and swamps spread out in the valley, and dinosaurs browsed on tropical vegetation. Over millions of years, the streams falling over the escarpment filled the basin with sediment. The currents carried enough debris to form the red sandstone, shale, and conglomerate that are characteristic south of the fault.

Wildlife. The formation is covered by a hardwood forest consisting of trees and vegetation typical for the area. As the area is privately owned, no wildlife survey has been done.

History. A village called Monroe existed nearby until the 1930s. A few businesses, a roadside inn, and some residences remain.

39

Ringing Rocks County Park

Every year, thousands of hammer-toting people come to rap on these 175-million-year-old rocks. After you've explored the boulder field, view the nearby High Falls, a ribbonlike cascade in a charming glen at the end of the main trail. Children find the rocks and waterfalls especially compelling.

Ownership. Bucks County Department of Parks and Recreation.

Size and Designation. 70 acres.

Nearby Nature Attractions. Silver Lake, Churchville, and Peace Valley nature centers; Bristol Marsh Preserve; David R.

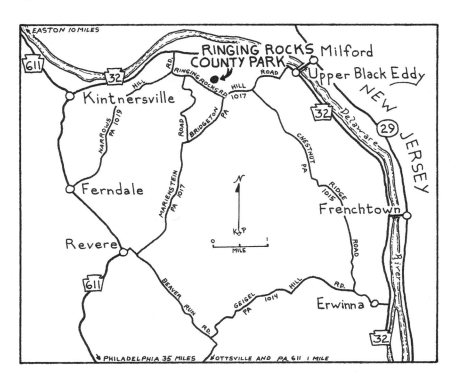

Johnson State Forest Natural Area; Honey Hollow Environmental Center; Monroe Border Fault; Bowman's Hill Wildflower Preserve; Delaware Canal, Nockamixon, Neshaminy, Ralph Stover, and Tyler state parks.

Features. The left fork of the hiking trail leads to the southern edge of the boulder field; the right fork (main trail) takes you to the boulder field and then to High Falls. To hear the rocks ring, make your way to the center of the field, beyond the range of shade, and lightly strike the stones with a hammer (or metal bar or wrench). Avoid using a sledgehammer or crowbar, which would chip and deface the rocks. A small hammer and light tap are sufficient. If the first rock does not ring—not all of them do—tap another one. Every third or fourth boulder rings, and has its own sound. Wear safety glasses; rock chips may cause injury.

High Falls is a 30-foot cascade in a large amphitheater, with a brook flowing over a pocked, solid rock streambed. Don't bother tapping the boulders along the trail to High Falls. They are all duds.

The park is open daily from dawn to dusk and has rest rooms and picnic tables.

For more information, contact the Bucks County Department of Parks and Recreation, Core Creek Park, 901 E. Bridgetown Park, Langhorne, PA 19047, telephone (215) 757-0571.

Geology. Long ago, this part of Bucks County was submerged beneath Lake Lockatong. As time progressed, the lake collected sediment (mostly mud and clay), which eventually hardened into shale. Later, about 190 million years ago, magma from the earth's interior was injected into the shale and formed thin horizontal shelves, or sills, of igneous rock known as diabase sandwiched between the shale beds. Over the years, erosion washed away the topmost less-resistant shale and exposed the diabase.

As the hot magma intruded, it caused the shale it touched to metamorphose into an impervious rock called hornfels. The boulder field now rests on a crust of hornfels.

Though continental glaciers never covered Bucks County, the frosty climate produced by ice masses only a dozen miles away contributed to the formation of the boulder field. The diabase was exposed to near glacial conditions similar to today's high alpine climates. Repeated freezing and thawing broke the diabase into flat boulders and frost heave pressed the boulders toward the surface. The chunks of diabase in this boulder field probably rolled off the edge of a sill and accumulated here. The cold temperatures, combined with rain washing away soil, prevented plant life from colonizing the field. What developed was a vast boulder-strewn field without soil or vegetation—a sea of rocks.

As the climate warmed and the glacier retreated, the forest gradually moved into the boulder field. The remaining barren boulder field is about 3.5 acres.

In 1965, scientists sought to learn why some of these boulders resonate. They discovered that water penetrated two to three inches into the boulders and reacted chemically with elements in the rock in a process called chemical weathering. Being an igneous rock, diabase contains a high concentration of pyroxene, a group of minerals known for their dark color and hardness. When contacted by water, pyroxene changes into a clay called montmorillonite. At the surface of the ringing boulders, montmorillonite had largely replaced pyroxene; deeper in the rock, less of the pyroxene had been transformed to montmorillonite. Montmorillonite takes up more space than pyroxene. As a result, the shells of these boulders have expanded and become tense. This stress produces the ring. Diabase also contains a big dose of iron, which helps produce sound waves. The uppermost sills of diabase cooled exceptionally fast because they were close to the surface. This factor also added stress.

Boulders stuck in soil or shaded by trees retain their water longer. Consequently, weathering occurs too fast and the rocks break up or never establish the state of stress needed to resonate. The sunbaked boulders in the middle of the field, on the other hand, don't retain water for a long time, so weathering and frost damage happen slowly, and these rocks build up the stress necessary to produce the ring. Buried or wedged boulders in the field do not ring, however, because their resonance is muffled.

At High Falls, note how the bedrock has been peeled away, and its odd slant toward the boulder field and the Delaware River.

Wildlife. Species of trees, shrubs, and vines in the park—numbering 44—include eastern hemlock, black birch, tulip tree, sugar maple, white oak, witch hazel, mapleleaf viburnum, and greenbriar. At least 11 kinds of ferns have been found here, notably rattlesnake, long beech, marginal shield, and little ebony spleenwort.

Wildflowers include white snakeroot *(Eupatorium rugosum),* wild geranium *(Geranium maculatum),* hepatica *(Hepatica americana),* Canada mayflower *(Maianthemum canadense),* white wood aster *(Aster divaricatus),* hog peanut *(Amphicarpa bracteata),* horse balm *(Collinsonia canadensis),* white baneberry *(Actaea pachypolda),* swamp saxifrage *(Saxifrage pensylvanica),* lion's-foot *(Prenanthes serpentaria),* and heal-all *(Prunella vulgaris).*

The wood thrush, blue jay, swallow, eastern wood pewee, downy and red-bellied woodpeckers, great-crested flycatcher, warblers, cardinal, crow, and great horned owl, have been observed among the hemlock.

History. Dr. J. J. Ott held a "rock concert" in June 1890, with members of the Buckwampum Historical Society as an audience. Ott had discovered an octave scale among the rocks, and tapped out a tune in the boulder field with a hammer. A brass band accompanied him.

The ringing rock field now is a county park.

Blue Marsh Lake Project

Primarily a haven for outdoor recreation, Blue Marsh offers a few quiet nature hikes and some 200 species of birds.

Ownership. U.S. Army Corps of Engineers, Philadelphia District.

Size and Designation. The area totals 6,200 acres. About 2,500 acres are leased to the Pennsylvania Game Commission, which assists the Corps of Engineers with wildlife management.

Nearby Nature Attractions. Hawk Mountain Sanctuary, Ruth Zimmerman State Forest Natural Area, Nolde Forest Environmental Education Center, French Creek State Park, and Tulpehocken Creek and the Schuylkill River, both state scenic waterways. The Appalachian Trail meanders through Weiser State Forest along the Berks-Schuylkill county line.

Features. Blue Marsh Lake, a Corps of Engineers project, appeals to swimmers, boaters (unlimited horsepower), water sport enthusiasts, picnickers, hikers, cross-country skiers, fishers, and hunters.

From the Dry Brooks Day Use Area, you can hike the 3/4-mile Great Oak Nature Trail on the east side of the area, and the longer Foxtrot Loop on the west side (accessible from the swimming beach).

Another interpretive trail, the Squirrel Run Nature Trail, branches from the State Hill Boat Ramp on the south shore. This 3/4-mile loop trail is usually quieter and less crowded than the Great Oak path, and more compelling. To get there from the Dry Brooks area, continue east (right) on Palisades Road, and turn right on Reber Bridge Road. After passing State Hill Road, the road becomes Brownsville Road. Just ahead, on the right, turn into the driveway for the boat ramp. The trailhead is at the left near the bottom of the hill. Before leaving the recreation area, stop at the hilltop overlook.

Ambitious hikers can take a 14.5-mile trail between Church Road and the dam at Stilling Basin. It roughly traces the southern shoreline of the lake. Begin at the State Hill Boat Ramp.

Trail maps and interpretive guides for the Great Oak and Squir-

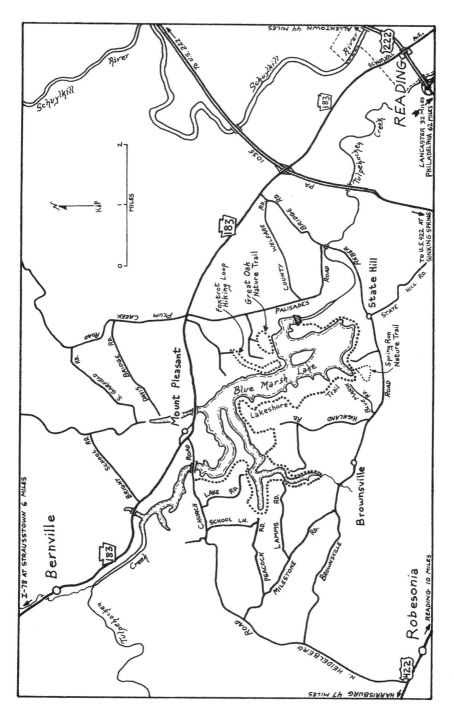

rel Run nature trails are available at the ranger station and administration building on Palisades Road, or contact Blue Marsh Lake Project, U.S. Army Corps of Engineers, Philadelphia District, R.D. 1, Box 1239, Leesport, PA 19533, telephone (215) 376-6337 or 6338.

Boaters can launch their craft from the Dry Brooks, State Hill, or Sheidy boat ramps. Check park rules before launching.

Geology. The impoundment built in the late 1970s altered the course and velocity of this section of Tulpehocken Creek. Before the dam was built, the stream twisted freely through rolling farmland. Fierce periodic flooding—all part of the natural process—destroyed human settlements on its fertile banks.

Today Blue Marsh Lake stretches for eight miles, with a surface area of about 1,150 acres, depending on the water level. The lake can hold 16 billion gallons; during the summer recreation period, it stores about 7.7 billion gallons.

Control gates (sluiceways) in the concrete tower beside the dam now regulate the Tulpehocken's flow. When the lake level approaches the crest of the dam, gates open and release water to control flooding. Releases also cool downstream water temperatures during the summer, which benefits stocked trout.

Wildlife. A quarter of the land remains wooded, with white and red oaks predominating. Other trees include black and chestnut oaks, shagbark hickory, tulip tree, beech, dogwood, sassafras, white ash, black cherry, black walnut, red and silver maples, American hornbeam, hackberry, and spicebush. There are also many areas of successional growth—meadows and former farmland in various stages of returning to forest.

Some 200 species of birds frequent the wetland, meadow, successional, and forest habitats. Pick up a bird checklist at the ranger station. Common residents include the Canada goose, mallard, red-bellied woodpecker, killdeer, eastern phoebe, belted kingfisher, wood thrush, and common yellowthroat warbler. Migratory birds, from waterfowl to warblers, arrive in spring, including the osprey, great blue heron, and egret. The black-crowned night heron, tricolored heron, tundra swan, snow goose, American bittern, hooded merganser, and bufflehead duck occasionally show up at the lake, and a bald eagle, peregrine falcon, or sharp-shinned hawk may soar above the shore. In the fields, look for ring-necked pheasant, woodcock, and an occasional bobwhite. Great horned, barn, and screech owls hoot at dusk.

History. In 1955, floods along several tributaries of the Delaware and Schuylkill rivers killed 90 people and caused $100 million in property damage. The devastation prompted a congressional flood control study of the Delaware River basin. Blue March

Lake was a product of that study. Construction of the earthen dam near the Dry Brooks Day Use Area started in 1974 and was completed in January 1979. During construction, the Corps of Engineers moved the historic Gruber Wagon Works to a site on higher ground five miles away. Erected in 1882, the shop produced hundreds of wagons before it closed in the 1950s. Today, Gruber Wagon Works is listed on the National Register of Historic Places, and the restored carpentry shop and foundry are the centerpiece of Berks County's Heritage Center.

41

Nolde Forest Environmental Center

In 1904, German immigrant Jacob Nolde bought 500 acres of played-out farmland. On one tract, a lone white pine that had avoided the logger's ax and the farmer's plow towered above the deciduous saplings. This was a sign to Nolde that a pine forest could be planted here. Today the tree, called the Inspiration Pine, still reigns over an evergreen and deciduous forest.

Ownership. Pennsylvania Department of Environmental Resources, Bureau of State Parks.

Size and Designation. 665 acres.

Nearby Nature Attractions. Hawk Mountain Sanctuary, Blue Marsh Lake Project, French Creek State Park, Ruth Zimmerman State Forest Natural Area, and the Schuylkill River and Tulpehocken Creek, both scenic rivers. The Appalachian Trail and Weiser State Forest straddle the Berks and Schuylkill county line.

Features. Nolde Forest is a natural area and an environmental education center with ten miles of hiking trails. Opportunities abound for bird-watching, nature photography, and field research. Fishing is permitted in Angelica Creek, but hunting is forbidden. Horseback riding is available on designated trails. The Inspiration Pine can be seen midway between the sawmill and the curator's home.

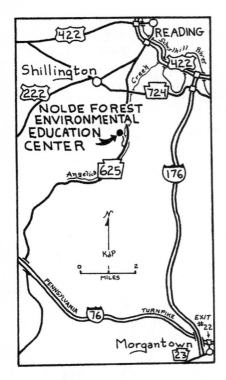

The Boulevard and Watershed trails begin at the teaching station on the road that runs behind the mansion. (This road is closed to motor vehicles.) The trails split a few steps into the woods, with the Boulevard Trail staying on the north side of a rill called Punches Run and the Watershed Trail weaving a path on the south side. At a landmark called Lower Reservoir, the Boulevard Trail starts a huge loop into the northwestern section of the property. Take the right leg of the loop to reach a rock outcrop of diabase. Visitors in wheelchairs can navigate two short, paved trails, one circling behind Nolde Mansion, the other following a loop near the sawmill entrance. The trails are open daily from dawn to dusk. Trail maps are available in the lobby of the mansion.

The Nolde Mansion, the center's administration building, and McConnell Hall are open Monday through Friday from 8 A.M. to 4 P.M. and on weekends and evenings when programs are held.

The center specializes in environmental and natural history classes for preschoolers through high school seniors. Teachers also attend workshops here, and the center helps school districts develop environmental education programs for classrooms. For more information, contact Nolde Forest Environmental Education Center, R.D. 1, Box 392, Reading, PA 19807, telephone (610) 775-1411.

Geology. Beneath Nolde Forest lie two very different types of bedrock dating back 193 to 230 million years (Late Triassic and Early Jurassic periods). A reddish brown sandstone, sprinkled with quartz pebbles and shale, underlays the southern and central section of the woods. This conglomerate is the sediment of an eroded mountain range.

Diabase, an igneous rock, lies beneath the northern third of the grounds. This rock can be seen on a slope along the Boulevard Trail. Once liquid molten rock deep inside the earth, it bubbled to the surface when a rift in the earth's crust occurred 200 million years ago.

The small brooks traversing this rolling terrain generally flow northeast and empty into Angelica Creek, which flows into the Schuylkill River about two miles downstream. Two small ponds on the property support aquatic life. North Pond is refreshed by runoff, and springs feed Painted Turtle Pond.

Wildlife. Though conifers were planted on 310 acres of Nolde Forest, they dominate on only 213 acres today, having lost some ground to the hardwoods. Healthy groves of Norway spruce and white pine preside over smaller stands of Douglas fir, Japanese larch, and red pine. A hardwood forest blankets the remaining 436 acres of the forest, chiefly tulip tree, red maple, black cherry, American beech, black and yellow birches, and red, white, chestnut, and black oaks. Ninety-two kinds of trees and shrubs thrive in these soils. Some, such as hackberry, white ash, black walnut, and shagbark hickory, are found only in small numbers.

Three hundred species of wildflowers brighten the forest floor, trail sides, wetland clearings, and small fields. Look for scarlet pimpernel *(Anagallis arvensis),* devil's walking stick *(Aralia spinosa),* field pussytoes *(Antennaria neglecta),* black mustard *(Brassica nigra),* dittany *(Cunila origanoides),* enchanter's nightshade *(Circaea quadrisulcata),* and two state-protected flowers: wild bleeding heart *(Dicentra eximia),* listed as rare, and ginseng *(Panax quinquefolius),* considered vulnerable.

The preserve boasts 45 kinds of grasses; 20 species of ferns, including northern maidenhair and hay-scented; 20 species of sedges; and patches of ground cedar, shining club moss, tree club moss, and ground pine.

Woodland inhabitants include the star-nosed mole, Norway rat, deer, opossum, long-tailed weasel, muskrat, and red bat. A couple of spots have been boxed off to determine the effects of overbrowsing by deer and the regenerative power of the forest.

Birdwatchers have spotted 110 species in the preserve, notably the northern goshawk (PA rare); sharp-shinned, Cooper's, red-tailed, broad-winged, and rough-legged hawks; pileated woodpecker; scarlet tanager; indigo bunting; eastern bluebird; yellow-bellied sapsucker; pine siskin; and golden-crowned kinglet. Warblers arrive in the spring, including the pine, blackpoll, Cape May, northern parula, black-and-white, magnolia, chestnut-sided, blue-winged, and Wilson's. A checklist is available in the lobby of Nolde Mansion.

Other residents include the northern spring peeper, snapping turtle, and black rat snake. Angelica Creek and Punches Run (no fishing) support native brown and brook trout. Rainbows are stocked in Angelica Creek. Waters in the preserve are also home to white sucker, redbreast sunfish, largemouth bass, and bluegill.

History. Before Europeans arrived, the slopes above Angelica Creek supported a lush oak-chestnut forest. Early settlers cleared the gentler slopes for subsistence farms. This logging was minor, however, compared with the clear-cutting that occurred after iron forges were built along Angelica Creek. The oaks were cut for charcoal to fire the forges. By 1870 the forges had vanished, and so had the hardwood forest.

Nolde bought 500 acres of the depleted land in 1904, desiring to restore the farmland into a pine forest. To that end, he hired a German forester in 1906 and began planting conifers. Over the years, Nolde continued to add to his holdings and plant trees. Between 1913 and 1929, 1.4 million conifers were rooted on 310 acres, 75 percent of them Norway spruce. Ninety percent of the plantings lived, a phenomenal survival rate. The forest stayed in the family until 1966, when the commonwealth of Pennsylvania purchased the property. In the early 1970s, an environmental education center was opened on the grounds.

42

Ruth Zimmerman State Forest Natural Area

As you hike through this trackless hardwood forest, be careful not to mistake a turtle for a stone and step on it. The cobbles are chips off the Reading Prong, a granite flake that toppled off an ancient mountain range.

Ownership. Pennsylvania Department of Environmental Resource, Bureau of Forestry.

Size and Designation. This 33-acre wetland forest became a state forest natural area in 1993.

Nearby Nature Attractions. Hawk Mountain Sanctuary, Nolde Forest Environmental Education Center, French Creek State Park, Blue Marsh Lake Recreation Area, Weiser State Forest, and the Schuylkill River and Tulpehocken Creek, both state scenic

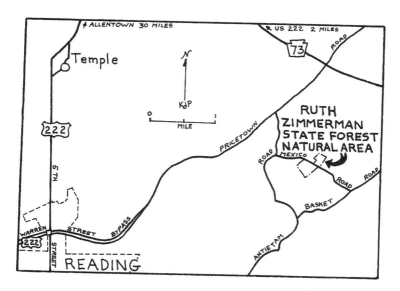

waterways. The Appalachian Trail follows the Berks-Schuylkill county line.

Features. This small, trackless preserve offers solitude and peace, but no accommodations. Note the signs on both sides of the road that mark the boundary of the preserve. Stay off private property, and do not block farm lanes.

Geology. The preserve sits at the southern edge of the Reading Prong, a ridge of granite that extends into New York. This thin slab likely slid off lofty mountains to the southeast during the mountain-building event that formed the Appalachians 290 million years ago.

The Reading Prong contains some of the oldest rock in Pennsylvania—granite dating back more than 570 million years. Granite is an igneous rock that originated as molten rock. Radioactive radon gas, a natural by-product of decaying uranium, rises from the ridge.

The brook flowing through the preserve is Antietam Creek. It trickles from a nearby farm pond, rolls down the ridge, and empties into the Schuylkill River a few miles southeast of Reading.

Wildlife. The moist forest here is mixed, with oaks, red and sugar maples, American beech, black cherry, tulip tree, shagbark hickory, flowering dogwood, hornbeam, and ironwood.

Bloodroot *(Sanguinaria canadensis),* spring beauty *(Claytonia virginica),* mayapples *(Podophyllum peltatum),* and various violets and ferns grow on the forest floor.

Tracks in the mud reveal the presence of deer. The preserve is also home to the fox, raccoon, and box turtle. Box turtles may live for 80 years in an area only 300 to 700 square feet. They nibble on small plants, mushrooms, berries, and dead aquatic animals. In winter, box turtles hibernate in pond bottoms, streambeds, or tree stumps, usually emerging in April.

History. The Pennsylvania Department of Environmental Resources designated this place a state forest natural area in 1993.

43

French Creek State Park

Hopewell Furnace National Historic Site

Pennsylvania's oldest and youngest rocks reach the surface in this area where hikers can experience the feeling of the "big woods."

Some of the state's purest water flows in French Creek. This state scenic river begins its journey to the Schuylkill River at Hopewell Lake. Pine Swamp, a rare, acidic broadleaf mire, drips into Pine Creek, a state-designated stream that feeds French Creek.

Ownership. Pennsylvania Department of Environmental Resources, Bureau of State Parks. Hopewell Furnace National Historic Site is managed by the National Park Service.

Size and Designation. 7,339 acres. French Creek, which drains the park's Hopewell Lake, has been designated a scenic river. The 98-acre Pine Swamp is a state park natural area.

Nearby Nature Attractions. Marsh Creek and White Clay Creek state parks, Nolde Forest Environmental Education Center, Valley Forge National Historic Park, Blue Marsh Lake Project, Ruth Zimmerman State Forest Natural Area, Great Valley Nature Center, the Serpentine Barrens, Hawk Mountain Sanctuary, and five state-designated scenic rivers: the Schuylkill River, and French, Brandywine, Tulpehocken, and Octoraro creeks.

Features. French Creek State Park has much to offer: campgrounds, cabins, equestrian camping, picnicking, swimming pool, cross-country skiing, boating, fishing, hunting, horseback riding, disc golf, and orienteering. Eight hiking trails totaling 35 miles are

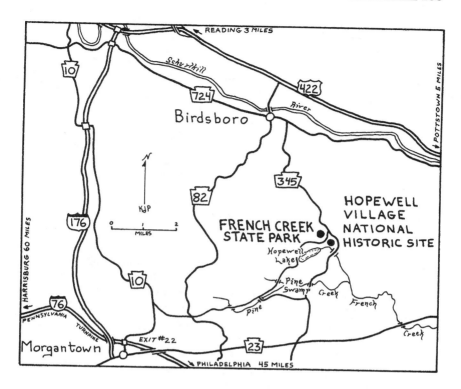

open every day from sunrise to sunset. The six-mile Boone Trail, named after Daniel Boone, who grew up nearby, leads to the Hopewell fire tower (now closed) and Hopewell Furnace. The Horseshoe Trail, a 120-mile walking and bridle trail from Valley Forge National Historic Park to Rattling Run Gap, goes through the park and the adjoining national historic site.

For more information, contact the Department of Environmental Resources, French Creek State Park, 843 Park Road, Elverson, PA 19520-9523, telephone (610) 582-9680.

Hopewell Furnace National Historic Site, a historic ironworks, is open daily 9 A.M. to 5 P.M. The entrance is a mile south of the state park main entrance on PA 345. There is a small admission fee. For more information, contact Hopewell Furnace National. Historic Site, 2 Mark Bird Lane, Elverson, PA 19520, telephone (610) 582-8773.

Geology. You can see three distinct rock groups as you hike to the Hopewell fire tower via the Boone Trail. Hopewell Lake, at the trailhead, lies on a pinkish, pebbly sandstone. Bands of red sandstone and shale appear at about the halfway point. The tower stands on Williams Hill, a ridge of grayish red conglomerate that originated as stream sediment 195 to 245 million years ago. Dinosaur tracks have been found in nearby rock of similar age.

To the southeast are older ridges of quartzite, such as Mount Pleasant. The Horseshoe Trail, heading southeast from the eastern end of Hopewell Lake, goes past a talus slope, or rock slide, of quartzite. These rocks likely broke off from an outcrop during the ice age 12,000 to 15,000 years ago. Though the Wisconsinan glacier stopped 50 miles to the north, the weather here was cold enough for ice crystals to form in fractures and break the outcrop into boulders.

The quartzite began as sandstone 500 to 570 million years ago. Some of the quartzite boulders on the west side of the slope, near PA 345, reveal sediment-filled tubes a quarter inch in diameter and a foot long. These tiny tunnels are skolithos, the excavations of soft-bodied worms that once burrowed in the sandy beaches.

At the summit, many quartzite boulders show the white vein markings of quartz injections. These veins are younger than the quartzite, as the injections filled cracks and fractures in the rock.

Precambrian gneiss boulders, the oldest rocks in the park, flank PA 345 in the southern end of the historic site. The surface of these igneous rocks is reddish brown because of the weathering of their iron content. In other words, they have rusted.

Miller's Point is a knob of diabase rock, the youngest rock in the park. Here, molten rock was injected into cracks and faults and crystallized into igneous rock deep within the earth's crust. This activity, called an intrusion, occurred 135 to 195 million years ago. In places, the diabase is more than a mile thick. This iron-rich rock is dark gray, but its surface is rust-colored. Weathering and erosion crumbled the diabase into hugh blocks.

The diabase was mined here in the late nineteenth and early twentieth centuries, hence the quarry in the north part of the park. Polished diabase, marketed as black granite, was a popular ornamental and architectural stone at the time.

From 1958 to 1977, Bethlehem Steel Corporation excavated 45 million tons of ore from a mine north of Morgantown. The iron-rich ore was used to fuel the stoves at Hopewell Furnace.

Wildlife. More than 500 different plants have been recorded in the Hopewell Furnace area, and 200 of them live in Pine Swamp. This area is a swampy forest with several meadows. Actually, no evergreens grow in Pine Swamp. Water from the swamp drains into Pine Creek, which gives the swamp its name. This waterway merges with French Creek a mile outside the park.

Pine Swamp is an acidic broadleaf swamp, an unusual habitat in the region. Swamp white oak, red maple, green ash, pin oak, arrowwood *(Virburnum recognitum),* highbush blueberry, and swamp rose *(Rosa palustris)* predominate. All totaled, 33 kinds of trees and shrubs can be found in the swamp.

A rare plant, bog bluegrass *(Poa paludigena,* PA threatened), hides in this protected spot. This small, wispy grass grows on hummocks that anchor trees and shrubs. Three state-endangered plants colonize Pine Swamp: branched bur reed *(Sparganium androcladum),* southern water plantain *(Alisma plantago-aquatica),* and short hair (fringed) sedge *(Carex crinita* var. *brevicrinis).* Bushy beardgrass *(Andropogon glomeratus)* and brown sedge *(Carex buxbaumii),* which are declining in population, find refuge here.

Pine Swamp abounds with 17 varieties of ferns, including rattlesnake, reddish lady, royal, and ebony spleenwort. Cinnamon and sensitive ferns predominate.

Blossoms abound from early spring through autumn. Look for the blueberry lily *(Belamcanda chinensis),* bog wrinkle-leaf goldenrod *(Solidago rugosa* var. *sphagnophila),* square-stemmed monkey flower *(Mimulus ringens),* hooked crowfoot *(Ranunculus recurvatus),* mad-dog skullcap *(Scutellaria lateriflora),* long-leaved chickweed *(Stellaria longifolia),* hog peanut *(Amphicarpa bracteata),* and Turk's-cap lily *(Lilium superbum).*

A mixed hardwood forest of predominantly white, black, chestnut, and red oaks covers the rest of the park and historic site. Other trees include the tulip tree, beech, sugar maple, black birch, flowering dogwood, black walnut, sassafras, black cherry, black willow, and hickory. The size of the trees here is fairly uniform, as the woods were clear-cut every 30 years to make charcoal for the iron furnaces. Smooth blackhaw, nannyberry, and arrowwood grow in the understory.

Under the dark canopy are jack-in-the-pulpit *(Arisaema triphyllum),* sweetflag *(Acorus calamus),* skunk cabbage *(Symplocarpus foetidus),* and arrowhead *(Sagittaria latifolia)* in wet sites, as well as dogtooth violet *(Erythronium americanum),* false Solomon's seal *(Smilacina racemosa),* Canada mayflower *(Maianthemum canadense),* showy orchid *(Orchis spectabilis),* ragged fringed orchid *(Habenaria lacera),* and nodding ladies' tresses *(Spiranthes cernua).*

Ferns and associates include cinnamon, interrupted, royal, Scott's spleenwort, marginal woodfern, bracken, Christmas, wood and field horsetails, and tree club moss.

Birders have observed some 185 species. Birds commonly sighted here include the osprey (PA endangered), American merganser, sharp-shinned hawk, northern harrier (PA at risk), long-eared owl, whippoorwill, horned lark, orchard oriole, yellow-bellied sapsucker, and worm-eating, magnolia, hooded, and chestnut-sided warblers.

Others are rarely sighted, like the bald eagle (PA endangered), common tern, loggerhead shrike (PA endangered), Henslow's sparrow (PA at risk), tundra swan, red-headed woodpecker, bobolink, evening grosbeak, and pine siskin. Canada geese overpopulate Hopewell Lake.

In Hopewell Lake are northern pike, chain pickerel, bass, walleye, muskellunge, and several kinds of panfish. Trout anglers will have better luck at the stocked Scott's Run Lake.

Animal inhabitants include the raccoon, fox, and skunk. Sightings of bobcats (PA at risk) remain unconfirmed.

History. During the French and Indian War, French soldiers occupied a garrison downstream on what the colonials referred to as "the French creek." The name stuck after hostilities ceased.

In 1771, Mark Bird built Hopewell Furnace to manufacture iron products. In those days, furnaces were built close to their fuel source, charcoal. Colliers cleared a section of forest, made huge mounds of charcoal, then hauled the fuel to the furnaces. The ruins of charcoal hearths are scattered in the forest.

Hopewell Furnace reached the peak of its prosperity in the 1830s. The Panic of 1837, however, weakened the business. The Civil War temporarily revived it, but by the end of the nineteenth century, iron manufacturing, now stoked by anthracite coal, had shifted to big cities like Pittsburgh. The furnace closed in 1883. Today guides at Hopewell Furnace explain the history of rural iron making.

The decline of the furnace enabled the forest and watershed to recover. French Creek State Park was established as a national park in the 1930s. The heir of Hopewell Furnace sold the ironworks to the federal government in 1935, and three years later the property was designated a national historic site. Additional park land was purchased in the 1930s, and the Civilian Conservation Corps and Works Progress Administration built roads and park facilities. The National Park Service transferred the land to Pennsylvania in 1946.

Peace Valley Nature Center

eace reigns here. The shore of Lake Galena was placid enough for a rare sandhill crane, an endangered bird, to stop by during its northern migration in April 1994.

Ownership. Bucks County Department of Parks and Recreation. Lake Galena is managed by the North Penn-North Wales Water Authority.

Size and Designation. The nature center encompasses about 300 acres of land and 20 acres of Lake Galena. The center is part of a 1,500-acre county park.

Nearby Nature Attractions. Churchville and Silver Lake nature centers; Ringing Rocks County Park; Nockamixon, Tyler, Ralph Stover, Theodore Roosevelt, and Neshaminy state parks; Bowman's Hill Wildflower Preserve; Honey Hollow Environmental Education Center; Bristol Marsh Preserve; and David R. Johnson State Forest Natural Area.

Features. Nine miles of paths lead through woods, fields, and thickets, and along streams, ponds, and the lakeshore. Trails

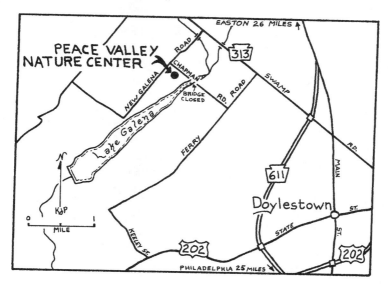

departing from the parking lot on the north side of Chapman Road visit a trio of creeks that refresh Lake Galena: the west and east branches of Hardiaken Creek and the north branch of Neshaminy Creek. These are also the most forested trails, and the coolest during summer hikes. The trails are open daily during daylight hours. Trail guides are available at the visitors center.

The south side features the solar-heated visitors center; a pond; a bird blind; wildflower, butterfly, and herb gardens; and trails leading to Lake Galena, meadows, woods, and fields. Much of the lakeshore is a wildlife refuge, a buffer zone that is off-limits to humans.

The visitors center, open Tuesday through Sunday from 10 A.M. to 5 P.M., has wildlife exhibits, Indian artifacts, rest rooms, drinking water, a classroom, a library, and a gift shop. Nature and environmental education programs are offered for both children and adults.

For more information, contact the Peace Valley Nature Center, 170 Chapman Road, Doylestown, PA 18901, telephone (215) 345-7860.

Geology. The Peace Valley Nature Center, like most of Bucks County, lies within a geological area know as the Newark Basin. About 210 million years ago, during the Triassic Period, as the supercontinent of Pangea began to break apart, rifts developed in the earth's crust. Many of these rifts lie beneath the Atlantic Ocean. The Newark Basin, however, is one valley that did not become submerged.

Over the years, the basin filled with sand, silt, and other sediments to form thick layers of sandstone, shale, and conglomerate. Water drained into the valley and formed lakes and ponds. Later, the strata were tilted in a northwesterly direction, and molten rock flowed upward into cracks, forming dikes and sills.

The youngest rock formation in the park is a yellow, red, and brown shale laced with sandstone. Other rocks are hard gray, black, and brown shales. These bedrocks can be seen along creek and lake beds. Both formations show wavy ripple marks and mud cracks, evidence that they probably were formed in shallow water. A fault line in the bedrock is visible from the Fallen Tree and Swamp trails. Lake Galena was named for the galena ore that was once mined here. This ore contains 80 percent lead and traces of silver. Bits of gold also were found in the New Galena mines—about a dime's worth for every ton of lead. Some of the old galena mines are submerged under 365-acre Lake Galena, an impoundment created for flood control, water storage, and recreation.

Wildlife. Wildflowers are abundant here. Try to find birdfoot trefoil *(Lotus corniculatus)*, Indian pipe *(Monotropa uniflora)*, and

Peace Valley Nature Center _____ 139

swamp rose (marsh) mallow *(Hibiscus palustris)*. More common are chicory *(Cichorium intybus)*, bloodroot *(Sanguinaria canadensis)*, pokeweed *(Phytolacca americana)*, and common mullein *(Verbascum thapsus)*.

In front of the visitors center, hummingbird moths hover over bee balm. Like the ruby-throated hummingbird, this moth sips the nectar of flowers. Other butterflies and moths at Peace Valley include the luna moth and banded hairstreak, red-spotted purple, and summer azure butterflies.

Two hundred sixty bird species have been sighted in the park, including sandhill crane, bald eagle, and osprey (all PA endangered); great egret (PA threatened); northern harrier (PA at risk); saw-whet and long-eared owls (both declining in population); common snipe (PA at risk); American coot (PA rare); red-throated and common loons; double-breasted cormorant; great blue heron; mallard and wood ducks; Tennessee, yellow, Blackburnian, bay-breasted, Canada, worm-eating, blue-winged, and mourning warblers; Philadelphia, solitary, white-eyed, and warbling vireos; ruby-throated hummingbird; goldfinch; red-bellied woodpecker; and common flicker.

Also found here are the white-tailed deer, red fox, mink, long-tailed weasel, raccoon, little and big brown bats, spotted and red-backed salamanders, Fowler's toad, redbelly turtle (PA threatened), and northern water snake.

Lake Galena is home to channel catfish, brown and yellow bullheads, golden and spotted shiners, sunfish, pumpkinseed, bluegill, white sucker, carp, largemouth bass, black crappie, and walleye.

History. Artifacts found on the property indicate that the Lenni Lenape lived in the area. The Lenape may have had a hunting camp at White Oak Crossing, a ford across the north branch of Neshaminy Creek.

The nature center opened in the northeast corner of Peace Valley Park in May 1995. Trees and shrubs, as well as herb, butterfly, and wildflower gardens, were planted, and in 1990 trails were built.

45

Honey Hollow Environmental Education Center

By 1939 the farmland in Honey Hollow showed the wear and tear of 235 years of cultivation. The U.S. Soil Conservation Service offered advice, and farmers in the entire Honey Hollow watershed began employing new conservation farming techniques. For the last half century, Honey Hollow has been a model of natural resources conservation and a vital regional education facility.

Ownership. The property is owned by the Heritage Conservancy (formerly the Bucks County Conservancy). The Bucks County Audubon Society operates the education center.

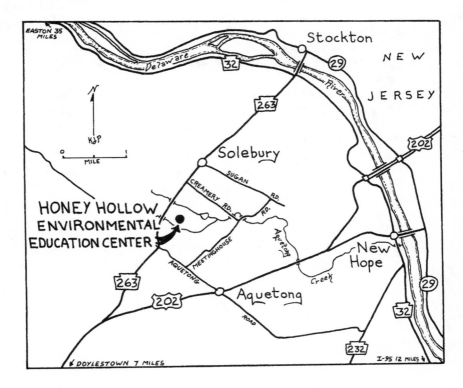

Size and Designation. The 200-acre center lies within the Honey Hollow watershed, which is designated a national historic landmark.

Nearby Nature Attractions. Delaware Canal, Tyler, Nockamixon, Ralph Stover, and Neshaminy state parks; Ringing Rocks County Park; Silver Lake, Churchville, and Peach Valley nature centers; Bowman's Hill Wildflower Preserve; Bristol Marsh Preserve; and David R. Johnson State Forest Natural Area.

Features. The five trails in the preserve can all be reached from the trailhead at the parking lot. Visit Many Springs Pond, then follow the red blazes of the wooded Brook Trail, along the west branch of Honey Hollow Brook. From there go to Audubon Pond. Another trail follows the edge of a small swamp.

Stop at the office to register and pick up a trail map before hiking. The trails are open Monday through Friday from 9 A.M. to 5 P.M.

For more information, contact Honey Hollow Environmental Education Center, 6324 Upper York Road, New Hope, PA 18938, telephone (215) 297-8266.

Geology. Honey Hollow watershed spreads out in the Piedmont, a land of fertile rolling hills situated between the coastal plain and the mountainous region to the northwest. The brook itself is barely a yard wide and just a few inches deep in midsummer.

Three types of rock underlay the watershed: sandstone, limestone, and a conglomerate containing quartzite pebbles. These rocks influence the soil above them. Seven types of soil, two of which were important to agriculture, characterize the watershed. Silt loam is fertile, slightly acidic to slightly alkaline soil that holds water longer during droughts, derived from the limestone. Gravelly loam, acidic and nutrient deficient soil that drains easily but dries up during droughts, covered the sandstone and conglomerate.

Wildlife. Early settlement and intensive farming reduced the original forest of oak, chestnut, and hickory. The logging appears to have been selective, rather than wholesale, wasteful clear-cutting. The area still boasts a mature, healthy woodland of deciduous trees dominated by oak and hickory. The chestnuts perished in the blight earlier in this century.

Seventy-two species of trees have been counted, including six kinds of oaks, black walnut, white and Scotch pines, cottonwood, tulip tree, white ash, various willows (including pussy willow), elm, sugar maple, sassafras, and shagbark, pignut, and bitternut hickories. Chestnut oak prefers the shallow soils on ridges; red maple, cottonwood, and sycamore like the deep, soggy soils along streams; hemlocks enjoy cool north-facing slopes. Flowering trees and shrubs include dogwood, mountain laurel, and rhododendron.

A total of 189 species of herbaceous wildflowers, both native and introduced, live here. These include bluets *(Houstonia caerulea)*, citronella horsebalm *(Collinsonia canadensis)*, fairy-candles *(Cimicifuga racemosa)*, monkeyflower *(Mimulus ringeus)*, poor-robin's-plantain *(Erigeron pulchellus)*, striped pipsissewa *(Chimaphila maculata)*, naked-flowered tick-trefoil *(Desmodium nudiflorum)*, wild madder *(Galium mollugo)*, and gill-over-the-ground *(Glechoma hederacea)*. Mayapples *(Podophyllum peltatum)* are abundant here and throughout Bucks County.

Ferns found at Honey Hollow include maidenhair, cinnamon, Christmas, and brittle. Hay-scented fern grows in the open fields, and marsh fern at the water's edge.

The many habitats in the watershed make it an excellent environment for birds. Cedar waxwings, towhees, cardinals, and catbirds like the berry patches, which were originally planted to curb erosion. Tall trees host the scarlet tanager, northern oriole, yellow-billed cuckoo, yellow-bellied sapsucker, rose-breasted grosbeak, red-bellied woodpecker, chestnut-sided, blue-winged, Wilson's palm, myrtle, Blackburnian, and blackpoll warblers streak through the forest canopy. They are best seen in the spring before the trees fully leaf out. Meadow dwellers, such as eastern meadowlark and bobwhite, are plentiful. Marshes attract the red-winged blackbird, common yellowthroat, little green heron, and swallows. Around ponds, look for the great blue heron, ducks, Canada geese, sandpipers, and common snipe (PA at risk). In early autumn, hawks glide on the thermal currents above the area. Butterflies, moths, dragonflies, and damselflies are plentiful at Honey Hollow. Butterflies and moths include the meadow fritillary, tawny-edged skipper, red admiral, Baltimore checkerspot, and Darling underwing. Eight kinds of dragonflies and damselflies fly here including green jacket and civil bluet.

Early settlers wiped out many mammals, such as the elk, mountain lion, wolf, and white-tailed deer, the latter abundant again after a reintroduction effort. Many animals in the watershed are nocturnal and are seldom seen by visitors. These include the short-tailed shrew, pine and meadow voles, opossum, striped skunk, raccoon, and a half dozen varieties of bats.

Star-nosed and eastern moles, which eat worms while burrowing in the topsoil, thrive in the woods. The hollow is also home to the longtail weasel; red and gray foxes; cottontail rabbit; spotted, wood, eastern box, snapping, and eastern painted turtles; black racer, red-bellied, water, milk, and northern ringneck snakes; bullfrog, spring peeper, pickerel, leopard, and green frogs; northern red, two-lined, red-backed, dusky, and long-tailed salamanders; and red-spotted newt.

Honey Hollow Brook and the ponds support bluegill, large-mouth bass, creek chub, and blacknose dace, as well as snails, mollusks, crustaceans, and numerous kinds of insects.

History. The Lenni Lenape (Delaware Indians) still lived in Honey Hollow when European settlers arrived with their plows in the early 1700s. Over the next two centuries, agriculture degraded the land. In the late 1930s, a local farmer sought the advice of the U.S. Soil Conservation Service to prevent further erosion. The federal agency told the farmers in the watershed that their problems could be solved if they participated in a land management plan and adopted new farming techniques. The farmers took that advice in 1939. It marked the first time in U.S. history that landowners in an entire watershed agreed to participate in a long-term conservation plan.

The plan included contour plowing, tree plantings, pond construction, soil analysis, and wildlife plantings, all new farming practices at the time. Within a decade, the productivity of the land improved, and the area boasted a richer and more diverse environment for wildlife. Honey Hollow became a model for the nation.

In 1969, the U.S. Department of the Interior honored the pioneering soil preservation effort by declaring the Honey Hollow watershed a national historic landmark. That year also marked the creation of the Honey Hollow Watershed Association and the Bucks County Audubon Society. These groups, along with the Bucks County Conservation District, established the environmental education center.

46

David R. Johnson State Forest Natural Area

This patch of untamed woods lies just north of New Hope. Do not come here for an easy stroll. Do come here, though, if you want to get away from the tourists on River Road.

Ownership. Pennsylvania Department of Environmental Resources, Bureau of Forestry.

Size and Designation. This state natural area encompasses 56 acres.

Nearby Nature Attractions. Bowman's Hill Wildflower Preserve; Bristol Marsh Preserve; Monroe Border Fault; Honey Hollow

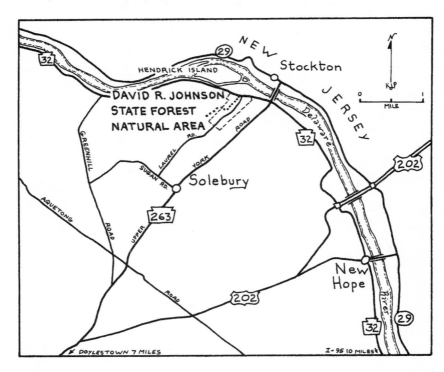

Environmental Education Center; Ringing Rocks County Park; Silver Lake, Peace Valley, and Churchville nature centers; and Delaware Canal, Neshaminy, Nockamixon, Ralph Stover, and Tyler state parks.

Features. This steep and wooded preserve is new and undeveloped with no designated trails or rest rooms. You can roam through the property or follow the wood road from a gate on PA 32. (From Laurel Road, cross the brook to reach this road.) Wear long pants and insect repellent for summer hikes.

Geology. An unnamed brook that empties into the Delaware River has cut a V-shaped ravine through the center of this property.

Wildlife. Thirty-one species of trees and shrubs grow here, as well as an assortment of wildflowers. Tall specimens of tulip tree and American beech grow on the lower slopes. White, chestnut, and black oaks thrive on the higher and drier parts of the ridge; black walnut, sycamore, and great rhododendron shade the brook that twists through the ravine. Other trees and shrubs include the red oak, red and silver maples, basswood, white ash, shagbark hickory, flowering dogwood, American hop hornbeam, witch hazel, black birch, hackberry, spicebush, black gum, speckled alder, sassafras, and bigtooth and quaking aspens.

Wildflowers include the yellow hawkweed *(Hieracium pratense)*, bluet *(Houstonia caerulea)*, spotted wintergreen *(Chimaphila maculata)*, tumble mustard *(Sisymbrium altissimum)*, naked miterwort *(Mitella nuda)*, and common winter cress *(Barbarea vulgaris)*. Hay-scented, New York, and Christmas ferns also grow here.

Tracks indicate the presence of deer, raccoons, and foxes. Squirrels and chipmunks are abundant.

History. The preserve is named after the former landowner, David R. Johnson. The Hartman family also donated land. The Pennsylvania Department of Environmental Resources designated the site a state forest natural area in May 1993.

47

Bowman's Hill Wildflower Preserve

More than 1,000 kinds of plants thrive in this 80-acre preserve. Come here in the spring, when the wildflowers are at their peak.

Ownership. The site is owned by the Commonwealth of Pennsylvania but administered by the Pennsylvania Historical and Museum Commission, the Washington Crossing Park Commission, and Bowman's Hill Wildflower Preserve Association.

Size and Designation. This 80-acre sanctuary is part of the Washington Crossing Historic Park.

Nearby Nature Attractions. Tyler, Delaware Canal, Neshaminy, Ralph Stover, and Nockamixon state parks; Bristol Marsh Preserve; Ringing Rocks County Park; and Silver Lake, Churchville, and Peach Valley nature centers.

Features. Get your bearings at the preserve headquarters. Twenty-six trails lead to various wildflower collections. First purchase the inexpensive trail map and blooming guide at the headquarters, then check the outdoor bulletin board to find out which flowers are in bloom. Labels along the trail help you identify plants.

For birders, a bird checklist is available at headquarters, and a collection of birds, eggs, and nests is housed in the basement.

Also at headquarters are a wildlife viewing window, a gift shop, rest rooms, and drinking water. Nature and horticultural programs are offered throughout the year. Ask for a schedule and for membership information. A picnic area, also with rest rooms, is located near the preserve entrance.

The grounds are open daily from 8:30 A.M. to sunset, and headquarters Monday through Saturday from 9 A.M. to 5 P.M. and Sunday from noon to 5 P.M.

The nearby Bowman's Hill Tower, commemorating a strategic lookout of the Revolution, features panoramic views of the Delaware River Valley. From the preserve, turn right (south) on River Road and follow signs to the tower. You also can walk to it from the preserve along a paved road now closed to auto traffic. The tower is open daily April through October from 10 A.M. to 5 P.M. (gates close at 4:30 P.M.). In November, it is open only on weekends. There is a small admission fee.

For more information, contact Bowman's Hill Wildflower Preserve Association, Washington Crossing Historic Park, P.O. Box 103, Washington Crossing, PA 18977, telephone (215) 862-2924.

Geology. Convulsions and rumblings in Earth's crust more than 200 million years ago explain why Bowman's Hill became a lookout point during the Revolutionary War. About 210 million years ago, the continental plates that had earlier collided to form the Appalachians began to drift apart. This movement caused rifts along fault lines south and east of the mountainous area, and huge slabs of bedrock broke off. The resulting basins captured eroded sediment, which became the sandstone and shale that underlie most of the lowlands.

The rifting allowed molten rock to seep into the cracks and joints. The magma formed sills and dikes in the sandstone and shale beds. Later, movement in Earth's crust crumpled the layers and tilted them northwesterly, exposing some of the igneous rock. Over the millennia, erosion carved the softer shale and sandstone into gentle lowlands. The igneous rock withstood erosion, creating ridges such as Bowman's Hill, which is made of diabase, a dark gray to black igneous rock derived from the magma.

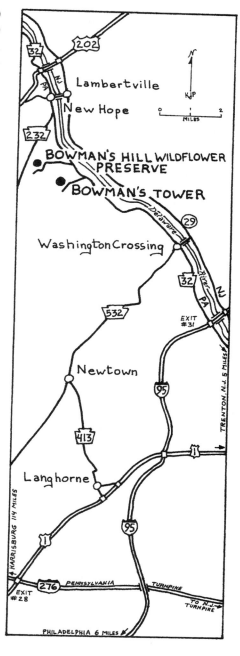

Pidcock Creek, which winds through the preserve, flows over a metamorphic rock called hornfels, or baked shale. As the hot magma seeped upward into faults and joints, its incredible heat metamorphosed red Brunswick shale into black hornfels. Outcrops of unaffected red shale are visible from the stone bridge over the creek. Look along the north bank downstream from the bridge.

Debris deposited by the Wisconsinan glacier covers some of the preserve. Although the ice sheet went no farther south than the Delaware Water Gap about 12,000 years ago, it made its mark on land to the south. As the glacier melted, it produced huge torrents of water, which carried till—a mixture of boulders, gravel, sand, and silt—down swollen rivers and streams. The debris was dumped on the banks of the waterways in terraces, or benches, that reveal the level and direction of the current.

Wildlife. Bowman's Hill Wildflower Preserve is the place to admire and enjoy Pennsylvania's herbaceous plants. Botanists have counted 3,319 kinds of wild plants growing in Pennsylvania, some 2,076 of which are native to the state. This preserve shows off 1,030 species, 800 of them native.

Many species have been planted here so that they can be protected. Bowman's Hill is a living outdoor museum, a zoo of sorts, for Pennsylvania's plants, all labeled and cultivated for preservation and propagation. The plants grow in natural settings—forest, meadow, bog, pond, or barren. Upon arrival, head to the exhibit on display—say, the Virginia bluebells *(Mertensia virginica)* in late April or early May—or simple browse.

Few places protect as many plants of special concern—species designated as endangered, threatened, or rare. Some rarities are glade spurge *(Euphorbia purpurea,* PA endangered); goldenstar *(Chrysogonum virginianum,* PA endangered); fringed bleeding heart *(Dicentra eximia,* PA endangered); Canby's mountain-lover *(Paxistima canbyi,* PA endangered); and box huckleberry *(Gaylussacia brachycera,* PA threatened).

The locations of these rare plants are not kept secret. Consult your printed guide or ask an employee. The box huckleberry, for example, is near the start of the Azalea Trail, on the right—the plant with white blossoms from late April through mid-June. The goldenstar is the yellow bloomer on the left, mid-April through July. Cliff-green, a rarity at its northern limit, sticks to high rocky cliffs.

Other flowers include showy skullcap *(Scutellaria serrata),* marsh marigold *(Caltha palustris),* celandine poppy *(Stylophorum diphyllum),* jack-in-the-pulpit *(Arisaema triphyllum),* yellow lady's slipper *(Aplectrum hyemale),* and elephant's foot *(Elephantopus carolinianus).*

Along the Fern Trail are some 30 varieties of ferns and associates, including Boott's wood, blunt-lobed woodsia, Susquehanna wood, Miss Slosson's wood, maidenhair, and Clinton's wood. Ferns grow throughout the preserve, but not in the abundance and variety as along the Fern Trail.

Labels at eye level help you identify the preserve's trees, which include Canadian hemlock, umbrella magnolia, tulip tree, river birch, slippery elm, pawpaw, witch hazel, fringetree (at the northern edge of its range), and American holly (PA threatened). In Penn's Woods, 65 varieties represent the state's native collection.

Birders have observed 151 species of birds at Bowman's Hill. Some, like the mourning warbler, northern saw-whet owl, and whippoorwill, are sighted occasionally. The ruby-throated hummingbird, red-bellied woodpecker, screech owl, American kestrel, rose-breasted grosbeak, and wood thrush, as well as the northern parula, golden-winged, prairie, cerulean, worm-eating, and black-throated green warblers, have established nests in the preserve. Hot spots are the Audubon Trail and pond (via Gentian and Fern trails), Pidcock Creek, and Bowman's Hill Tower, a good vantage point for spying migrating raptors and warblers.

History. Bowman's Hill has served as a landmark for centuries. The Lenni Lenape called the place *Wund-achga-chunick* or "hill near the water." An Indian village by the same name stood in the bottomland between the hill and the river.

Nobody seems to know exactly how Bowman's Hill got its name. It may have been derived from the French *beau mont* meaning "pretty mountain." More romantic storytellers say the hill honors Dr. John Bowman, who sailed as a surgeon for the pirate Captain Kidd. They say that Bowman retired to this area and that his bones lie beside pirate treasure on the hill.

The most believable story has the place named after English merchant Thomas Bowman, who traded in the valley in the 1600s.

In the early 1700s, Pidcock Creek, which twists through the preserve, divided John Pidcock's plantation from the London Tract. Now it marks the boundary between Solebury and Upper Makefield townships.

In December 1776, Gen. George Washington and his army camped on the grounds now occupied by the wildflower preserve. From Bowman's Hill, the Continental Army could relay messages and detect British movements. Washington feared that a successful British attack on his position would end the revolution. The army's morale was low, desertions were high, and supplies were scarce. But instead of hunkering down for the winter, Washington boldly led his troops to Trenton, about 14 miles from the preserve.

On Christmas night, Washington made his famous crossing of the ice-clogged Delaware River, hoping to catch Hessian mercenaries off guard. He was supposed to meet two other divisions, posted south of Trenton, on the outskirts of town, but a storm kept them from crossing. It did not matter. Washington surprised the Hessians and the victory boosted the rebel cause.

Washington Crossing Historic Park was established in 1917. The state acquired Bowman's Hill in 1923. The 110-foot tower was built in 1930 from local fieldstone, and in 1934 the wildflower preserve took form, as trails were laid and beds of wildflowers were planted.

48

Susquehanna River Overlooks

Chickies Rock County Park
Conejohela Flats
Turkey Hill Overlook
Susquehannock State Park

East Shore Overlook
Pinnacle Overlook
Face Rock Overlook

Twice a year, the gorge of the lower Susquehanna River Valley hosts the mass migration of millions of birds. From overlooks along the Lancaster County shore, you can watch this miracle unfold.

In March, if you are lucky, you might witness the arrival of thousands of tundra, or whistling, swans on the Conejohela Flats. They may linger here a day or two, then vanish northward, toward the tundra.

Ownership. *Chickies Rock:* Lancaster County Department of Parks and Recreation; *Conejohela Flats* and *East Shore Overlook:* Safe Harbor Water Power Corporation; *Pinnacle* and *Face Rock Overlooks:* Pennsylvania Power and Light Company; *Susquehannock State Park:* Pennsylvania Department of Environmental Resources, Bureau of State Parks, (PECO Energy manages the Conowingo Islands); *Turkey Hill Overlook:* The Lancaster County Conservancy leases the property.

Size and Designation. Chickies Rock County Park encompasses more than 400 acres. The Conejohela Flats is a collection of

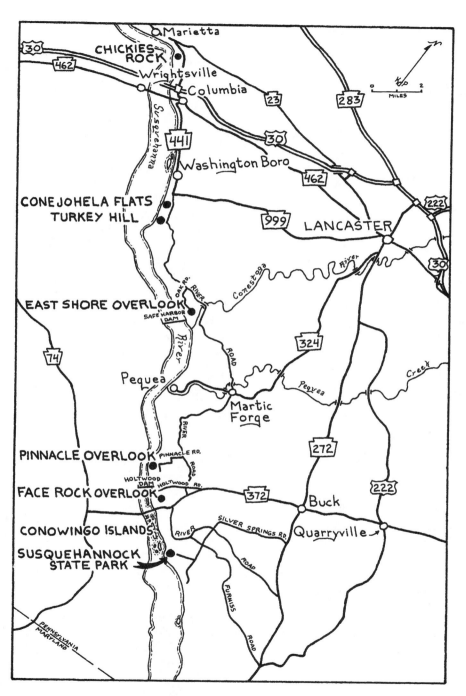

low islands in calm water along the eastern shore of the Susquehanna River. The largest island, and the one closest to shore, is Rookery Island (sometimes called Middle or House Island). The Pennsylvania Game Commission has designated Rookery Island as a state game-propagation area, and it is off-limits to visitors from March 1 to July 31. East Shore Overlook is part of 2,330 acres offered by Safe Water Power Company for recreational pursuits. Pinnacle and Face Rock overlooks are part of the 5,000-acre Holtwood Recreation Area managed by Pennsylvania Power and Light Company. The Susquehannock State Park encompasses 224 acres.

Nearby Nature Attractions. Kelly's Run, Pequea Creek, Tucquan Glen, and Trout Run Preserves; Shenk's Ferry Wildflower Preserve; Muddy Creek Recreation Park; Lancaster Central Park; and Tucquan and Octoraro creeks, both state scenic rivers.

Features. *Chickies Rock County Park:* An easy, half-mile trail leaves the parking lot and roughly follows the utility line to the outcrop. A wooden, waist-high fence encourages visitors to stay back from the edge of the sheer, two-hundred-foot drop. Climbing on the cliff is dangerous and is prohibited.

Rest rooms, picnic tables, drinking water, ballfields, and a playground are located in the Breezyview section of the park. The county also runs a campground a mile north of Chickies Rock. From here, anglers can try their luck in Chickies and Donegal creeks (the latter for fly-fishing only).

For more information, contact the Lancaster County Department of Parks and Recreation, 1050 Rockford Road, Lancaster, PA 17602, telephone (717) 299-8215.

Conejohela Flats: This is a choice spot to view egrets, herons, and other nesting shorebirds, especially on a midsummer evening. There are marinas and launching sites on the York County shore for those who want to explore the islands by boat. The nearby Manor Lions Club Park has a small playground for children. Safe Harbor Park (south on River Road) offers picnic accommodations, rest rooms, drinking water, playgrounds, tennis courts, ballfields, and fishing. The East Shore Overlook is nearby.

For more information, contact the Safe Harbor Water Power Company, P.O. Box 97, Conestoga, PA 17516, telephone (717) 872-0291.

Turkey Hill Overlook: For picnic tables, rest rooms, fishing, and other outdoor activities, head south on River Road to Safe Harbor Park. For more information, contact the Lancaster County Conservancy, P.O. Box 716, Lancaster, PA 17608, telephone (717) 392-7891.

East Shore Overlook: This is the place to go if you like to look at dams and hydroelectric power plants. Nevertheless, gulls, ducks, and herons are common, and bald eagles have been seen hunting for fish in the tailrace, the channel below the dam.

Lake Clarke spreads out north of the dam and Lake Aldred to the south. Although these impoundments on the Susquehanna are called lakes, it still looks very much like a river.

There are picnic tables and rest rooms here. Safe Harbor Park, a few miles farther south, also has picnic tables, rest rooms, drinking water, play areas, and fishing.

For more information, contact the Safe Harbor Water Power Corporation, P.O. Box 97, Conestoga, PA 17516, telephone (717) 872-0291.

Pinnacle Overlook: This overlook is one of the wildest, quietest, most scenic panoramas of the lower gorge. Trails to the left (downstream) lead to the nearby Kelly's Run Nature Preserve. The last 200 yards of pavement are closed to traffic in the winter; simply park at the end of the road and hike to the vista. There are picnic tables and toilets at the parking lot.

For more information, contact the Pennsylvania Power and Light Company, Holtwood Land Management Office, 9 New Village Road, Holtwood, PA 17532, telephone (717) 284-2278.

Face Rock Overlook: Here you glimpse the Holtwood Dam and power plant, the Norman Wood Bridge (PA 372) over the river, and Piney Island, one of the northern Conowingo Islands. The Conestoga Trail, a cross-country hiking path (orange blazes), connects this vista with Pinnacle Overlook to the north. Healthy hikers should try the rocky, rugged trail between these points.

For more information, contact the Pennsylvania Power and Light Company, Holtwood Land Management Office, 9 New Village Road, Holtwood, PA 17532, telephone (717) 284-2278.

Susquehannock State Park: The Conowingo Islands, pristine island outcrops, lie in the middle of the river though they are not part of the park. Upper Bear Island, upstream, is the largest and least disturbed island. Mount Johnson, a former Audubon Society bald eagle sanctuary, is the dome-shaped island far downstream and close to the eastern shore.

The state park has five miles of hiking trails, a bridle trail, historic ruins, a large picnic area (two pavilions), a play area, rest rooms, and drinking water.

For more information, contact the Pennsylvania Department of Environmental Resources, Susquehannock State Park, 1880 Park Drive, Drumore, PA 17518, telephone (717) 548-3361; or PECO Energy, Muddy Run Recreation Park, R.D. 3, Box 730, Holtwood PA 17532, telephone (717) 284-4325.

Geology. Several different continental glaciers blanketed much of North America during the ice age. Though none of them reached as far south as Lancaster County, they still had a profound influence on the land and on the Susquehanna River.

Each freeze was succeeded by a warm period, during which the ice sheet would retreat northward. Enormous amounts of meltwater propelled boulders, rocks, and finer sediments. This powerful debris-laden torrent carved the gorge, cut channels, drilled the unique potholes on the Conowingo Islands, and scooped out the peculiar deeps, 130-foot-deep clefts, in the east channel of the river.

The narrow northern section of the gorge, from Turkey Hill to Susquehannock State Park, is made up of Wissahickon schist, an extremely hard and erosion-resistant metamorphic rock. This rock began as a muddy sediment on an ocean floor 500 million years ago. It later hardened into shale. Then 470 million years ago, the shale experienced intense pressure and heat when continental plates collided. This metamorphosed the shale into schist.

At Turkey Hill, the river narrows and enters a gorge. Here the river crosses the Martic Line, believed to be a line that divides two distinct groups of rock. This is a thrust fault where ancient rock slid over younger rock.

The vistas at Turkey Hill, East Shore, Pinnacle, Face Rock, and Susquehannock State Park sit atop Wissahickon schist. Many tributaries have carved picturesque and steep ravines through this schist.

Chickies Rock (including Breezyview Overlook) and Conejohela Flats, north of the gorge, have different geological stories.

Chickies Rock is a massive 200-foot-high cliff of Chickies quartzite dating back 500 to 570 million years. Quartzite originally was sandstone laden with the mineral quartz. When the mountains were uplifted, the sandstone metamorphosed into the harder quartzite rock. Chickies quartzite is highly resistant to erosion. As the Susquehanna River strikes Chickies Rock, the waterway bends sharply to the right. The hard, ancient rock is also responsible for the rapids beneath the cliff.

If you look at the Chickies Rock overlook from the middle of the river, you will see that it rides the crest of an anticline, a ridge or swelling with the bedrock layers folded upward, that stretches several miles eastward. The anticlinal ridge is cut here to expose a cross section.

Between Chickies Rock and the Maryland state line, two power plant dams—Safe Harbor and Holtwood—block the current of the Susquehanna. The body of water behind Safe Harbor Dam is called Lake Clarke; Lake Aldred lies behind Holtwood Dam.

At the Face Rock Overlook, notice the rocks and small islands just below the dam. These are called the Sculptured Rocks, because the American Indians carved inscriptions in them. Many figures have disappeared due to weathering and vandalism. Other inscriptions appeared on rocks south of the Maryland border. The meaning of the inscriptions remains a mystery.

Five to six miles downstream from Chickies Rock, the Susquehanna broadens and becomes shallower. Along the calm eastern shore, low-lying islands and marshy areas have developed around sand and gravel bars, mud flats, and debris piles. These are the Conejohela Flats, which annually attract thousands of migratory birds.

Wildlife. The Susquehanna River Valley is a main artery of an avian migratory route known as the Atlantic Flyway. Hundreds of thousands of birds use this north-south corridor annually. There is hardly a pause in activity here—just as the spring-early summer northbound flights for some species conclude, others begin their late summer-autumn southbound journeys. There is also a good number of year-round residents.

From any of the lookouts you might see the following: hooded and common merganser, oldsquaw, mallard, black, blue-winged teal, brant, scoter, American wigeon, pintail, scaup, common goldeneye, canvasback, bufflehead, ruddy, and redhead ducks; common loons; horned and pied-billed grebes; and double-crested cormorants.

Yellow-crowned night, black-crowned night, and green-backed herons gather on the Conejohela Flats, along with cattle, great, and snowy egrets and glossy ibis. Some 10,000 tundra swans have also been seen there, and some of these swans winter on the flats. Also look for Canada and snow geese, and glaucous and herring gulls.

Shorebirds include the greater and lesser yellowlegs; least, western, semipalmated, and spotted sandpipers; dowitcher; and killdeer.

Predatory birds such as the bald eagle, osprey, peregrine falcon (all PA endangered), red-tailed and rough-legged hawks, American kestrel, and turkey and black vultures have been observed. Eagle nests were common in the gorge in the nineteenth century, but their numbers declined drastically in the early twentieth century because of habitat loss, poisoning, and shooting. Mount Johnson Island was one of the first bald eagle sanctuaries established by the National Audubon Society; however, eagles have not nested there since 1948.

The eagles have been making a comeback recently, thanks to cleaner river water, legal protection, release of eaglets by the Pennsylvania Game Commission, and the slow northward movement of a reestablished Chesapeake Bay colony. A pair built a nest near the Conowingo Dam in Maryland in 1986. Three nesting couples were observed along the lower Susquehanna in Pennsylvania in 1989. Eagles hunt in the tailraces of the dams in the winter.

Swarms of smaller birds, such as swallows and warblers, also follow the Susquehanna flight path. Southbound swallows—rough-winged, barn, tree, cliff, bank, and purple martins—come through in August. Warblers, including the hooded, Kentucky, yellow-throated, worm-eating, Connecticut, and Wilson's, stay in the woods a little longer.

If you explore the Conejohela Flats or Conowingo Islands, study the vegetation. The calm-water flats allow aquatic vegetation, crustaceans, and mollusks to flourish. Egrets and herons nest in the silver maples. Box elder and river birch stand on the bigger islands.

Upper Bear Island, the emperor of the Conowingo group, is made up of several unspoiled small habitats. This island is close enough to shore to be influenced by its flora and fauna. Eastern hemlock grows in wet, shady sites right beside red and chestnut oaks, which prefer drier locations. Elsewhere, trees that like moderately moist soil thrive, including American beech, white ash, black birch, black gum, red maple, and tulip tree. In the understory grow flowering dogwood, sassafras, hornbeam, and pawpaw, which attracts the zebra swallowtail butterfly, more common in southern states.

The island supports two plants found at their northern extreme: American holly (*Ilex opaca,* PA threatened) and indigobush *(Amorpha fruticosa)*. Migrating birds that ate the fruits of these plants farther south probably dispersed their seeds on the island.

Rainwater has filled potholes, creating ponds ringed with cattails, reeds, and spatterdock *(Nuphar advena)*. The water holes attract frogs, snakes, and turtles. Mammals include the skunk, opossum, rabbit, mole, raccoon, beaver, and even deer, which have been seen swimming the short distance back and forth to the island.

Sportsmen enjoy game fishing along this section of the river, which holds walleye, carp (a favorite of the bald eagle), channel catfish, bullhead, eel, white crappie, and largemouth, smallmouth, rock, and striped bass. Minnows, darters, shiners, and sunfish also inhabit the waters. Pennsylvania's only endemic fish (a species living nowhere else), the Maryland darter (US endangered), may be present.

Eighty-eight kinds of fish live in the Susquehanna watershed, 27 of which have been introduced. One variety, the African blue tilapia, got into the river accidentally and began breeding. It survives the winter by living near the warm discharge currents from nuclear power plants.

History. The petroglyphs found on the Sculptured Rocks indicate that the Indians spent time on the Susquehanna River. No doubt they netted and speared fish on the rocks and temporarily camped on shore or on the bigger Conowingo or Conejohela islands.

The lower Susquehanna Valley originally was inhabited by the Shenk's Ferry Indians, but by the late 1500s, the Susquehannocks had overpowered and absorbed them. At the time of European contact, the Susquehannock nation occupied a large area.

Europeans began to settle the valley in the late seventeenth century, establishing farms, villages, fishing and trading camps, and later, various industries, including iron, charcoal, and dynamite making. In the 1840's, the village at Safe Harbor became a major ironworks center. (Safe Harbor was so named because of the calm water near the mouth of the Conestoga River, where boatmen could relax in a safe harbor after negotiating the turbulent rapids by Turkey Hill.) The town managed to recover from a series of floods along the Conestoga and Susquehanna rivers, but then the high water of 1918 took away too much, and Safe Harbor rapidly declined. Downstream, at the site of Holtwood Dam, McCall's Ferry operated from 1740 to 1936.

Holtwood Dam now spans the river where a wooden bridge once stood. The project, begun in 1905 by the McCall's Ferry Power Company, was completed in 1910 by the Pennsylvania Water and Power Company (PW&P). Turbines spun by the river's current still produce electricity. In 1955, Pennsylvania Power and Light (PP&L) merged with PW&P, and PP&L assumed control of the Holtwood hydroelectric plant. The Philadelphia Electric Company (now PECO Energy) also built a hydroelectric plant, Muddy Run, a few miles downstream in 1968. The Safe Harbor Power Company finished its dam and power plant in 1932. Besides the power plants, the utilities have also established natural areas, wildlife sanctuaries, and outdoor recreation facilities.

49

Lancaster Central Park

C entral Park has it all—quiet hiking trails, woods, fields, wild-flowers, dozens of bird species, meandering streams, (the Conestoga River and Mill Creek), historic sites, a nature center, and plenty of outdoor recreation activities.

Ownership. Lancaster County Department of Parks and Recreation.

Size and Designation. A county-owned park encompassing 544 acres.

Nearby Nature Attractions. Chickies Rock County Park; Pequea Creek; Shenk's Ferry Wildflower Preserve; Kelly's Run, Hauer-Trout Run, and Tucquan Glen preserves; Susquehanna

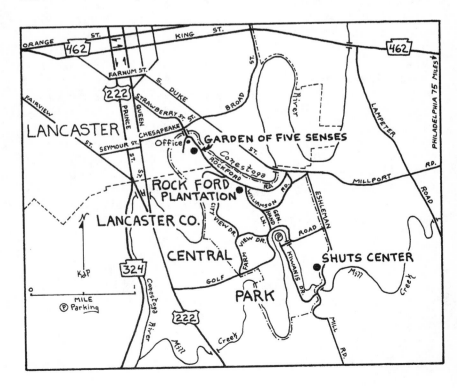

Overlooks; and Tucquan and Octoraro creeks, both state scenic rivers.

Features. Central Park offers facilities for tennis, soccer, meetings, swimming, picnics and parties, playgrounds, sledding, archery, skiing, snowmobiling, horseback riding, primitive camping, volleyball, and baseball, as well as a fitness trail. Also located here is the Rock Ford Plantation, the restored eighteenth-century estate of Edward Hand, adjutant general for George Washington's Continental Army. Naturalists conduct programs and classes at the Shuts Environmental Center and throughout the park. The Garden of Five Senses is located near the park office. Pick up a park guide at the park office or Rock Ford house when you arrive.

The most natural paths in the park are the 1.5-mile Mill Creek Trail, which circles through the Kiwanis Natural Area, beginning at the covered bridge and following the hairpin course of Mill Creek, and the half-mile Wildflower Trail, which starts atop a ridge near the junction of Kiwanis Road and Kiwanis Drive and joins the Mill Creek Trail.

A three-mile portion of the Conestoga Trail traverses the park. It is a challenging hike that crosses Mill Creek via a wire bridge. The Scout Trail runs from Indian Rock in the Williamson Area of the park to the primitive camping area near the nature center. Indian Rock offers a striking view of the Conestoga River and Lancaster. The trails are open daily from dawn to sunset.

For more information, contact the Lancaster County Department of Parks and Recreation, 1050 Rockford Road, Lancaster, PA 17602, telephone (717) 299-8215.

Geology. Lancaster is smack in the middle of Pennsylvania's fertile Piedmont, a landscape of gently rolling hills south and east of the Appalachian Mountains that generally slopes southeasterly toward the ocean. This region has some of the most agriculturally productive land in the eastern United States. Its soils derive from the erosion of metamorphic rock ridges formed 290 million years ago.

Water is plentiful in the Piedmont, both in the form of numerous streams (no natural lakes) and precipitation, an average of 40 to 50 inches a year. The growing season exceeds 180 days, 60 percent of which are sunny.

Indian Rock sits atop a wall of 500-million-year-old limestone indicating that this portion of Pennsylvania was once covered by an ocean.

Mill Creek empties into the Conestoga River, which meanders to the Susquehanna River just below the Safe Harbor Dam.

Wildlife. Because of the Piedmont's fertility, it has been heavily developed for farming and other enterprises. This led to fast deforestation. At one time about 95 percent of the area was under the plow. Today roughly half the region remains cultivated.

There are 72 species of trees in Lancaster Central Park, though many of them are not natives. Growing here are white, chestnut, red, yellow, pin, and scarlet oaks; tulip trees; beech, bitternut and mockernut hickories; black walnut; butternut; green and white ashes, slippery and American elms; eastern red and northern white cedars; silver, norway, red, and sugar maples; hemlock; basswood; catalpa; white, red, pitch, Austrian, and Scotch pines; pawpaw; sassafras; sweet gum; black cherry; American hornbeam; and hop hornbeam. Stately sycamores arch over Mill Creek and the Conestoga River.

Wildflowers bloom in the forest in the spring and summer, especially in the Kiwanis Natural Area. These include the spring beauty *(Claytonia virginica)*, Dutchman's breeches *(Dicentra cucullaria)*, mayapple *(Podophyllum peltatum)*, violets *(Viola* spp.*)*, Virginia bluebell *(Mertensia virginica)*, trout lily *(Erythronium americanum)*, and wild blue phlox *(Phlox divaricata)*. A colony of wild columbine *(Aquilegia canadensis)* thrives at Indian Rock. Various ferns also grow throughout the park.

Many creatures hide from predators beneath rocks, logs, and piles of debris in the streams, including the crayfish, fingernail clam (which resembles the size and shape of a fingernail), and river snail. Insects include water pennies (a beetle larvae shaped like a penny) and mayfly larvae, distinctive for their three tail-like gills.

Birds observed here include the yellowleg, white-winged crossbill (sporadic), yellow-bellied sapsucker, indigo bunting, Swainson's thrush (PA rare), red-headed woodpecker, pine siskin, northern oriole, blue grosbeak (rare in the park), cedar waxwing, Philadelphia vireo, great horned owl, and chestnut-sided, cerulean, baybreasted, Wilson's, American redstart, Blackburnian, prothonotary (PA at risk), yellow-rumped, and black-throated green warblers.

History. The Rock Ford Plantation is the eighteenth-century estate of Edward Hand, adjutant general under George Washington. The Shuts Environmental Center is the restored eighteenth-century stonehouse of a local gunsmith. Robert Fulton, the inventor of the steam-powered paddle wheel boat, began his navigation experiment on the Conestoga River along the park's Rockford Road.

The original section of the park, known as the Williamson Area, was donated to the borough in 1903. In 1918, 94 acres more, known today as the Kiwanis Area, were added. Lancaster County established a parks department in 1966 and acquired 397 additional acres, which were added to Central Park in 1971.

An Indian burial ground was discovered in the Williamson area in 1979.

50

Shenk's Ferry
Wildflower Preserve

The wooded banks that flank Grubb Run burst into a splendid profusion of wildflowers in the spring. Some 70 varieties bloom by the end of May, and another five dozen show off in summer and early fall.

Ownership. Pennsylvania Power and Light Company.

Size and Designation. The preserve is part of the utility company's Holtwood Recreation Area, comprising more than 5,000 acres. The sites of American Indian villages at Shenk's Ferry have been placed on the National Register of Historical Places.

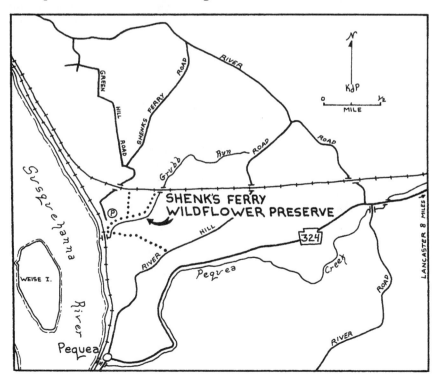

161

Nearby Nature Attractions. Susquehanna River Overlooks; Kelly's Run, Pequea Creek, Trout Run, and Tucquan Glen preserves; Muddy Run Recreation Park; and Lancaster Central Park.

Features. The main event is the annual blossoming of wildflowers, a rainbow of more than 130 varieties. The peak months are April and May.

The trail through the glen begins at the parking area and heads upstream. Midway, the path splits. The right fork continues along Grubb Run and goes to the preserve's boundary at a railroad arch. The left fork concludes at a power line and railroad bed. Rest rooms and an information board with preserve guides are at the trailhead.

Nearby Pequea Creek Campground has camping, picnic tables, food, and drinking water. Return to River Road and follow the signs heading south.

Geology. Grubb Run has cut a valley into the eastern bank of the Susquehanna River. Unlike nearby Kelly's and Tucquan runs, which flow over hard Wissahickon schist, Grubb Run washes over a slab of limestone. The nutrient-rich soil derived from the limestone makes this preserve a nursery for wildflowers.

The presence of limestone suggests that an ocean once covered the region. This sedimentary rock is made of the remains of shelled sea creatures that settled on the ocean floor.

Since limestone is less resistant to erosion than schist, the slopes above Grubb Run generally are not as steep as those found at Kelly's Run and some others. The valley is more U-shaped than V-shaped

Wildlife. In April and May, the peak blooming months, you'll find Dutchman's breeches *(Dicentra cucullaria),* false Solomon's seal *(Smilacina racemosa),* miterwort *(Mitella diphylla),* shepherd's puree *(Capsella bursa–pastoris)* and squirrel corn *(Dicentra canadensis),* as well as wood betony *(Pedicularis canadensis),* and wild columbine *(Aquilegia canadensis),* both red bloomers.

Blue flowers include the Virginia bluebell *(Mertensia virginica),* Venus' looking-glass *(Specularia perfoliata),* speedwell *(Veronica officinalis),* bluet *(Houstonia caerulea),* heal-all *(Prunella vulgaris),* ground ivy *(Glechoma hederacea),* and blue phlox *(Phlox divaricata).*

Yellow blossoms include the trout lily *(Erythronium americanum),* coltsfoot *(Tussilago farfara),* golden corydalis *(Corydalis micrantha),* and celandine *(Chelidonium majus),* a member of the poppy family.

Also look for blue cohosh *(Caulophyllum thalictroides),* a diminutive greenish flower in spite of its name; Philadelphia fleabane *(Erigeron philadelphicus);* jack-in-the-pulpit *(Arisaema tryphyllum),* which grows in damp woods; and wild ginger *(Asarum canadense).* Picking or collecting flowers and plants is forbidden.

Birds sighted here include the wood pewee, Philadelphia vireo (becoming a rarity), yellow-breasted chat, and pileated woodpecker. Warblers such as the yellow-throated, northern parula, cerulean, worm-eating, Kentucky, and hooded arrive in the spring to nest in the tree canopy.

History. A mass grave of Shenk's Ferry Indians found here is evidence of warfare among tribes before European settlement. Historians believe that Susquehannock warriors led the massacre. The Susquehannocks migrated to this territory in the 1500s, driven south by the Iroquois. Competition between the Susquehannocks and the Shenk's Ferry tribes probably resulted in warfare, with the Susquehannocks the eventual victor, only to later be overwhelmed by the Iroquois and arriving Europeans.

Shenk's Ferry was the location of a river ferry. Early industries in the area were charcoal making and iron ore mining. The woodlands were extensively logged to support these businesses. The hiking trail through the glen is a former narrow-gauge railroad track used for hauling ore to an iron furnace. Later, dynamite manufacturing became a major enterprise.

Pennsylvania Water and Power Company purchased much land on both banks of the Susquehanna to construct the Holtwood Dam and hydroelectric plant downstream. The plant went into service in 1910. In 1955, this company merged with Pennsylvania Power and Light, which now manages the site, as well as all the recreational facilities associated with Lake Aldred (the lake behind the Holtwood Dam).

51

Pequea Creek Preserve

If you are lucky, a blue-winged teal will flush from a quiet pool in the creek. Downstream, in an eddy pool below some rapids, a female, mindful of your presence, may huddle with her ducklings until you pass.

Ownership. Pennsylvania Power and Light Company.

Size and Designation. The Pequea Creek area is part of the 5,000-acre Holtwood Recreation Area.

Nearby Nature Attractions. Shenk's Ferry Wildflower, Kelly's Run, Trout Run and Tucquan Glen preserves, Susquehanna River Overlooks, Lancaster Central Park, Muddy Run Recreation Park, and Tucquan and Octoraro creeks, both state-designated scenic rivers.

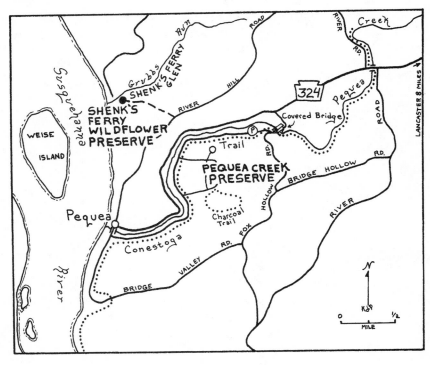

Features. Pequea Creek has much to offer: hiking trails, a boat ramp, fishing, a campground, a small store, rest rooms, drinking water, showers and laundry facilities, a playground, picnic tables, and a group pavilion.

For more information, contact the Pequea Creek Campground and Recreation Area, 86 Fox Hollow Road, Pequea, PA 17565, telephone (717) 284-4587.

Geology. Pequea Creek slices through Wissahickon schist. This rock started as muddy sediment on an ocean floor and later hardened into shale, probably during the Cambrian Period 500 to 570 million years ago.

Intense heat and pressure changed it into schist. Schist resists erosion, so the banks along Pequea Creek are steep. In places, walls of schist jut into the stream creating narrows and rapids.

Wildlife. Eastern hemlock, birch, American beech, tulip tree, and sycamore grow along this section of the Conestoga Trail. A few sycamores fall into the stream each year. Amazingly, the branches above the water level continue to thrive. On the nature trail, you will find more birch and hemlock, oak and hickory on higher ground, and mountain laurel.

Birds in the Pequea Creek area include great blue heron, red-bellied and pileated woodpeckers, and cerulean and yellow-throated warblers. Gulls congregate near the boat launch at the confluence of the creek and the Susquehanna River.

Deer, raccoons, mice, foxes, skunks, and opossums inhabit the woods. Look for their tracks on the nature trails.

History. During the American Revolution, charcoal was made near the campground and hauled by mules to the ironworks in Martic Forge.

Charcoal making required a lot of hardwood. First, four-foot logs were stacked upright. Workers then packed leaves and sod around the wood to form an airtight mound, poured hot coal in a hole at the top of the mound and allowed it to smoulder for two weeks. The remnants of three mounds can still be seen along the Charcoal Trail.

The Colemanville Covered Bridge on Fox Hollow Road is the second-largest single-span wooden bridge in Lancaster County. The original span, built in 1856, was damaged by floods in 1938 and 1972. Each time it was repaired. In 1990, the bridge was determined unsafe and torn down. The new one stands 70 feet downstream and on higher ground.

Construction of the Holtwood Dam across the Susquehanna River created Lake Aldred in 1905. Pennsylvania Power and Light established several recreational facilities on both sides of the river.

52

Tucquan Glen Preserve

The verdant glen cooled by the winding Tucquan Creek supports an abundance of ferns and groves of stately hemlocks. This is a refreshing hike on a hot day.

Ownership. Lancaster County Conservancy.

Size and Designation. This nature preserve encompasses more than 142 acres. Tucquan Creek is a state scenic river.

Nearby Nature Attractions. Shenk's Ferry Wildflower Preserve; Trout Run, Kelly's Run, and Pequea Creek preserves; Susquehanna River Overlooks; Lancaster Central Park; Muddy Run Recreation Park; Alexander-King and Boyer Nature preserves; Greider's Run; and Octoraro Creek, another state scenic river.

Features. The preserve straddles Tucquan Creek from River Road to the railroad tracks near the mouth. An old road that fords the creek a half dozen times serves as the main trail along this state scenic river. It begins at the main parking lot and heads downstream to the railroad tracks, the preserve boundary line. The fords are shallow, but wet feet are likely.

The hike is easy at the outset but, as you approach the river, the walk becomes difficult. The last third of the trail enters the narrowest, wildest, and rockiest part of the glen. Backtrack when you reach the railroad tracks. A thinner path traces the north streambank, but in spots it disappears into the stream.

There are no established trails leading upstream from the smaller parking lot. Rest rooms are not available, and you'll have to supply your own drinking water.

For more information, contact the Lancaster County Conservancy, P.O. Box 716 (128 East Marion Street), Lancaster, PA 17608-0716, telephone (717) 392-7891.

Geology. Like most nearby tributaries flowing into the Susquehanna River, Tucquan Creek washes over a metamorphic rock called Wissahickon schist before it empties into the river.

Wissahickon schist developed from the muddy sediment on an ocean floor at least 500 million years ago. When the ocean receded, the sediment hardened into shale. It was metamorphosed

166

into schist and shoved north on top of other bedrock 440 million years ago.

A striking outcrop of schist rises behind the small parking lot on the east side of River Road. Upstream from that point, the valley widens. Springs on the north side trickle into the creek and create a narrow wetland.

From the outcrop to the confluence with the Susquehanna River, about 1.5 miles, the current traces fault lines, or cracks, in the schist. Just before it empties into the river, the creek tumbles wildly down small cascades and wraps around huge boulders of moss-covered schist.

Wildlife. Tall, stately hemlocks inhabit cool, shady spots in the glen. Other giants include red and chestnut oaks, red maple, black and yellow birches, hickory, tulip tree, and pawpaw. Spicebush, viburnum, and flowering dogwood grow in undisturbed areas upstream from River Road, and rhododendron thickets are found near the mouth of the creek.

Ferns abound, with 21 species represented. Polypody ferns often grow on the crown of the ledges. Ground pines and mosses carpet the forest floor, and mosses and lichens grow on the schist outcrops.

More than 40 species of wildflowers grow here, including cut-leaved toothwort *(Dentaria laciniata),* dwarf ginseng *(Panax trifolius),* wild geranium *(Geranium maculatum),* false hellebore *(Veratrum viride),* bloodroot *(Sanguinaria canadensis),* early saxifrage *(Saxifraga virginiensis),* false Solomon's seal *(Smilacina racemosa),* and large flowered trillium *(Trillium grandiflorum).*

Worm-eating warblers, Acadian flycatchers, wood thrushes, and phoebes are among the warm-weather nesters. When cold weather arrives, they head for Central and South America. Pileated woodpeckers and great horned owls are year-round residents.

Red-backed, slimy, two-lined, and dusky salamanders inhabit the preserve. The stream supports trout, minnows, crayfish, and northern water snakes. Insect life includes the damselfly and the waterstrider.

History. The Lancaster County Conservancy, founded in 1969, purchased the core tract of the preserve (97 acres) in 1983. Since then, it has acquired more land, and the preserve has grown to more than 142 acres.

53

Trout Run Preserve

Trout Run flows through a tunnel and a cool hemlock grove lush with ferns and other foliage. Wildflowers brighten the forest in May. Trout swim in the chilly stream, and give the preserve its name.

Ownership. Lancaster County Conservancy.

Size and Designation. This nature preserve encompasses 46 acres.

Nearby Nature Attractions. Tucquan Glen, Pequea Creek, and Kelly's Run preserves; Shenk's Ferry Wildflower Preserve; Lancaster Central Park; Susquehanna River Overlooks; Alexander-King and Boyer Nature preserves; and Octoraro and Tucquan creeks, both state-designated scenic rivers.

Features. Enter the preserve via the tunnel or hike over the abandoned railroad bed. Paths lead along both sides of the creek. There are no facilities here.

For more information, contact the Lancaster County Conservancy, P.O. Box 716 (128 East Marion Street), Lancaster, PA 17608-0716, telephone (717) 392-7891.

Geology. The ragged Wissahickon schist rock outcrops flanking the gentle run date back 440 to 500 million years. The metamorphic schist was originally shale.

Trout Run journeys just a few miles. It flows into Climbers Run on the north side of Pennsy Road. Climbers Run empties into Pequea Creek, a tributary of the Susquehanna River.

Wildlife. In early May, wildflowers add color to the preserve.

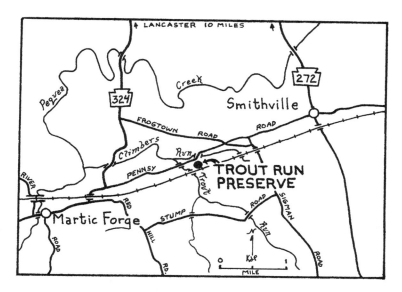

The spring display includes skunk cabbage *(Symplocarpus foetidus)*, wild ginger *(Asarum canadense)*, spring beauty *(Claytonia verginica)*, mayapple *(Podophyllum peltatum)*, trout lily *(Erythronium americanum)*, hellebore *(Veratrum viride)*, bloodroot *(Sanguinaria canadensis)*, round-lobed hepatica *(Hepatica americana)*, Indian cucumber root *(Medeola virginiana)*, jack-in-the-pulpit *(Arisaema triphyllum)*, wood anemone *(Anemone quinquefolia)*, and rue-anemone *(Anemonella thalictroides)*.

The preserve supports one of only a few habitats in Lancaster County for dwarf ginseng *(Panax trifolius)*, and Canada mayflower *(Maianthemum canadense)*. Look for ground pine and shining club moss creeping up the slopes, and the evergreen foliage of striped wintergreen, partridgeberry *(Mitchella repens)*, and checkered rattlesnake plantain *(Goodyera tesselata)* declining in population).

Ferns appear everywhere—alongside fallen logs, rock cracks, beneath ledges, spreading across boulders. Christmas, wood, and maidenhair ferns are the most numerous. Polypody ferns share their habitat on boulders and ledges with colonies of mosses. Pincushion and sphagnum mosses flourish in the preserve.

Bald cypress grows near the railroad tracks. This species of southern swamps and bayous resembles the tamarack and has knees, or modified roots, that stick out from the base of the trunk. The knees help the tree to breathe in its wet habitat.

Yellow birch is abundant here because of the shady, moist habitat. Its glossy, yellowish bark peels off in curls. Sniff a scarred twig.

The wood gives off a wintergreen odor (the smell of birch beer), though fainter than that of black birch.

The gnarly roots protruding from the banks provide nesting sites for Louisiana waterthrushes. Phoebes, which feed on insects that they snatch from the air, often nest on the rock ledges.

History. Fred and Florence Hauer and Charles Hauer donated this land to the Lancaster County Conservancy in 1976.

54

Kelly's Run Natural Area

The clutter, chaos, and wildness in this steep ravine are engaging. Great rhododendron intertwines with toppled hemlocks and birches. Boulders lie in random, jumbled heaps, requiring the brook to follow a plunging, slalom course to the Susquehanna.

Ownership. Pennsylvania Power and Light Company.

Size and Designation. Kelly's Run is part of the electric company's 5,000-acre Lake Aldred-Holtwood Recreation Area and has been set aside as a natural area. Its 7.5-mile trail system has been designated a national recreational trail.

Nearby Nature Attractions. Shenk's Ferry Wildflower Preserve; Pequea Creek, Tucquan Glen, and Hauer-Trout preserves; the Susquehanna River Overlooks; Muddy Run Recreation Park; Lancaster Central Park; and Tucquan and Octoraro creeks, both state scenic rivers.

Features. The overlook above the Susquehanna River Valley has one of the best views along the river, especially at sunrise and sunset. In spring and fall, birders come here to observe migrating birds, which on some days number in the thousands.

From April through October, rest rooms, drinking water, and picnic tables are available at the overlook. Five interconnecting hiking trails that vary in difficulty depart from this spot. The Conestoga Trail is a tough climb; the Pine Tree Trail is easier.

Most of the trails eventually descend into Kelly's Run, a wild,

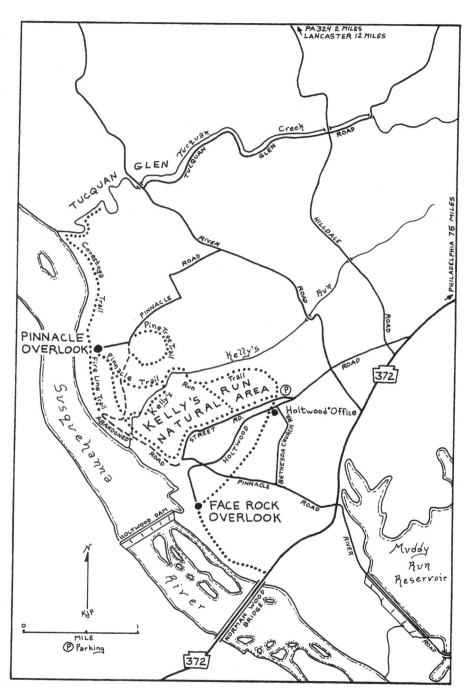

PA 324 2 MILES
LANCASTER 12 MILES

TUCQUAN GLEN

Tucquan

GLEN

Creek

ROAD

PHILADELPHIA 75 MILES

TUCQUAN

Conestoga Trail

RIVER

ROAD

HILLDALE

ROAD

Run

PINNACLE
OVERLOOK

PINNACLE

Pine Tree Trail

Pinnacle Trail

Fire Line Trail

ABANDONED

Susquehanna

Kelly's Run Trail

KELLY'S NATURAL RUN AREA

Trail

Kelly's

ROAD

372

P

Holtwood Office

STREET

HOLTWOOD RD.

BETHESDA CHURCH RD.

ROAD

PINNACLE

ROAD

FACE ROCK
OVERLOOK

HOLTWOOD DAM

N

KJP

River

Muddy
Run
Reservoir

RIVER

NORMAN WOOD BRIDGE

ROAD

0   MILE   1

P Parking

372

steep ravine. The most popular path to the creek is the white-blazed Pinnacle Trail and then the blue-blazed Kelly's Run Trail, which traces nearly the entire course of the creek.

Kelly's Run also can be reached from trails departing from the arboretum near the Holtwood Land Management Office on Old Holtwood Road, off River Road.

Geology. Kelly's Run has cut its deep gash through some of the oldest and hardest rock in Pennsylvania—Wissahickon schist. This metamorphic schist probably developed from muddy ocean-floor sediment dating back 500 to 570 million years. This sediment first hardened into shale and later into schist.

Pinnacle Overlook sits atop a massive anticline (bell-shaped fold or wrinkle in bedrock) of schist running east-west. Kelly's Run follows the east-west trend on the south slope of the anticline.

Schist resists erosion, hence the V shape of the gorge, which from Pinnacle Overlook plunges 300 to 500 feet down rocky, rugged terrain. All of the sculpting has been done by a small stream just a few miles long. The gorge is still wild because its severe terrain is simply too tough for loggers, farmers, or developers.

Downstream, the Holtwood Dam blocks the flow of the river to form Lake Aldred. In the river are trenches known as deeps, some of which are two miles long, several hundred feet wide, and 125 feet deep. Nobody knows for sure how they formed. They may be troughs cut by enormous volumes of water melting from glaciers during the ice age, or faults in Earth's crust.

Wildlife. The lower Susquehanna Valley supports an unusual beech-maple forest community, but Kelly's Run natural area seems to have its own mix of trees, in which oaks are predominant.

Chestnut oaks flourish on the rocky, higher slopes, with their dry, sunbaked soil. Other oaks include red, white, and black. Sugar maples, tulip trees, and beech also grow here, along with eastern hemlock, which favors cool, shady sites like deep ravines. Dense stands of cone-bearing hemlocks can shade out most life in the understory, and their shed needles acidify the soil. Stands of mountain laurel, which favors dry, acidic soil, bloom in late May and early June.

Careful observers here find clumps of Virginia and mountain pines, the latter an indicator of dry soil. The two trees are similar, but they can be distinguished by their pine cones: Mountain pine cones have thorny spines; Virginia pine cones have thin, stubby ones.

Great rhododendron has become an impenetrable thicket in places along the run. Like the mountain pine, the great rhododendron is usually found at higher elevations. Its rose-purplish flowers emerge in June and July.

The poisonous, northern copperhead likes rocky, wooded hillsides like Kelly's Run. These snakes hunt for rodents, birds, and amphibians at night, but during the early spring and late fall they may be active during the day. They usually lie motionless when approached.

Birds observed here include the nuthatch (probably white-breasted); pileated, hairy, red-bellied, and downy woodpeckers; yellow, worm-eating, and hooded warblers; Philadelphia and warbling vireos; and barred and great horned owls. Pinnacle Overlook, at the parking lot, is an ideal spot to observe spring and autumn migrants.

History. American Indians inhabited Reed and Duncan islands, which you can see from Pinnacle Overlook. Duncan Island has been listed on the National Register of Historic Places.

McCall's Ferry, located a little south of the mouth of Kelly's Run, operated across the Susquehanna from 1740 to 1936.

In 1815, McCall's Ferry Bridge opened as the longest single-arch wooden span ever built, but ice jams destroyed the bridge in 1818.

Construction of a hydroelectric project was started in 1905 by McCall's Ferry Power Company. The Pennsylvania Water and Power Company took over the project in 1907, and the utility began generating power in 1910. The village of Holtwood grew around the dam, but by the 1960s it had largely been torn down. Philadelphia Power and Light assumed control of the project in 1955.

In 1992, the U.S. Department of the Interior designated the Kelly's Run-Pinnacle Trail System a national recreational trail.

Muddy Run Recreation Park

Ferncliff Wildflower and Wildlife Preserve
Haines Station Natural Area

Two zebra swallowtail butterflies cruise over the drooping ferns along the banks of boulder-strewn Rock Creek. Far above the ferns, tall beeches and hemlocks reign in this wild, craggy ravine called Ferncliff.

The scene changes at Muddy Run, where land that has been cultivated and manipulated for two centuries is slowly returning to forest, and wetland is developing where a stream meets a lake.

Ownership. PECO Energy.

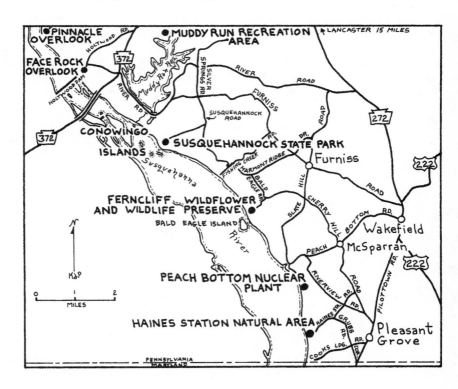

Size and Designation. Muddy Run Recreation Park is 700 acres. The 65-acre Ferncliff Wildflower and Wildlife Preserve has been designated a national natural landmark.

Nearby Nature Attractions. Susquehanna River Overlooks; Shenk's Ferry Wildflower Preserve; Kelly's Run, Tucquan Glen, and Trout Run preserves; Lancaster Central Park; and Octoraro and Tucquan creeks, both state-designated scenic waterways.

Features. Muddy Run Recreation Park has much to offer: a 100-acre man-made lake, Muddy Run Reservoir, for fishing and boating (gas-powered motorboats and swimming are prohibited), hiking trails, picnic tables, a playground, boat and bike rentals, a camp store, and ballfields.

Nature trails branch from the campground. The Wetlands Interpretive Trail wanders through a swampy area east of the campground. The Lakeshore Hiking Trail encircles the reservoir. Pick up trail brochures at the information center.

Benton Hollow Road, a rough gravel road for weekend residents, serves as the trail through Ferncliff preserve. Rock Creek flows over the road in places, but it is rarely ankle-deep, except after a heavy rain. Stay away from the cottages. Haines Station Road is the trail for the natural area, though you can wade in Haines Branch.

The park's information center has exhibits, slide shows, films on natural history and energy, and environmental programs. The center is open 9 A.M. to 4 P.M. Tuesday through Saturday, December to March; Wednesday through Sunday, April to November.

For more information, contact PECO Energy, Muddy Run Recreation Park, 172 Bethesda Church Road West, Holtwood, PA 17532, telephone (717) 284-2538.

Geology. Until 1968, Muddy Run flowed down a valley and emptied quietly into the Susquehanna River. Then PECO dammed the stream, pumped a billion gallons of river water into the basin, and created a 100-acre reservoir for its power plant. In places the lake is 80 feet deep.

On the Trail of Changing Landscapes, there is a block of rock known as Wissahickon schist. This rock started as fine sediment on an ancient seafloor more than 500 million years ago and later hardened into shale. About 470 million years ago, when continental plates collided, the shale experienced intense pressure and heat which changed the shale into schist.

Rock Creek, running through Ferncliff preserve, tumbles over schist in small, scenic waterfalls en route to the Susquehanna River.

On the Wetlands Interpretive Trail, a fuzzy yellow substance known as yellow boy appears on rocks at one spring. Yellow boy is produced when water sources of different pH values meet. Iron is dissolved in the water and filters out as iron oxide.

Wildlife. Muddy Run park is a changing landscape. Fields are slowly returning to the forest that greeted pioneers. In a process called succession, grasses and sedges lose out to shrubs and vines, which then are overtaken by trees.

There are three kinds of wetlands in the park: emergent cattail swamp, shrub swamp, and swamp forest. Cattails and reeds dominate the freshwater cattail marsh. Sweetflag *(Acorus calamus),* which grows partly submerged, blossoms here too. Willow and alder prevail in the shrub wetland. These give way to elm, ash, and red maple in the swamp forest, located between two streams. Spring floods bring nutrients into the wet woods.

Other trees in the park include flowering dogwood, chestnut, white, red, and black oaks, black walnut, sycamore, tulip tree, black cherry, black gum, hackberry, and red cedar. Walnut trees favor wet areas, like streambanks. Their shells float downstream to shores and gravel banks. Seedlings spread their roots on this shifting ground.

Black raspberry, staghorn sumac, Virginia creeper, greenbrier, wild grape, and maple-leaved viburnum are also found here.

Thirty-seven bird species have been sighted, including the American kestrel, ruby-throated hummingbird, ring-necked pheasant, northern oriole, purple martin, wood duck, great horned owl, goldfinch, and red-winged blackbird, the last found in the cattail marsh.

Carolina chickadees live year-round in Ferncliff. They resemble black-capped chickadees but are slightly smaller. In this area, the ranges of the two birds overlap.

Box turtle and water, black rat, and garter snakes also live here. The wetlands shelter spring peepers, bullfrogs, leopard frogs, and dusky salamanders.

Deer wander into the park. Other residents are the cottontail rabbit, woodchuck, red fox, striped skunk, raccoon, gray squirrel, and meadow mole.

Muddy Run Reservoir contains 34 species of fish. Most entered the lake when PECO pumped river water into the basin. Largemouth bass, sunfish, and crappie made the transition from river to lake. Brook trout and northern pike are stocked every year.

A virgin beech-maple forest (or a mixed hardwood forest according to some sources) flourishes at Ferncliff and Haines Station. American beech, maple, and hemlock dominate; tulip tree, white ash, sugar maple, basswood, and chestnut, scarlet, and red oaks are found in lesser numbers.

Various trilliums, including the purple trillium *(Trillium erectum)*, bloom in the ravines in May. Some species are unusual for the area. Also look for Dutchman's breeches *(Dicentra cucullaria)*, jack-in-the-pulpit *(Arisaema triphyllum)*, Virginia bluebells *(Mertensia virginica)*, and dwarf ginseng *(Panax trifolium)*. Common polypody, Christmas, hay-scented, spinulose wood, and marginal wood ferns grow throughout the preserve.

History. Muddy Run Recreation Park opened in 1969. Ferncliff was designated a national natural landmark in 1972.

◆ 56 ◆

Serpentine Barrens

Goat Hill State Forest Natural Area
Nottingham Park
Chrome Barrens

Early settlers called these odd openings in the Piedmont *barrens* because they could not coax crops from the thin, dry soil. These areas are not really barren, however, but are refuges for many unusual and endangered plants. The heavy-metal, low-nutrient bedrock that defeats corn and the common foliage of the surrounding Piedmont allows rarities such as the mouse-eared chickweed, serpentine aster, and glade spurge to flourish. Pennsylvania's largest virgin stand of pitch pine, a scrubby conifer usually found on the windswept summits of the Appalachian Mountains, dominates the barrens.

Ownership. Pennsylvania Department of Environmental Resources, Bureau of Forestry, owns Goat Hill. Nottingham Barrens belongs to the Chester County Department of Parks and Recreation. The Pennsylvania Chapter of the Nature Conservancy transferred the land title of the Chrome Barrens to Elk Township.

Size and Designation. The Goat Hill preserve is a state forest natural area totaling 803 acres. Part of the property has been nominated as a national natural landmark. Octoraro Creek, which

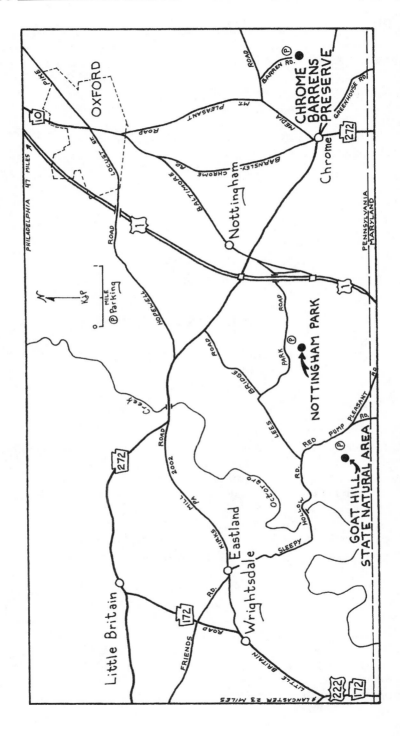

forms the western boundary of the preserve, is a state scenic river. Chester County designated two-thirds of Nottingham Park, which encompasses 651 acres, a natural area in 1977. Chrome Barrens covers about 160 acres.

Nearby Nature Attractions. French Creek, Marsh Creek, and White Clay Creek state parks; Warwick and Hibernia parks; Springton Manor Farm; Great Valley Nature Center; Valley Forge National Historic Park; and Brandywine, Octoraro, and French creeks, all state scenic rivers.

Features. To explore Goat Hill, first hike down the abandoned road that begins above the parking lot and heads in the direction of the power line. The main trail follows the power line. Keep track of your course, because trails are unmarked and maps are not available. Several fire lanes also cut through the preserve, and there are many routes you can take. Stay off private property. There are no rest rooms or drinking water. For more information, contact the Bureau of Forestry, Valley Forge District Forester, 1132 Ridge Road, Pottstown, PA 19464, telephone (610) 469-6217.

Nottingham Park offers eight miles of bridle and hiking trails that lead to pitch pine forests, serpentine outcrops, and brooks, camping, fishing, picnic areas, playgrounds, rest rooms, and drinking water. Pick up a trail guide at the information board in front of the park office. For more information, contact Nottingham County Park, 150 Park Road, Nottingham, PA 19362, telephone (610) 932-9195.

In the Chrome Barrens, many fire lanes branch from the main path that departs from the parking lot. Choose your own paths, but remember your route. There are no facilities at this location. For more information, contact the Pennsylvania Chapter of the Nature Conservancy, 1211 Chestnut Street, 12th Floor, Philadelphia, PA 19107-4122, telephone (215) 963-1400.

Geology. Geologists may have uncovered the origin and movement of serpentine rocks that contain hydrated magnesium silicates and were formed along cracks in the ocean floor.

During the ancient mountain-building periods, molten rock, called peridotite, from Earth's mantle, seeped and squeezed into fractures at the vanguard of colliding continental plates. Near the surface of the ocean floor, the dense, dark peridotite wedged into the formations of lighter hydrated silicates and cooled. Here ocean water reacted with olivine and pyroxene, the main ingredients of peridotite. The enormous heat and pressure produced by the collision of the continental plates metamorphosed the peridotite and silicates along these faults in a process called serpentinization.

The new rock, serpentinite, contained various ingredients, determined by the composition of its parent rocks, the temperatures and pressure during the transformation, and the duration of the metamorphosis. Consequently, serpentine rocks in the same location show shades of green (the predominant color), blue, and black, and the texture of the rock varies.

Exactly how serpentine moved from the ocean floor to the eastern coast of North America remains a mystery. The best theory is that it moved northwest with the continental plates.

The Chester County barrens lie along a string of serpentine sites stretching from Georgia to Newfoundland. Other bands of barrens run from central California to Alaska, Quebec to Manitoba, and Guatemala to Cuba. Each regional serpentine barren has a different ecosystem. The barrens between Georgia and New York are temperate serpentine barrens. More than 90 percent of the temperate barrens lie within Pennsylvania and Maryland. A dozen or so tiny serpentine barrens developed in Pennsylvania. Chester County has nine of them, and the three largest examples.

The underlying bedrock in the Nottingham, Chrome, and Goat Hill barrens consists of gneiss and schist, both metamorphic rocks. Talc, asbestos, chromite, and soapstone are often found here.

The soil of a barren, derived from the serpentine rock, is not fertile enough for crops or the natural vegetation typical of the surrounding Piedmont. It is rich in magnesia and heavy metals, such as chromium, iron, and nickel, but low in nutrients, such as potash and lime. Because there is little accumulated decayed vegetation, or humus, the soil is thin and susceptible to erosion. Though the region may receive 50 inches of rainfall a year, the water drains away quickly, and the barrens stay dry. Serpentine rock has a high heat capacity, meaning it can absorb much heat and retain it longer, and this also discourages most vegetation. Because of these factors, only xerophytes—plants that have adapted to these harsh conditions—succeed in the barrens.

Soil conditions differ among the barrens, largely because the metal content in the serpentine varies. This may explain why the mouse-eared chickweed grows only at Goat Hill and not at Nottingham or Chrome. Similarly, Chrome Barrens is the only known location in Pennsylvania for Curtiss' milkwort.

Octoraro Creek snakes around the western boundary of the preserve. It has carved steep cliffs (200 feet high in some places) on the northwest face of Goat Hill. Black Run is the only reliable water source for wildlife in the Nottingham barrens.

Although farmers and loggers dismissed the barrens, the mining industry saw profit in these stark ridges. Magnesite was extracted from Goat Hill between 1835 and 1871, and again briefly in 1921. Chrome Barrens and the crossroads hamlet of Chrome earned their names from the local chromite mines in the nineteenth century. Abandoned chromite and feldspar quarries are attractions at Nottingham Park (Mystery Hole and Nature Trail).

Wildlife. The barrens are grassy openings with scrubby pitch pines or blackjack and post oaks, sprinkled with wildflowers, and impenetrable jungles of smilax briers that suffocate the understory and conceal many endangered plants.

Goat Hill protects 220 plant species, of which 16 are endemic, or exclusive, to the area. This is the only known habitat of the state endangered mouse-eared chickweed (*Cerastium arvense* var. *villosissimum*), a star-shaped white flower with fuzzy leaves that grows along Octoraro Creek. The hairy leaves keep the plant from dehydrating and overheating. Another endangered plant, the glade spurge *(Euphorbia purpurea),* occupies a swampy area near the confluence of an unnamed brook and the Octoraro. This specimen grows in only four other colonies in the state.

Other endemic rarities are the serpentine chickweed (*Cerastium arvense* var. *villosissum*), serpentine aster (*Aster depauperatus,* PA threatened), diminutive sedge *(Fimbristylis darlingtoniana),* Aleutian maidenhair fern (*Adiantum pedatum* var. *aleuticum*), moss pink (*Phlox subulata,* PA endangered), pink milkwort (*Polygala incarnata,* PA endangered), prairie dropseed (*Sporobulus heterolepsis,* PA endangered), and round-leaved fameflower (*Talinum teretifolium,* PA threatened). Small's ragwort *(Senecio smallii)* is not found north of Virginia, except in the barrens. The lyre-leaved rock cress *(Arabis lyrata),* and whorled milkweed also reach their northernmost range at Goat Hill.

Serpentine aster and fameflower have developed special adaptations to resist scorching temperature and drought. The aster's rosette of leaves, which spreads across the ground, protects the fragile green parts from wind and from harsh sunlight that reflects off rocks. The ground-hugging fameflower is a succulent, meaning that it stores water. Unlike a cactus, however, which holds water in the stalk, the fameflower uses its cylindrical leaves as reservoirs.

Chrome Barrens conceals Pennsylvania's only community of Curtiss' milkwort (*Polygala curtissii,* PA endangered), a petite plant with delicate rose or purple blossoms more common in sandy soil. Here also are some of the best surviving specimens of staggerbush (*Lyonia mariana,* PA endangered), plain ragwort (*Senecio anonymus,* PA rare), Bicknell's hoary rockrose (*Helianthemum bicknellii,* PA endangered), and arrow-feather red, three-awned (*Aristida purpurascens,* PA threatened), whose flowerhead resembles the feathers on an arrow. Look for a few-flowered nutrush (*Scleria pauciflora,* PA threatened), with berries shaped like tiny golf balls, and annual fimbry (*Fimbristylis annua,* PA threatened), also found in Arizona deserts.

At Nottingham, 54 kinds of grasses and 20 varieties of sedges survive. Some are species of special concern in the state, including cluster fescue (*Festuca paradoxa,* PA endangered), field paspalum (*Paspalum laeve* var. *philosum,* declining in numbers), prairie dropseed, slender spike rush (*Eleocharis tenuie* var. *verrucosa,* PA endangered), and clustered beak rush *(Rhynchospora capitellata).*

Other imperiled plants found here are the sandplain wild flax (*Linum intercursum,* PA endangered), southern wood rush (*Luzula bulbosa,* declining), umbrella magnolia tree (*Magnolia tripetala,* PA threatened), Spanish (southern red) oak (*Quercus falcata,* PA endangered), spring ladies'-tresses (*Spiranthes vernalis,* PA endangered), maidenhair fern (*Adiantum pedatum* ssp. *calderi,* declining), and American holly (*Ilex opaca,* PA threatened). Some of these rare plants grow in all three preserves.

In Goat Hill, a stand of red oak with light bark grows on the cliff above the Octoraro. Scientists think this tree grove, nominated for national natural landmark status, is an example of an ecotype, a subspecies that has somehow adapted to survive in an inhospitable location. Hay-scented, Christmas, maidenhair, marginal, and interrupted ferns spread out beneath the oaks.

Oddly, Goat Hill safeguards the state's largest and healthiest colony of pitch pine, a conifer usually found on mountaintops. Eastern red cedar and blackjack, bear, and dwarf chinquapin oaks also grow here. Smilax briers, dwarf gray willow, black huckleberry, and deerberry make up the understory.

The bird population at Goat Hill shows diversity because there are several habitats in the preserve: pine barrens, scrub growth, stream, prairie, and the edge between mature hardwood and open savanna. Seventeen kinds of warblers have been spotted here, notably the prairie, cerulean, parula, pine, worm-eating, and yellow-throated. The whippoorwill, a nocturnal insect hunter declining in numbers because of habitat loss, thrives in the barrens although it is uncommon elsewhere in the region.

The saw-whet owl, Pennsylvania's smallest owl and a species of special concern, favors the pines in the barrens for nests. Other typical birds in the barrens include the yellow-breasted chat, hermit thrush, prairie warbler, fox sparrow, white-eyed vireo, gray catbird, rufous-sided towhee, and sharp-shinned, Cooper's, and red-shouldered hawks.

Barrens are also prime habitats for rare butterflies and moths, such as the pink devil moth, cobweb skipper, barrens buckmoth, frosted elfin, and black-waved flannel moth.

From time to time the preserve owners start prairies fires, called prescribed burns, to clear away the tangle that threatens rare flora. The fires restore the health of the habitats. For instance, fire stimulates the germination of prairie dropseed.

Dense thickets and pines help conceal deer at Goat Hill and Chrome. Beavers construct lodges on the banks of the Octoraro Creek, and bobcats (PA at risk) reportedly roam at Goat Hill, though some naturalists dispute the sightings.

History. American Indians used the barrens for hunting grounds and gathering places. The sharp boundary in vegetation made the barrens a distinct landmark. Here the Indians easily obtained soapstone, a stone they carved.

European settlers saw no potential for agriculture in the barrens, so they left them undisturbed. Around 1810, chromite was discovered on a barren near Baltimore. The discovery inspired Isaac Tyson, son of the landowner, to mine the ore for paint makers in Philadelphia. Tyson found other barrens, and by 1828 he was extracting chromite and magnesite from mines in Chester County. Tyson probably controlled the world's supply of chromite from 1828 to 1850. A village called Chrome grew up near the richest chromite mines in the nineteenth century.

Magnesite and chromite were mined at Goat Hill between 1828 and 1871. Chrome and feldspar mining occurred at Nottingham from the mid-1800's to 1930. Today, mine openings, water-filled abandoned quarries, and sinkholes along the trails recall the area's mining past.

Today suburban sprawl is the biggest threat to the barrens. Many barrens have become the sites of housing and commercial developments. In 1958, the Chester County Commissioners established a parks department and the Nottingham barrens were determined to be worth preserving. That led to the creation of Nottingham Park.

The effort to preserve Goat Hill intensified in 1979 when an excavating firm sought local zoning board approval to quarry stone in these barrens. Although the board denied the request, residents feared that another company might seek a variance. In 1983, the Pennsylvania Chapter of the Nature Conservancy purchased 592 acres on Goat Hill and later turned it over to the Pennsylvania Department of Environmental Resources. The department declared the barrens a natural area in 1993, and also designated Octoraro

Creek a scenic river. The conservancy later purchased a 93-acre tract and has management agreements on 118 acres.

In a series of transactions in 1991 and 1992, the Nature Conservancy bought the Chrome Serpentine Barrens. The land title has since been transferred to Elk Township.

Valley Forge
National Historical Park

Valley Forge recalls images of the hardships of the encamped Continental Army, the unrelenting winter chill, General Washington's devotion and leadership.

Today Valley Forge is more than a national shrine. As the population and development increase in the area, the value of the park's natural setting grows too.

Ownership. U.S. Department of the Interior, National Park Service.

Size and Designation. This national historic site totals 3,500 acres.

Nearby Nature Attractions. Briar Bush Nature Center; Riverbend Environmental Education Center; Fort Washington, Evansburg, French Creek, Marsh Creek, and White Clay Creek state parks; the Serpentine Barrens; Great Valley Nature Center; French, Brandywine, and Octoraro creeks, all state scenic waterways. The Schuylkill River, a state scenic river, passes through Valley Forge.

Features. Be sure to visit the historic sites. Begin at the visitors center and view the 15-minute orientation movie. Drive the one-way auto route to the various landmarks, or pedal a bike or hike on a paved 6.4-mile path. You can also hike on ten miles of bridle trails, a mile-long footpath along the west bank of Valley Creek between the covered bridge on Yellow Springs Road and Washington's Headquarters, and the two-and-a-third-mile Schuylkill River

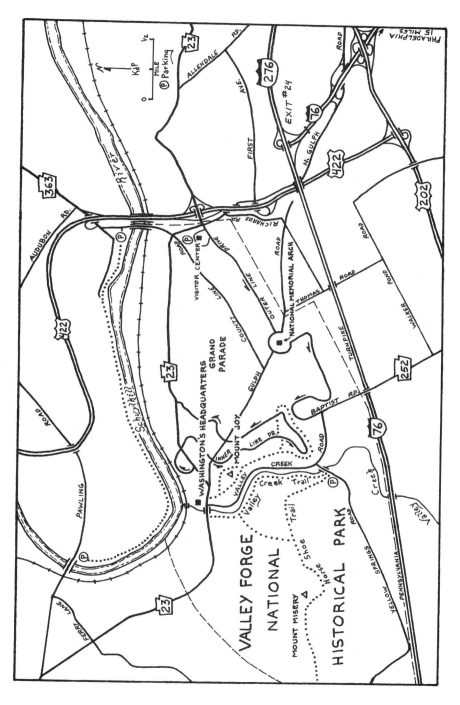

Trail at the Betzwood Picnic Area. The Schuylkill River Trail traces the towpath of the Schuylkill Canal, which operated from 1825 to the 1920s. Part of the Horseshoe Trail goes through the park; the trail begins at Washington's Headquarters. Pick up trail maps at the visitors center before departing. Guides in the center can direct you to specific destinations.

The auto route is open daily from 6 A.M. to 10 P.M. The visitors center and most buildings are open daily from 9 A.M. to 5 P.M. Between April 1 and November 30, there is a small admission fee to enter Washington's Headquarters. Visitors can picnic at the Betzwood, Varnum's Woods, or Wayne's Woods Picnic Areas.

For more information, contact the Superintendent, Valley Forge National Historic Park, P.O. Box 953, Valley Forge, PA 19481-0953, telephone (610) 783-1000.

Geology. The topography around Valley Forge made it an ideal defensive location. King George's redcoats lodged in Philadelphia. Washington cleverly camped close enough to the city to keep them from raiding the interior and far enough away to avoid a sudden attack. From Mount Joy and Mount Misery, lookouts observed British movements and the progress of supplies on the river. The army bivouacked on high ground. If necessary, it could cross the river at Fatland's Ford or on Sullivan's log bridge.

Washington's soldiers constructed their barracks on karst topography, a limestone-based plateau with sinkholes, pits, ravines, caves, and underground streams. At Valley Forge, the ground is supported by dolomite, a calcite-rich bedrock similar to limestone. Precipitation, which is usually slightly acidic, soaks through the topsoil and dissolves the underlying limestone or dolomite. Surface water eventually drains thorough an enlarging network of seeps and channels in the dolomite. Tunnels and caves also take shape. Sometimes the roofs of underground structures collapse, forming sinkholes on the surface.

In karst terrain, sinkholes are always opening and closing. Some sinkholes seen by soldiers during the Revolution have been plugged by sediment and vegetation. Small depressions with clusters of trees on the Grand Parade Ground are probably filled sinkholes. New sinkholes develop suddenly. A few brooks, like the one flowing near General Varnum's Headquarters, disappear into sinkholes and freshen the underground water system.

The visitors center stands in an abandoned dolomite quarry. The long rock on the south side of the parking lot and another rock 500 feet north of the lower parking lot are dolomite. Dolomite began as sediment that accumulated in horizontal layers off the coast of an ancient ocean 500 million years ago. Its high concentration of calcium carbonate derives from the remains of primitive marine creatures.

Long wavy sheets, or laminations, in the rock show the presence of microbial mats (algal colonies) struggling in a scummy, shallow sea. When ocean tides and storms covered the mats with sediment, the mats stacked themselves one atop the other, reaching upward to cleaner water and sunlight.

Bottom layers compressed into rock called stromatolites. Sometimes they appear as layered spheres, or cabbage heads. Stromatolites served as the foundation for the topmost algae beds. The mats may have been the only conspicuous life forms on earth at the time.

Hikers on the Valley Creek path will see bedrock from the Chickies and Antietam formations. Note the piles of Chickies quartzite on the west slope of Valley Creek near the Upper Forge footbridge.

Chickies quartzite started as sand on an ocean beach more than 580 million years ago. During a mountain-building period, the sand bed was folded beneath offshore sediments, pushed inland, and metamorphosed into quartzite. This rock forms the foundation of Mount Misery.

Though resistant to weathering by precipitation, Chickies quartzite weakens from the freezing and thawing of water. Water enters tiny cracks in the rock. When it freezes, it acts like a wedge to break the rock along fractures. The talus near the Upper Forge bridge resulted from such weathering. Some of these rocks show circular impressions. These are the tunnels of worms that lived in the sand 570 million years ago.

Antietam formation underlays Mount Joy. This rock started as an offshore deposit of sand and mud 580 million years ago. It folded over the Chickies rock and was also metamorphosed during the mountain-building period. Examples of Antietam rock lie near the covered bridge. This rock is finer grained than Chickies quartzite and breaks off in plates or tablets. The shiny specks in the rock are mica.

Wildlife. Valley Creek Gorge, the summit of Mount Joy, and the Schuylkill River are good outposts for birders. More than two hundred species have been sighted here. Pick up a bird checklist at the visitors center.

Spring visitors include the spotted sandpiper, turkey vulture, chimney swift, red-bellied woodpecker, red-eyed vireo, yellow-rumped warbler, and American redstart. In summer, look for the indigo bunting, wood thrush, goldfinch, eastern meadowlark, green-backed heron, and great crested flycatcher. The black duck, killdeer, common goldeneye, black-and-white warbler, cedar waxwing, and an occasional Philadelphia vireo are spotted in the autumn. Few birds linger here during the winter. Still, you may see a pied-billed grebe (PA rare), ring-necked duck, screech owl, American kestrel, red-tailed hawk, and dark-eyed junco.

The bald eagle and osprey (each PA endangered) fly by occasionally. The northern harrier, Swainson's thrush, northern goshawk, and prothonotary warbler (all PA at risk) also appear at Valley Forge.

History. Valley Forge was a pastoral community of farms, forests, and forges at the start of the War of Independence. The place got its name from the iron-making forges built along Valley Creek in the 1740s. Hessian soldiers, mercenaries for the British, wrecked these valuable enterprises in September 1777, then camped there for a while.

General Washington's haggard and ill-equipped army of 12,000 men arrived at Valley Forge in a snowstorm on December 19, 1777. In a few days, six inches of snow covered the parade ground.

Soldiers cut down trees for huts, stables, fuel, defense works, and other structures. Mud from the river sealed the cracks in the shelters. The troops were overcrowded, malnourished, and poorly clothed. Typhus, typhoid, dysentery, and pneumonia swept through the camps. At one time 4,000 soldiers, a third of the army, were listed as too sick for duty. Some 2,000 soldiers died that winter in camp. The Continental Congress seemed unable to adequately supply them.

The Continental Army pulled out of Valley Forge on June 19, 1778, in pursuit of the British, who were heading for New York. By persevering and staying in the field, the Continental Army had won a major victory.

The Schuylkill Canal, running 108 miles from Port Clinton to Philadelphia, opened in 1825. Mule teams pulled 180-ton barges on a towpath. The canal closed in the 1920s because it could not compete with the Reading Railroad, which passed through the park.

Alexander Kennedy, an Irish immigrant, dug the first quarry in 1805. He also built a lime-burning business in Port Kennedy, south of Valley Forge. In 1846, quarrymen uncovered a huge cavern with stalagmites and stalactites, columns, and other formations. One room was big enough to be a dance hall for Fourth of July celebrations in 1846 and 1847. Eventually, the cave was quarried.

In 1871, miners found a mastodon tooth in a 40-foot tunnel descending from a quarry floor. This became known as Bone Cave, or Port Kennedy Cave. Parts of mammals, reptiles, bugs, and plants stuck in the black mud that coated the cave wall. The biggest find was a four-foot mastodon tusk. Bone Cave remained undisturbed until a deeper chamber was blasted open in 1894.

Scientists discovered 34 species in the cave, including fragments of mastodons (most of them calves), giant sloths, black bears, wolverines, badgers, peccaries, and deer. Paleontologists painstakingly recorded their treasures, but amazingly they failed to mark the exact location of the cave. After the last excavation in 1896, Bone Cave disappeared beneath a landfill and thick vegetation. Park officials believe the cave still entombs rodents, insects, and other animals overlooked in earlier excavations and hope to find its location.

Valley Forge became Pennsylvania's first state park in 1893. The property was later turned over to the National Park Service. Mining continued in the park until 1976. The Pennsylvania Chapter of the Nature Conservancy helped the park service purchase a 46-acre tract at the eastern end of the park.

The privately owned Washington Memorial Chapel and Museum of the Valley Forge Historical Society, located in the park, are worth a stop.

Great Valley Nature Center

When Arnold Bartschi announced in 1974 that he was donating ten acres of land to the township for a nature center, officials thought he wanted to start a nudist camp. What he really had in mind was the Nature Center of Charlestown, which later became the Great Valley Nature Center.

Ownership. Great Valley Nature Center is a nonprofit organization emphasizing nature and environmental education.

Size and Designation. Ten acres.

Nearby Nature Attractions. Valley Forge National Historical Park; the Serpentine Barrens; French Creek, Marsh Creek, and White Clay Creek state parks; and three state-designated scenic rivers: Brandywine, Octoraro, and French creeks.

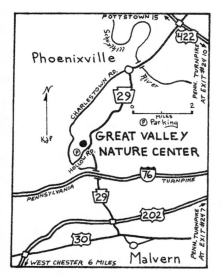

Features: Great Valley is a compact nature center designed as a natural history learning center. Long-distance travelers should not choose this site as a primary destination. Instead, think of the center as a place for a brief encounter with nature.

Offices, exhibits, a gift shop, rest rooms, and indoor classrooms have been crammed into an old, quaint fieldstone barn, built around 1800, but major renovation is under way to improve the facilities.

A half-mile foot trail departs from either the parking lot or the nature center. The land was once a dairy farm, so it has been logged and grazed. A few big trees are scattered on the grounds, including a giant 300-year-old white oak, but there is no lush woodland. Instead, the trail leads through meadows and thickets; to a stream, pond, and wildflower garden; and past a restored two-story stone springhouse that has a milking house on the second level.

Families with small children should begin at the nature center, where they can play with the animal bones, skulls, and shells located in outdoor bins. Next, head to the observation deck overlooking a swampy brier patch and to the giant old white oak.

The center is open Monday through Saturday from 9 A.M. to 5 P.M. and Sunday from noon to 5 P.M. For more information, contact the Great Valley Nature Center, P.O. Box 82, Route 29 & Hollow Road, Devault, PA 19432, telephone (610) 935-9777.

Geology. Great Valley refers to a huge ditch created 210 to 230 million years ago, when the continental plates that had fused to create a supercontinent called Pangea began to drift apart. As that happened, huge chunks of bedrock slid or dropped along fault lines, creating clefts or rift valleys.

Hartman Creek, the stream that runs through the nature center, flows into Pickering Creek, which empties into the Schuylkill River. The land has been farmed for more than two centuries.

Wildlife. Among the scattered trees gracing the property are white oak, black walnut, black cherry, flowering dogwood, pine, spruce, holly, redbud, eastern red cedar, witch hazel, and fringe-tree. Iris blooms along the pond in the spring.

In the wildflower garden, dozens of beauties flourish in the cultivated beds. Here's a sample of the treats in the garden: the perfoliate bellwort *(Uvularia perfoliata)*, sweet (licorice scented) golden-rod *(Solidago odora)*, boneset *(Eupatorium perfoliatum)*, barberry *(Berberis vulgaris)*, butterfly weed *(Asclepias tuberosa)*, New York aster *(Aster novi-belgii)*, New England aster *(Aster novae-angliae)*, sweet white violet *(Viola blanda)*, beardtongue *(Penstemon* spp.), sweet William, *(Phlox divaricata)*, crested dwarf iris *(Iris cristata)*, bleeding hearts *(Dicentra eximia)* and herb Robert *(Geranium robertianum)*.

History. Before the arrival of Europeans, circa 1680, this land was inhabited by the Lenni Lenape. In 1683, this property was part of a 5,000-acre estate given to Charles Pickering by William Penn.

Instead of farming, Pickering hatched a get-rich-quick scheme with a miner named John Tinker. The duo lived in a cave on Tinker Hill and mined along Pickering Creek. They tried to pawn off their ore as silver. The provincial council in Philadelphia charged Pickering with counterfeiting—the "quoining of Spanish bitts"—and ordered him to pay a fine. Pickering supposedly paid his debt, then practiced law in Philadelphia and was elected to the state assembly.

The land upon which the nature center now sits passed through numerous families during the next two centuries, before ending up in the hands of Arnold Bartschi, a businessman and owner of the nearby Japanese garden called Swiss Pines. In 1974, he donated ten acres of the old Pickering estate to Charlestown Township. The nature center opened in the autumn of 1976.

59

Tyler Arboretum

Tyler Arboretum is an exotic, global gallery of trees: a giant sequoia from the Pacific coast, a cedar of Lebanon from Asia Minor, a magnolia from central China, and a ginkgo, whose Asian ancestors date back 200 million years. Native species from Penn's Woods reach the sky here, too.

A healthy population of bluebirds flies in this green, quiet realm. The arboretum's Pink Hill section, a rare serpentine barren,

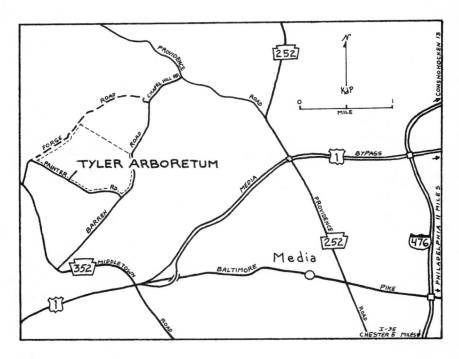

in one of the last strongholds of the endangered moss pink (*Phlox sublata* ssp. *brittonii*).

Ownership. The Tyler Arboretum is a nonprofit educational institution partially supported by memberships.

Size and Designation. 700 acres.

Nearby Nature Attractions. Ridley Creek State Park (premium bird-watching during the spring and autumn migrations).

Features. The arboretum's 20 miles of trails go to woodlands, ponds, streams, and open fields. You also can wander around collections of magnolias, lilacs, rhododendrons, hollies, flowering cherries, conifers, and crab apples, and explore specialty gardens, such as the fragrant, butterfly, and bird gardens.

The ten-mile Wilderness Trail leads to all the habitats. Figure on spending five or six hours on this walk. Hike through the barrens on the two-mile Pink Hill Trail in late April, when the moss pinks bloom. The wooded 2.7-mile Dismal Run Trail traces Dismal Run and visits Indian Rock, a disc of rock on which a mysterious cross is carved. The 3.8-mile Painter Brothers Trail is enjoyable every season, and goes to the giant sequoia, through the Pinetum and Old Arboretum, past dogwoods and rhododendrons, and across Rocky Run at Indian Rock.

The buildings of the former estate owners stand near the parking lot. A restored barn serves as the visitors center, bookstore, gift shop, and exhibit area. The butterfly, bird, and fragrant gardens, the last specially designed for sight-impaired visitors, surround the barn. The Old Arboretum features the cedar of Lebanon and a score of other trees planted in the early nineteenth century. North of the center is the North Woods and a bike trail to Ridley Creek State Park.

The arboretum holds special events throughout the year, plus many natural history and horticultural programs and outings. Trail maps, brochures, a schedule of events, and membership information are available at the visitors center. The arboretum opens daily at 8 A.M. and closes at dusk. The gift shop and bookstore are open Monday through Saturday from 10 A.M. to 4 P.M. (3 P.M. in July and August), Sunday noon to 4 P.M. There is a small admission fee.

For more information, contact the Tyler Arboretum, 515 Painter Road, Media, PA 19063-4424, telephone (610) 566-9133.

Geology. The Pink Hill Barrens is an unusual geological feature. A rock called serpentine lies beneath its thin, pale earth. For more details about serpentine barrens, see the Geology section of the Serpentine Barrens chapter.

Wildlife. Between 1849 and 1876, two Quaker bachelors, Jacob and Minshall Painter, planted nearly 1,000 kinds of trees and shrubs here. About 20 of these original plants survive, including the lone giant sequoia (1859), the cedar of Lebanon, the ginkgo, a Corsican pine, and a towering Oriental spruce, said to be the tallest of its kind in the area.

Learn to identify trees in the Pinetum and along the Native Woodland Walk. The Pinetum is a collection of conifers—pines, spruces, hemlocks, cedars, larches, cypresses—spread out over an 85-acre parcel. The Native Woodland Walk displays more than 50 species of trees and shrubs for easy identification. Look for the bottlebush buckeye (native of Alabama and Georgia), yellowwood, sassafras, fringetree, spicebush, American holly (PA threatened), summersweet, and Virginia sweetspire. Wildflowers include yellow perfoliate bellwort *(Uvularia perfoliata),* cut-leaved toothwort *(Dentaria laciniata),* common fleabane *(Erigeron philadelphicus),* and purple-brown beechdrops *(Epifagus virginiana).*

Naturalists head to Pink Hill to see the unusual vegetation on a serpentine barren, a rare habitat. Though Pink Hill is barren for farmers, it is not a barren place for the pink and lavender blossoms of the endangered moss pink. The orange blossoms of the wood lily *(Lilium philadelphicum)* appear in June and July. Barren aster, three varieties of chickweed (*Cerastium* spp.), blackjack oak, whorled milkweed *(Asclepias verticillata),* slender mountain mint *(Pycnanthemem tenuifolium),* and New Jersey tea *(Ceanothus americanus)* are plants typically found in places with dry, sandy soil such as this one.

Beech, hickory, black birch, black cherry, and black, scarlet, swamp white, and white oaks grow along streams enriched by alluvial soils. Elsewhere, tulip trees, young red maples, witch hazel, maple-leaved viburnum, rhododendron, flowering and red osier dogwood, and ironwood flourish.

Other wildflowers include Jacob's ladder *(Polemonium vanbruntiae),* wood anemone *(Anemone quinquefolia),* and skunk cabbage *(Symplocarpus foetidus).*

The bird garden at the west end of the barn attracts, feeds, and shelters birds. Trumpet creeper *(Campsis radicans)* and bee balm *(Monarda didyma)* are planted for ruby-throated hummingbirds, an occasional nester at the arboretum; cotoneasters, dogwood, and hawthorn for cedar waxwings; and holly and shadbush for hermit thrushes and mourning doves.

Birds and bird-watchers flock to the arboretum. The arboretum's pioneer bluebird project—putting up nesting boxes—has been successful, and the eastern bluebird, rare in some places, is a common year-round resident. As many as 50 pairs of bluebirds have been counted, most of them in open fields near the Pinetum. Forty-one species of warblers and vireos have been recorded. Warblers such as the pine, cerulean, chestnut-sided, hooded, worm-eating, common yellowthroat, black-and-white, blue-winged, Louisiana, Kentucky, yellow-breasted chat, American redstart, ovenbird, and northern parula nest in the woodlands. The northern (Baltimore) oriole, rufous-sided towhee, indigo bunting, scarlet tanager, cedar waxwing, chimney swift, wood duck, American kestrel, red-bellied woodpecker, great crested flycatcher, eastern screech owl, and wood thrush are other nesters.

Several imperiled birds have appeared, notably the peregrine falcon (PA endangered), northern harrier (PA at risk), prothonotary warbler (PA at risk), Swainson's thrush (PA rare), northern goshawk (PA rare), yellow-bellied flycatcher (PA threatened), and osprey (PA endangered). Pick up a bird guide at the visitors center.

History. In 1681, Thomas Minshall, an English Quaker, acquired this property from William Penn. From that time until 1944, the land was held by seven generations of Minshall's descendants.

The most celebrated owners were brothers Minshall and Jacob Painter, who planted nearly a thousand kinds of trees and shrubs, including 200 fruit trees, on the grounds. Their collection, known as the Painter Trees, decorated the small valley behind the barn and Lachford Hall.

John J. Tyler, nephew of the Painter brothers, inherited the estate and increased its acreage. In 1944 his widow bequeathed the land for a public arboretum, which opened in 1945.

60

John Heinz National Wildlife Refuge at Tinicum

The John Heinz National Wildlife Refuge is home to some of Pennsylvania's rarest and most secretive animals, and hundreds of geese, ducks, and herons convene here, even though the refuge lies just a mile from the Philadelphia International Airport.

Ownership. U.S. Department of the Interior, Fish and Wildlife Service.

Size and Designation. This preserve, formerly the Tinicum National Environmental Center, is a national wildlife refuge encompassing 1,200 acres.

Nearby Nature Attractions. Little Tinicum Island State Forest Natural Area, Ridley Creek State Park, Tyler Arboretum, Wissahickon Valley, Pennypack Environmental Center, Schuylkill Center for Environmental Education, and Riverbend Environmental Education Center.

Features. Nine miles of hiking trails explore the impoundment, tidal marsh, lagoons, and Darby Creek. Pick up a trail map at the visitors center.

The 3-mile Impoundment Trail, used by hikers, birders, joggers, fishermen, and cyclists, is a level, wide gravel path that skirts the impoundment. Near the trailhead, a boardwalk crosses the shallow impoundment. A quarter mile down the path, a double-deck observation platform overlooks the water, which often abounds with geese, ducks, and other waterbirds. Ahead, another blind lets you observe the creatures in the tidal marsh. Beyond the

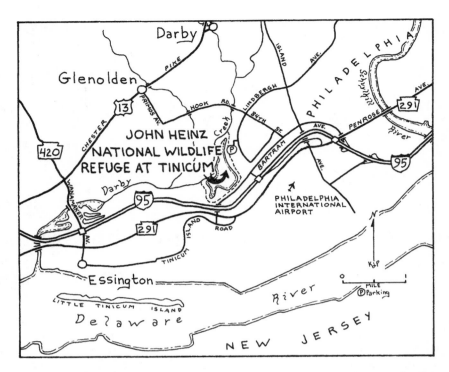

blind, the left trail fork completes the loop around the pond; the right fork winds through the western two-thirds of the refuge—through the tidal marsh and lagoons and along the south bank of Darby Creek. There are two more blinds along this route.

The blinds and observation platform are ideal lookouts for wildlife observers. A bird list is available at the visitors center.

Another way to experience the refuge is by navigating Darby Creek. Canoeists can launch near the visitors center. Tides influence the water level in Darby Creek, which is only navigable within two hours before and after high tide. Call the refuge at (215) 365-3118 for tide information.

Fishing is allowed except where restrictions are posted. The shore of the impoundment is popular. Hunting and trapping are forbidden. Insect repellent is essential in summer.

The grounds are open from 8:30 A.M. to sunset every day, the center from 9 A.M. to 4 P.M. daily.

For more information, contact the John Heinz National Wildlife Refuge at Tinicum, Refuge Headquarters, Suite 104, Scott Plaza, Philadelphia, PA 19113, telephone (610) 521-0662, or (215) 365-3118 (visitors center).

Geology. The refuge safeguards Pennsylvania's largest remaining freshwater tidal wetland. This region is part of the coastal plain, a narrow flatland running across the southeastern sections of Delaware, Philadelphia, and Bucks counties and continuing through New Jersey and Delaware to the Atlantic Ocean.

Underlaying the wetland, about 60 feet down, is Wissahickon schist of the Cambrian Period (500 million years ago). Beds of gravel, sand, silt, and clay cover the schist. Water carried these eroded sediments from uplands. The deposits thicken as you go southeasterly in the refuge.

During the ice age, the sea level fell, because huge amounts of water were trapped in the continental glaciers. When the ice melted, the sea level rose, and salt water flooded the mouth of the Delaware River, forming today's Delaware Bay. High tides pushed salt water into the coastal plain marshes and up the Delaware and Schuylkill rivers to their fall lines. The marshes became soggy, brackish estuaries.

Tinicum Marsh stretched east to the Schuylkill River and comprised about 5,700 acres when Swedish settlers arrived. Urban development has reduced it over time to about 200 acres. The lagoons at the western end of the refuge were gravel pits excavated in the early 1970s for the construction of I-95.

Darby Creek was once part of a braided delta that included the Schuylkill and Delaware rivers.

Wildlife. Birds are the main attraction here, and 288 species have been counted. Pick up a bird list at the visitors center. To ducks, geese, herons, and sandpipers, Tinicum Marsh is an important resting and feeding spot on the Atlantic Flyway, a north-south air route flown by migratory birds. Birds pass through in the spring heading north and return in the autumn en route to their southern wintering grounds.

Among the birds observed are the bald eagle (PA endangered), peregrine falcon, osprey, least and black terns, short-eared owl, loggerhead shrike, (which impales its prey on sharp branches or thorns), plus the upland sandpiper (PA threatened), yellow-crowned night heron (PA threatened), yellow-bellied flycatcher (PA threatened), northern shoveler, gadwall, American wigeon, ruddy duck, common nighthawk, northern bobwhite, northern goshawk (PA rare), common snipe (PA at risk), whippoorwill, Swainson's thrush (PA rare), and Henslow's sparrow (PA rare).

Eighty-five species nest here, including the king rail (PA endangered), American and least bitterns (both PA threatened), sedge wren (PA threatened), snowy egret (PA at risk), pied-billed grebe (PA rare), green-winged teal (PA rare), marsh wren (PA rare), and barn owl (PA at risk).

Thirty-five kinds of warblers and vireos visit the area, notably the prothonotary (PA rare), yellow-rumped, Cape May, cerulean, and black-throated green warblers. Seven nest here: the yellow warbler, American redstart, common yellowthroat, yellow-breasted chat, white-eyed, warbling, and red-eyed vireos. They arrive in early May and depart in October.

The refuge may be the only habitat in Pennsylvania where the coastal plain leopard frog (PA endangered) is common. This small amphibian (two to three inches) gets its name from the round brown spots on its body. More common are the bullfrog, green, wood, and pickerel frogs, and spring peeper. American and Fowler's toads, rare in this part of Pennsylvania, live here too.

The redbelly turtle (PA threatened) occasionally basks in the sun beside painted turtles. Reclusive eastern mud turtles may still lurk in the muck, though none have been seen for years. The northern diamond-backed terrapin, which favors the brackish water of estuaries, sometimes travels up Darby Creek on a high tide. The red-eared slider, a turtle named for a distinctive red line on each side of its head, is common here, as are snapping and musk turtles. Don't handle these reptiles; snappers' powerful jaws can injure fingers and hands,and musk turtles emit a foul odor when picked up.

Northern water snakes, often mistaken for the poisonous water moccasin, and eastern garter snakes are also residents of the refuge. Neither of them is venomous.

Butterflies, dragonflies, and damselflies also can be seen at the sanctuary. Common butterflies include the viceroy, red admiral, red-spotted purple, painted lady, and Aphrodite fritillary. Mourning cloaks emerge from hibernation in late March. Monarchs migrate into the area in May; in September, they head for central Mexico.

Golden acres of marsh marigold, or cowslip *(Caltha palustris),* are visible in late spring. The attractive and opportunistic magenta-colored wildflower around the pond is purple loosestrife *(Lythrum salicaria).* It appears in June along with spatterdock *(Nuphar advenum),* a yellow water lily. Other summer blossoms include common mullein *(Verbascum thapsus),* bladder campion *(Silene cucubalus),* and New York ironweed *(Vernonia noveboracensis).* The pink and white blooms of marsh mallow *(Hibiscus palustris)* brighten the marsh shores in late summer.

Red maple, various willows, green and white ash, sweet gum, black gum, sassafras, staghorn sumac, viburnum, and flowering dogwood grow in wooded spots. Mulberry can be found by the second bird blind on the Impoundment Trail.

Clusters of wild rice (*Zizania aquatica,* PA rare) go to seed in late summer. *Phragmites,* a type of reed, and cattails both provide the material for muskrat lodges. Tracks show the presence of the nocturnal weasel, raccoon, and opossum. Scores of rabbits live here as well. Fishers catch yellow perch, blue-backed herring, golden shiner, and carp.

History. The Lenni Lenape called their settlement at the mouth of the Schuylkill River Passyunk (from *Pachsegink*), meaning "in the valley." Tinicum comes from the Lenape word for island, *menatey.*

When Swedish settlers arrived here in 1634, the marsh measured 5,700 acres. Over the years, the marsh was drained, diked, dredged, dumped on, and developed down to a mere 200 acres.

Preservation of the wetland began in 1955, when Gulf Oil Corporation donated 145 acres of the eastern end of Tinicum Marsh to Philadelphia. This site became known as Tinicum Wildlife Preserve. In 1969, citizens' groups and conservation organizations rallied to protect the open-water section, which was threatened by construction of I-95 and a sanitary landfill. After hearings and legal actions, the interstate was rerouted north of the wetland and garbage dumping ended.

In 1972, Congress authorized the U.S. Department of the Interior to buy 1,200 acres for the Tinicum National Environmental Center. In November 1991, the refuge was renamed the John Heinz National Wildlife Refuge at Tinicum to honor the late senator, who had been instrumental in preserving this place.

61

Little Tinicum Island
State Natural Area

This green oasis in an unnatural and inhospitable urban environment is an important stopover for birds during spring and fall migrations on the Atlantic flyway. The birds congregate here because there are few other undisturbed places for them to go in the Delaware Valley.

Ownership. Pennsylvania Department of Environmental Resources, Bureau of Forestry.

Size and Designation. This 200-acre island is a state forest natural area with Valley Forge State Forest. The Pennsylvania

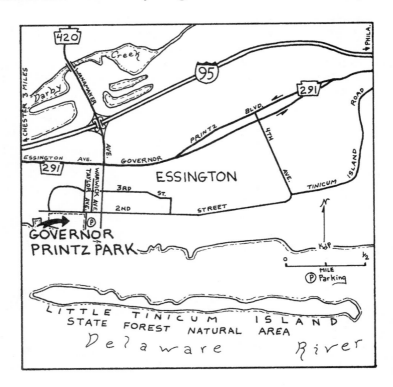

Fish Commission has designated the island a reptile and amphibian protection area.

Nearby Nature Attractions. John Heinz National Wildlife Refuge at Tinicum, Tyler Arboretum, Ridley State Park, and the Schuylkill River, a state scenic river.

Features. This is an island accessible only by canoe, rowboat, or light motorized boat; do not try to swim to the island. Be sure to beach your watercraft above the tide line, and anchor it with slack. The difference between low and high tides in this estuary is nearly six feet. This island has no trails nor accommodations for humans. Primitive camping is permitted, but don't expect quiet with the airport nearby. Hunting and fishing are allowed, except in posted areas.

The less adventuresome can observe the island from Essington; Governor Printz Park may be the best vantage point.

Geology. As temperatures warmed at the end of the ice age, 10,000 to 12,000 years ago, the ice melted and raised the level of he Atlantic Ocean, which backed up into rivers like the Delaware River, creating a broad estuary as far upstream as Philadelphia. An estuary, found near the mouth of a river, is influenced by both ocean tides and the river's current. Its water is brackish, a mix of fresh water from the river and salt water from the ocean. The salinity of an estuary fluctuates, depending on the river's flow and the strength of tides.

Little Tinicum Island may once have been part of a marsh in a delta between the mouths of the Schuylkill River and Darby Creek. A small channel may have split the island from the mainland. When the estuary's level rose at the end of the ice age, some of the marsh probably became flooded. Much of Little Tinicum Island also was swamped and was isolated in the main river current.

Wildlife. Two hundred and six species of birds have been observed at Little Tinicum Island, including occasional sightings of federal and state endangered birds such as the bald eagle and peregrine falcon. Other rarities seen here are the common tern (believed to be extirpated in Pennsylvania), osprey (PA endangered), short-eared owl (PA endangered), black tern (PA endangered), and American bittern (PA threatened.) Sightings of birds designated at risk in the state include the barn owl and northern harrier. The marsh wren, a rarity, is seen from time to time.

Waterbirds flock to the island. Look for the great blue heron; snowy and common egrets; tundra swan; double-crested cormorant; common loon; mallard, black, blue-winged teal, and pintail ducks; Forster's tern; and various gulls. Swallows, purple martin, snow bunting, American kestrel, northern oriole, horned lark, yellow-billed cuckoo, and myrtle, Cape May, parula, and black-and-white warblers are common residents.

A few species of small mammals—the rabbit, rat, mouse, vole, red bat, short-tailed weasel, and muskrat—live on the island.

The water around the island, especially the calm back channels, is a vital nursery and spawning ground for anadromous fish—marine fish that spawn in fresh water—such as shad, bay anchovies, blue-backed herring, and striped bass (the latter diminishing in numbers). Catfish, eel, bullhead, white perch, silver minnow, and banded killifish also inhabit the waters.

The island's vegetation must withstand fluctuations in tides, strong currents, and heavy waves. Three-square bulrush *(Scirons americana)* holds up against the waves on the south shore mud flats. Water lily and arrowhead have strong leaves and hardy flexible stems, enabling them to stand erect, float, or be immersed. Water hemp *(Acnida cannabina)*, false pimpernel *(Lindernia dubia)*, lamb's-quarters *(Chenopodium album)*, and marsh hoarhound *(Lycopus europaeus)* help retain the soil on the island.

Plants that tolerate pollution have established themselves on Little Tinicum, including purple loosestrife, Japanese knotweed, and Norway maple.

The state's healthiest community of Walter's barnyard grass *(Echinochloa walteri)*, an endangered plant, grows here. Wild Indian rice *(Zizania aquatica,* PA rare), another plant dwindling in number, flourishes in soggy spots.

There are 18 kinds of trees, including red maple, tree of heaven, willows, white mulberry, and sycamore, and nine varieties of shrubs, including buttonbush, false indigo, and common alder.

History. The New Sweden Company established a colony, Essington, on Tinicum Island in 1643. Governor Printz Park in Essington honors Sweden's first colonial governor.

Pieter Stuyvesant seized New Sweden for Holland in 1655, but in 1664 the Dutch were forced out by the English. The Dutch regained the territory in 1673, but they lost it forever the following year. English colonists arriving with William Penn in 1681 built settlements along the Delaware River.

Before the American Revolution, a series of dikes was constructed on the island so that crops could be cultivated. The dikes were destroyed in 1777, but it is not known whether the vandals were British soldiers or American patriots. Pennsylvania grabbed the title to the island in 1783.

The U.S. Army Corps of Engineers rebuilt dikes using sediments dredged from the river. In May 1993, the island became a state forest natural area.

62

Riverbend Environmental Education Center

W hat Riverbend Environmental Education Center lacks in post-card scenery, it makes up with hundreds of little daily dramas and details of nature. Nearby, some acrobatic swallows dip, swirl, and flutter. Just beyond them, two small birds face off over territory. Leaves and feathers fly, and squeals resound. A dragonfly skims the surface of a quiet pool in Saw Mill Run.

Ownership. Riverbend Environmental Education Center is a nonprofit educational organization.

Size and Designation. 28 acres.

Nearby Nature Attractions. Briar Bush Nature Center, Valley Forge National Historic Park, Fort Washington and Evansburg state parks, and the Schuylkill River, a state scenic river.

Features. The center's resources include a pond, stream, field, forest, bird blind, gardens, and two miles of paths, which are open

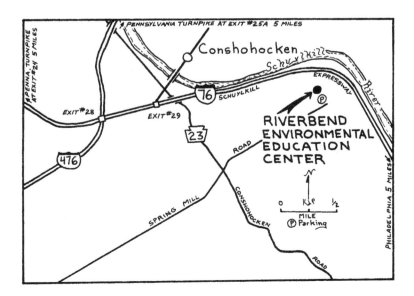

to the public from dawn to dusk. Part of the Aloha Trail passes through private property; always stay on the trail.

The headquarters, a big red barn, serves as a classroom, office, library, and discovery room. Rest rooms are located here.

The center's primary focus is education for schoolchildren, and it offers a summer day camp. Bird-watchers and star-gazers also favor the site.

For more information, contact Riverbend Environmental Education Center, P.O. Box 2, Spring Mill Road, Gladwyne, PA 19035, telephone (610) 527-5234.

Geology. The center's name comes from a 90-degree bend in the Schuylkill River known as the Conshohocken Curve. Here the river, which had been heading southeast over limestone and dolomite, hits a resistant wall of granite and gneiss. It turns northeast for a mile, then swings southeast again. Riverbend sits on heights above the latter bend.

The Schuylkill River cuts through a gorge once feared by boatmen because of the rapids at Rummell's Falls. Downstream, the Falls of the Schuylkill, another obstacle, marks the fall line dividing the Piedmont region and the Atlantic coastal plan.

Wildlife. Sixty-two species of birds have been observed, including the ruby-throated hummingbird, osprey (PA endangered), red-bellied woodpecker, northern parula, northern (Baltimore) oriole, indigo bunting, eastern phoebe, mourning dove, American redstart, and yellow-rumped and black-and-white warblers.

Tracks along Saw Mill Run indicate the presence of raccoons. Raccoons are omnivorous, meaning they eat just about anything. Their diet partly explains why this nocturnal prowler can survive in urban settings.

Much of the acreage around the center was farmland. The tulip tree is the most prevalent hardwood, though oak and hickory also grow here. Many of these trees are draped in ivy and other vines. From time to time, areas must be cleared of foreign invaders such as tree of heaven and akebia vine. White pine, spruce, and hemlock have been planted in these cleared spots.

History. The Lenni Lanape fished at the rapids and falls in the Schuylkill gorge. They called the river "ganshowahanna," meaning "falling waters," probably a reference to the Falls of the Schuylkill, and *manayunk,* or "where we drink."

William Penn, accompanied by Indian guides and a band of settlers, once admired the Schuylkill gorge from the eastern heights above Hagy's Ford.

In 1857, Alan Wood built iron works in Conshohocken, which

means "pleasant valley" in Lenni Lenape. Succeeding generations of the Wood family built a mansion called Woodmont on the estate, a three-story stone house called Aloha, and in 1924, the Sears Roebuck barn. In 1974, the family deeded the estate to the newly formed Riverbend Refuge Inc., the original name of the center.

63

Schuylkill Center for Environmental Education

The Lenni Lenape referred to the Schuylkill River as *manayunk,* or "where we drink." In their day it was safe to drink the water. The river flows through a scenic gorge in northwestern Philadelphia before joining the Delaware River. The Schuylkill Center for Environmental Education, located in Upper Roxborough, on the eastern heights just below the Conshohocken Curve, offers environmental and natural history education for residents of metropolitan Philadelphia.

Ownership. The Schuylkill Center for Environmental Education is an independent, nonprofit organization.

Size and Designation. 500 acres.

Nearby Nature Attractions. Wissahickon Valley, Pennypack Environmental Center, Fort Washington State Park, Riverbend Environmental Education Center, and the Schuylkill River, a state scenic river.

Features. The Schuylkill Center for Environmental Education has developed several innovative education programs, such as the Ecovan, an RV classroom and laboratory. It also has audiovisual programs, weekend nature programs for families, and loan boxes for teachers, self-contained teaching units lent to schools. Many classes and programs for children, teens, and adults are held at the center.

You can, if you wish, just drop in and stroll on the six miles of trails, which visit woodlands, meadows, thickets, streams, and

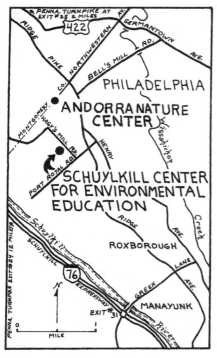

ponds. A couple of blinds with feeders offer year-round opportunities to see birds.

The mile-long Gray Fox Loop heads to Wild Dance Pond, traverses a pine plantation, and passes by a stone farmhouse built in 1754. The mile-long Ravine Loop is a more difficult trail that follows a stream and navigates a few slippery slopes and a marsh. Look for garnets in the rock outcrops. On clear days, for a view of the Philadelphia skyline, take the quarter-mile Upper Fields Trail. The Widener Trail, which passes through a forest, field, and thicket and visits a pond, is accessible to disabled visitors. Staff teachers also lead classes on this popular path.

The center also houses the Schuylkill Wildlife Rehabilitation Center, which yearly provides medical care and temporary refuge for 3,000 wild animals from the Delaware River Valley. The animals need quiet and solitude while they recover, so visitors are not allowed.

An interpretive education building houses a library and resource center, the Discovery Room (featuring hands-on exhibits), a bookstore, a gift shop, rest rooms, and drinking water. The center is open Monday through Saturday from 8:30 A.M. to 5 P.M. and Sunday 1 to 5 P.M. (closed Sundays in August). The bookstore closes a half hour earlier. There is an admission fee for nonmembers to enter the grounds.

For more information, contact the Schuylkill Center for Environmental Education, 8480 Hagy's Mill Road, Philadelphia, PA 19128-9975, telephone (215) 482-7300.

Geology. The center is located atop the eastern heights of the Schuylkill River gorge. The rock is Wissahickon schist, flanking the river formed 440 million years ago. It started as clay sediment on an ocean floor and later hardened into shale. As the mountains were uplifted, the pressure metamorphosed the shale into schist. This schist contains a large amount of the flaky, silvery mineral mica and is known as mica schist.

Quartzite is also found in the preserve; this rock was sandstone before its transformation. Phyllite also underlays the center. Like schist, phyllite started as shale. It has been metamorphosed more than slate (another metamorphic rock derived from shale) but not as mush as schist. Its luster comes from fine grains of mica.

Settlers had difficulty navigating boats in the gorge, especially over the rapids at Rummell's Falls. The Falls of the Schuylkill, downstream near the Philadelphia Museum of Art, mark the boundary between the Piedmont region and the Atlantic coastal plain.

Wildlife. There are plenty of trees here—tulip tree, sycamore, silver maple, birch, black walnut, white oak, buttonwood, sassafras, black cherry, aspen, and American beech. Dense thickets of briers and vines show that the land, now slowly reverting to forest, was once farmland. Blackberry, blueberry, poverty grass, and mountain laurel indicate acidic soil.

Overbrowsing by deer is decimating the center's wildflowers. The best floral displays are found in the moist ravines.

The center has been keeping track of birds since 1965, with an annual winter census taken around Christmas and a nesting census in early June. Among the species commonly observed here are the gray catbird, robin, starling, crow, house wren, cardinal, grackle, Carolina chickadee, tufted titmouse, mourning dove, ring-necked pheasant, rufous-sided towhee, red-tailed hawk, downy woodpecker, barn swallow, Canada goose, northern mockingbird, American redstart, yellow-breasted chat, common yellowthroat, and blue-winged warbler. Pick up a bird checklist at the nature center. More than 150 species have been observed.

Other inhabitants include the squirrel, deer, mouse, mole, fox, opossum, skunk, raccoon, and groundhog. Dragonflies and damselflies hover over the center's four ponds, and are plentiful in early summer. In mid-July, at the end of the Upper Fields Trail, look for the dogbane leaf beetle. Their shiny, coppery bodies resemble the polished helmets of palace guards.

History. The Lenni Lenape blazed a trail from the fords on the Schuylkill to fords on the Susquehanna River near Harrisburg. Europeans called it the Allegheny Path.

In the seventeenth century, the Dutch and Swedes established settlements along the Delaware River and at the mouth of the Schuylkill, their main interest being furs. By 1674, the British had gained control of the area, and in 1682, William Penn arrived to set up a colony.

The rapids and falls that made the Schuylkill unnavigable were overcome by the Schuylkill Canal, which opened in 1825 and connected Philadelphia with Reading.

The Schuylkill Center for Environmental Education was established in 1965 to serve a five-county region.

Wissahickon Valley

Wissahickon Gorge
Andorra Natural Area
Carpenter's Woods

Benjamin Franklin and John Greenleaf Whittier wrote about the charm of the Wissahickon Valley. Today the valley is a refreshing oasis of green in busy Philadelphia. Here, trees older than the Declaration of Independence stretch toward the sky, and vegetation covers the vestiges of the industrial era. Wissahickon Creek is cold enough and clean enough for stocked trout.

Ownership. All three sites are located in Fairmount Park, owned by the Fairmount Park Commission, city of Philadelphia.

Size and Designation. Fairmount Park totals more than 8,000 acres, of which Andorra Natural Area comprises 210, and Carpenter's Woods roughly 100. The Wissahickon Valley was designated a national natural landmark in 1964.

Nearby Nature Attractions. Pennypack Environmental Center, Schuylkill Center for Environmental Education, Riverbend Environmental Education Center, Tyler Arboretum, Briar Bush Nature Center, Little Tinicum Island State Forest Natural Area, and the John Heinz National Wildlife Refuge at Tinicum.

Features. Fairmount Park offers Philadelphians opportunities for enjoying nature and outdoor recreation. The most natural sections of the park include Carpenter's Woods and the northern half, from the confluence of Cresheim and Wissahickon creeks to Northwestern Avenue, of which Andorra Natural Area is part.

Andorra Natural Area: A network of hiking trails spreads out from the Tree House Visitor Center, which serves as a nature center and headquarters. The Central Loop Trail has interpretive signs on natural history. Most of the preserve's scheduled natural history programs begin at the Tree House, and trail maps, rest rooms, and drinking water are found there.

The preserve also can be reached via a trail branching from Forbidden Drive at Bell's Mill Road. Andorra Hill is one of the highest elevations in Philadelphia County.

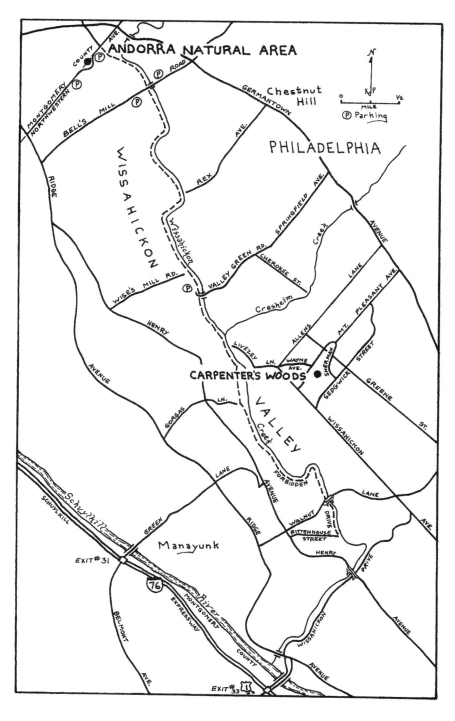

For more information, contact Andorra Natural Area, telephone (215) 685-9285.

Wissahickon Gorge: The best way to see the gorge is to hike Forbidden Drive, an old carriage road along the creek between Bell's Mill Road and Valley Green Inn. Trails north and south of those destinations lead to geological attractions (see Geology section). Look for picnic tables at the Bell's Mill Road bridge. Rest rooms, telephone, and drinking water are available at Valley Green Inn.

For a trail map, contact the Friends of the Wissahickon, 8708 Germantown Avenue, Philadelphia, PA 19118-2717, telephone (215) 247-0417.

Carpenter's Woods: Wissahickon Avenue, Mount Pleasant Avenue, Sherman Street, and Sedgwick Street border the woods. Unnamed trails crisscross through the woods, and you will find a picnic table in a field in the middle. There are no rest rooms or drinking water. Be warned that neighborhood dogs often roam through the woods, and some growl and intimidate hikers. Carry a sturdy walking stick.

Geology. The bedrock in the gorge, appropriately called Wissahickon formation, consists of schist, quartzite, gneiss, and pegmatite, a coarse granite. Schist, quartzite, and gneiss are metamorphic rocks. Under intense heat and compression, shale metamorphosed into schist and sandstone into quartzite. The Wissahickon gneiss probably formed when schist experienced extreme pressure and heat and welded with molten rock oozing into the earth's crust. Pegmatite, a light-colored igneous rock, contains mica, feldspar, and quartz crystals. It started as molten rock deep in the earth that seeped into the overlaying layers of bedrock. Other intrusive igneous rocks found in the gorge include serpentine, anthophyllite, amphibole gneiss, and granite.

Wissahickon schist is the predominant rock in the Philadelphia area. The schist may sparkle with silvery muscovite mica or shiny black biotite mica; beads of ruby red garnet, some a quarter inch in diameter; specks of black tourmaline; needles of glossy blue kyanite; or dark red, trapezoidal crystals of staurolite. The rock also contains chlorite and talc. Just which mineral is found in the schist depends on how much heat and pressure were exerted on the shale during its metamorphosis and how quickly it cooled.

Some schist contains branching white veins of quartzite. These were formed when cracks developed in the schist after metamorphosis and water laden with quartz crystals filled the openings. When the water cooled, the quartz crystals consolidated into the white veins.

The following are several specific locations at which to view some of these rocks and to study the geological history of the gorge.

1. From Bell's Mill Road, walk north on Forbidden Drive to these sites: an outcrop containing chlorite and talc; an old quarry where serpentine is exposed; wrinkled schist containing mica; another quarry, with a vertical band, or sill, of granite; and a pinkish layer of gneiss, perhaps a billion years old, running across the creek.

From Bell's Mill Road walk south on Forbidden Drive to the first small rise. Schist outcrops here contain garnet drops and quartzite veins.

2. From Valley Green Road, walk north on the east side of the creek. Rock with alternating strata of schist and quartzite lies opposite a shelter house. Ahead at a cliff on the right, look for garnet and staurolite. Cross a bridge and stroll up a path on the right about 500 feet, where there is some schist with wavy, white pegmatite intrusions. Return to the main trail and continue north to more cliffs with pegmatite and gemstones. Beyond Magargee Dam, a cliff exposes prominent layers of pegmatite, schist, and quartzite. Continue north to vertical beds of pegmatite and schist. Small trees grow from some rock cracks. At the Rex Avenue bridge, there is a pegmatite sill between dark layers of schist. The sill stands next to steps that climb to Council Rock, the highest point in the gorge.

3. From Valley Green Inn, walk north on Forbidden Drive, along the west side of the creek. A thick bar of pinkish rock composed of feldspar, mica, and quartz goes across the stream below Magargee Dam. Xenoliths—gray quartzite enwrapped by pegmatite—appear in this formation. Upstream there is a public spring, but don't drink the water. Continue to a tiny waterfall plunging over a quartz vein.

4. From Valley Green Road, walk south along the east bank to Cresheim Creek (less than half a mile), where you will find mica schist with garnets. On the hillside are brown, ten-foot boulders of anthophyllite and talc. Nearby, extending to the stream, injections of schist, quartzite, pegmatite, and quartz swirl in a band of gneiss. At the mouth of Cresheim Creek, a cascade falls into Devil's Pool, a pothole formed by the water-powered agitation of pebbles and grit.

5. Park at the end of Gorgas Lane, off Ridge Avenue, and follow the trail along Oil Mill Run into the gorge. Look for cave openings on the north side of the path that leads to Forbidden Drive. A few caves are natural; miners dug the others in the 1760s. The caves are easier to find in winter when vegetation does not conceal the openings. One cave measures ten feet in diameter and is forty feet

deep. Revolutionary War soldiers hid supplies in the caves, and runaway slaves found refuge in them before the Civil War.

Wildlife. Eighteenth-century naturalist John Bartram, from Philadelphia, and Thomas Nuttall and Frederick Pursh, two flora experts from the nineteenth century, studied the area. Four scientists explored the region in the second half of the nineteenth century and three more in the first half of the twentieth. The latest inventory of plants lists 654 species.

Eastern hemlock and scrub, Austrian black, pitch, eastern white, and scotch pines represent the conifers. Hardwoods include white, swamp white, scarlet, pin, chestnut, red, and black oaks; box elder, Norway, silver, red, sugar, and mountain maples; black, silky, and weeping willows; and American and slippery elms. Great specimens of American beech, black walnut, shagbark hickory, sycamore, river birch, and tulip tree rise in the valley. In Carpenter's Woods, Ohio buckeye, sweetbay magnolia (near its northern limit in Pennsylvania), flowering dogwood, sassafras, red mulberry, gray birch, and quaking and bigtooth aspens also grow.

Andorra Natural Area has 232 species of trees, including exotics like Japanese cryptomeria and Chinese cedrela. A cluster of bigleaf magnolias, a tree common in the Deep South, grows near a grove of cucumber magnolias.

Wildflowers are abundant. Look for Jacob's ladder *(Polemonium reptans)*, blue-flowered lettuce *(Lactuca floridana)*, pearlwort *(Sagina procumbens)*, bladder campion *(Silene cucubalus)*, blue cohosh *(Caulophyllum thalictroides)*, and yellow fumewort *(Corydalis flavula)*. Orchids include adder's-tongue *(Malaxis unifolia)* near Devil's pool, autumn coralroot *(Corallorhiza odontoriza)* in dry woods, slender ladies'-tresses *(Spiranthes gracilis)* along Thomas Mill Road, and pink lady's slipper *(Cypripedium acaule)* and purple five-leaved orchid *(Isotria verticillata)* along Bell's Mill Road.

Late summer bloomers at Andorra include Asiatic dayflower *(Commelina communis)*, evening primrose *(Oenothera biennis)*, Hercules-club *(Aralia spinosa)*, sweet everlasting *(Gnaphalium obtusifolium)*, cocklebur *(Xanthium strumarium)*, white wood aster *(Aster divaricatus)*, and six kinds of goldenrod. At Carpenter's Woods are jack-in-the-pulpit *(Arisaema triphyllum)*, false Solomon's seal *(Smilacina racemosa)*, clearweed *(Pilea pumila)*, common chickweed *(Stellaria media)*, kidneyleaf buttercup *(Ranunculus aborvitus)*, rose-of-Sharon *(Hibiscus syriacus)*, primrose-leaved white violet *(Viola primulifolia)*, striped pipsissewa *(Chimaphila maculata)*, bluet *(Houstonia caerulea)*, and mountain laurel.

More than 30 kinds of ferns and associates grow in the valley, among them the netted chainfern (declining in PA), marsh cinnamon, interrupted, rattlesnake, sensitive, Christmas, and ostrich ferns; and the silvery and ebony spleenworts. Bamboo, a grass, rises eight feet in a clearing in Andorra Natural Area.

Carpenter's Woods is one of the best birding spots in Philadelphia, especially for warblers, which include the black-and-white, blue-winged, Blackburnian, bay-breasted, magnolia, yellow-rumped, yellow, chestnut-sided, northern parula, black-throated blue, American redstart, black-throated green, and common yellowthroat. They arrive in May and leave in late August through mid-September. Sometimes rarities such as the cerulean, worm-eating, Tennessee, and Wilson's warblers visit the woods. These birds usually migrate on the Mississippi Flyway rather than the Atlantic Flyway, the route for birds in this region.

The veery, thrush, vireo, cardinal, robin, blue jay, and crow also appear in these woods.

Wissahickon Creek supports 30 species of fish, including the American eel, carp, goldfish, shiner, dace, darter, bass, and sunfish. Trout are stocked in the creek in April, but fishermen catch most of them, and few survive to breed.

Deer, which have no natural enemies here, overpopulate the valley. The raccoon, rabbit, squirrel, chipmunk, mouse, mole, and fox also live here.

History. The Lenni Lenape and their ancestors once lived in the valley. They hunted, farmed, and caught shad and catfish that swam upstream to spawn. Wissahickon may derive from the Lenape word *wisamickan,* meaning catfish stream, or it may come from *wissauchsikan,* meaning yellow-colored stream. They held meetings at Council Rock, the highest spot in the gorge.

The valley attracted religious idealists. Johannes Kelpius and a band of 40 mystical Pietists holed up in a cave in 1695. Most abandoned the place after Kelpius' death in 1708. In the 1730s, Dunkers held baptisms in the creek.

By the Revolutionary War, two dozen mills operated in the valley. The creek was contested during the 1777 Battle of Germantown. Defeated patriots retreated to Valley Forge. Gen. George Washington, camped at Valley Forge, set up a spy network in the valley to keep an eye on British movements. Patriot guerrilla bands protected the spies and challenged British approaches.

The mills enjoyed a golden era after the war, but their importance waned by the 1860s. Today, nature has nearly reclaimed the factory ruins. In the first half of the nineteenth century, the bucolic gorge appealed to wealthy Philadelphians, who built roads, mansions, and inns such as Valley Green. But like the factories, the estates eventually were abandoned.

Philadelphia began acquiring parkland in 1812. Fairmount Park slowly grew in size and popularity. The zoo opened in 1874. Fairmount Park was the site of the Centennial Exposition in 1876, marking the hundredth anniversary of the Declaration of Independence.

Andorra Natural Area got its start in the early 1970s, when the city purchased 100 acres from private landowners. Another parcel was acquired in 1981. Half the natural area was once Andorra Nursery.

65

Pennypack
Environmental Center

Tall tulip trees and arching sycamores grace the steep east bank of an S curve along Pennypack Creek. The grounds at Pennypack Environmental Center, located on a bluff above the curve, offer Philadelphians glimpses into the natural and historical past.

Ownership. Fairmount Park Commission.

Size and Designation. Pennypack Park is 1,600 acres; the grounds of the environmental center about 100.

Nearby Nature Attractions. Schuylkill Center for Environmental Education, John Heinz National Wildlife Refuge at Tinicum, Little Tinicum Island State Forest Natural Area, and Briar Bush Nature Center.

Features. The park has more than two miles of hiking trails, an equestrian trail, a bike path, and picnic areas and two bird blinds, which are open daily from dawn to dusk. Be sure to pick up a brochure and trail map. The visitors center offers nature programs, wildlife displays, aquariums, rest rooms, and drinking water. The operating hours of the visitors center vary; call ahead.

Other points of interest include the eighteenth century Verree House, as well as the ruins of mills, quarries, barns, wells, and other homes.

For more information, contact the Pennypack Environmental Center, Verree Road at Pennypack Creek, Philadelphia, PA 19115, telephone (215) 671-0440.

Geology. Pennypack Creek begins in the Piedmont near the border of Montgomery and Bucks counties and flows south across the Atlantic coastal plain into the Delaware River at Philadelphia. The creek meanders through the sanctuary. Ballard Brook empties into the creek north of the nature center.

Wildlife. Besides tulip trees and sycamores, the park has black walnut; bitternut hickory; red, sugar, and silver maples; and white, red, black, and pin oaks.

Deer have overbrowsed on the wildflowers. Nevertheless, you can still find ladies'-tresses *(Spiranthes cernua)*, trout lilies *(Erythronium americanum)*, mayapples *(Podophyllum peltatum)*, bloodroot *(Sanguinaria candensis)*, cut-leaved toothwort *(Dentaria laciniata)*, and Greek valerian *(Polemonium reptans)*.

More than 50 kinds of birds nest in the park, notably ringnecked pheasant, common flicker, indigo bunting, red-bellied woodpecker, chimney swift, kingbird, cedar waxwing, and veery. Crows are common; in winter flocks gather in the thousands.

Other inhabitants include the raccoon; squirrel; skunk; red fox; garter, ring-necked, and water snakes; snapping, box, musk, painted, red-bellied, and red-eared slider turtles (the last an escaped pet).

History. Pennypack Park was home to the Lenni Lenape when the Europeans arrived. William Penn bought land on both sides of Pennypack Creek from the Lenni Lenape in 1684.

Early settlers, many from Sweden, quickly cleared the land for rye, wheat, corn, and livestock. In 1687, Morris Gwynne erected a water-powered gristmill at this spot. As business improved, roads were built to the milling complex, which enlarged to include a sawmill and another mill for cloth production.

Gwynne's Mill fell into ruins before the Revolutionary War.

Robert Verree bought the property and built new mills. The industrial site was now called Verreeville. British troops may have raided Verreeville during the Revolutionary War, but the raid did not destroy Verree's enterprise. His son James opened an ax and shovel factory. John P. Verree, born in 1816, was the last male heir in the Verree family. He was an abolitionist and a member of Congress.

As steam replaced running water as the energy source for powering mills, the Verreeville mills fell into decline. Flour and feed grain from the Great Plains made local mills obsolete.

The city purchased the property in 1918 and tore down most of the abandoned structures. The grounds of the environmental center were dedicated in 1958 as a bird sanctuary, and later as a sanctuary for wildlife. The visitors center opened in 1970.

66

Briar Bush Nature Center

For 50 years, Everett and Florence Griscom practiced "benign neglect" on this 12-acre patch in suburbia. The grounds became a refuge for plants and animals. In the early 1960s, local folks persuaded the township to buy the sanctuary.

Ownership. Abington Township. The township's Bureau of Parks and Recreation manages the nature center with the help of the Friends of Briar Bush, a nonprofit organization.

Size and Designation. 12 acres.

Nearby Nature Attractions. Valley Forge National Historical Park, Riverbend Environmental Education Center, and Fort Washington and Evansburg state parks. The Schuylkill River, a state-designated scenic river, flows through the county.

Features. Briar Bush, both an environmental education center and a suburban wildlife sanctuary, is a perfect spot for a family outing, especially for parents with small children. The nature center has hands-on exhibits, natural history displays, live animals, an observation beehive, a library, a gift shop, rest rooms, and a special area designed for young children. Nature education programs, workshops, and member outings are offered throughout the year.

The former Griscom cottage now serves as a bird observatory. A windmill, built by Amish craftsmen in 1979, pumps water from an underground spring into a four-foot-deep pond.

Trails lead to a wildflower garden, meadow, pond with overlook, thicket, field, and mature woodland. An informative guide is available at the center.

The nature center, bird observatory, and pond overlook are open Monday to Saturday from 9 A.M. to 5 P.M. The nature trail is open daily from dawn to dusk. Hours may change on holidays (call first). For more information, contact the Briar Bush Nature Center, 1212 Edge Hill Road, Abington, PA 19001, telephone (215) 887-6603.

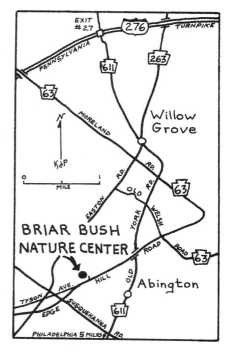

Geology. Briar Bush is located in the Piedmont physiographic province and supported by bedrock, mostly Wissahickon schist of the Lower Paleozoic Era (430–570 million years ago).

Wildlife. There are many small habitats within Briar Bush. The best way to view them and learn about them is to wander on the center's nature trails with the accompanying guide.

Start in the wildflower garden. In the spring and summer, you'll find mountain laurel, bloodroot *(Sanguinaria canadensis,* lesser celandine *(Ranunculus ficaria),* grape hyacinth *(Muscari botryoides),* Jacob's ladder *(Polemonium van-bruntiae),* and maidenhair fern. In late summer and autumn, observe Christmas and ostrich ferns, cardinal flower *(Lobelia cardinalis),* turtlehead *(Chelone glabra),* and false dragonhead *(Physotegia virginiana).* Farther up the trail, look for wild ginger *(Asarum canadense)* growing on a stone outcrop, and clusters of jewelweed *(Impatiens capensis),* with orange cornucopia-shaped blossoms dangling from the stems. The latter plant's seedpods open when touched, hence its other common name, touch-me-not.

The trail leads through a developing forest of maple, tulip tree, oak, beech, larch, and pine. Crab apples, silverbells, and redbuds blossom in April and May. Dead trees are home to red-bellied wood-peckers, yellow-shafted flickers, and yellow-bellied sapsuckers. Raccoons and squirrels may enlarge these holes for their own use.

At the pond, you may see bullfrogs, leopard frogs, painted and red-bellied turtles, dragonflies, and damselflies.

In early April, spatterdock, or cow lily *(Nuphar variegatum)*, spreads out on the water. The yellow flag iris *(Iris pseudacorus)* blossoms in May. Twelve-foot-tall plumes of reed grass *(Phragmites communis)* line the edge of the pond. Near the pond grow eastern white pine, witch hazel, American holly, eastern red cedar, azalea, multiflora rose, crab apple, and staghorn sumac.

Chickadees, downy woodpeckers, nuthatches, mourning doves, finches, pigeons, and tufted titmice frequent the feeders at the bird observatory. On the grounds you also may see robins, wood-thrushes, eastern pewees, brown creepers, flickers, gray catbirds, bluejays, and crows.

The mature woodland consists of white oak, beech, white birch, American holly, shagbark hickory, great rhododendron, white pine, red cedar, and sugar, red, and silver maples. In the spring, look for jack-in-the-pulpit *(Arisaema triphyllum)* in wet, shady areas. Woodland inhabitants include the white-footed mouse, red fox, groundhog, and brown snake.

History. Florence and Everett Griscom, devoted nature lovers and conservationists, moved into the cottage (now the bird observatory) on 12 acres in Abington in 1908. While neighboring land became suburbanized, the Griscoms allowed their plot to return to its natural state and become a wildlife sanctuary. In 1962, a group of local citizens persuaded Abington Township to buy the Griscom refuge for a nature center. Since them, Briar Bush has become a learning center as well.

67

Churchville Nature Center

O ne way to learn about nature, and our ancestors, is to study the people whose survival depended on their knowledge of nature. You can do that at the Churchville Nature Center, where life in a Lenni Lenape (Delaware Indian) village before European contact is reenacted.

Ownership. Bucks County Department of Parks and Recreation.

Size and Designation. 172 acres.

Nearby Nature Attractions. Silver Lake and Peace Valley nature centers, Ringing Rocks County Park, Bowman's Hill Wild-

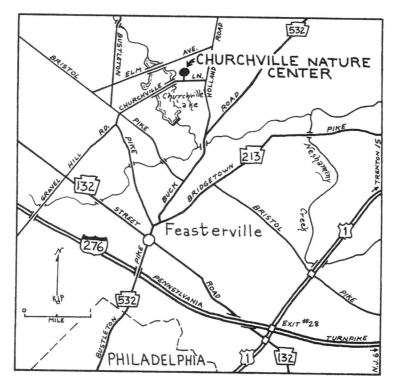

flower Preserve, Bristol Marsh Preserve, David R. Johnson State Forest Natural Area, Monroe Border Fault, Honey Hollow Environmental Education Center, and Tyler, Delaware Canal, Neshaminy, Nockamixon, and Ralph Stover state parks.

Features. Two miles of hiking trails wander through fields and forests, past a lake and a pond, and into a Lenni Lenape village. Pick up a trail map at the visitors center, where you also will find wildlife exhibits, a library, a gift shop, rest rooms, and drinking water.

The center offers nature, environmental, and outdoor recreation programs for children and adults, including bird walks, canoe trips, field trips to other locations, and special events such as a pumpkin festival and maple syrup day. Several clubs, such as beekeepers, woodcarvers, and orchid growers, meet here. Churchville also has a picnic area, apiary, bird blind, wheelchair-accessible trail, and edible wildflower garden.

Life among the Delaware Indians in the sixteenth century, a century before Europeans arrived on the scene, is reenacted in a recreation of a Lenni Lenape village. The structures in the village were constructed with primitive tools and natural materials. A canoe, for instance, was dug out with stone tools. A 25-foot longhouse framed with red maples is covered with bark from tulip trees. The village also has a grass-thatched bark wigwam, sweat lodge, garden, and areas for demonstrating pottery making, fire building, cooking, and hunting. Interpreters dress in buckskin.

There is no charge to visit the village, but a fee is charged for interpretive programs to large groups and for weekend programs. Interpreters are often on hand during the week to answer questions.

The trails are open daily from dawn to dusk. The visitors center is open Tuesday through Sunday from 10 A.M. to 5 P.M. For more information, contact the Churchville Nature Center, 501 Churchville Lane, Churchville, PA 18966, telephone (215) 357-4005.

Geology. Churchville Nature Center lies within the Piedmont physiographic province, a hilly region underlain (in this area) by schist and quartzite. A few shallow quarries in the preserve provided foundation stones for local buildings. Churchville Reservoir is a man-made lake created by damming Trout Works Creek.

Wildlife. Wildflowers include fairy candles *(Chamaelirium luteum)*, several kinds of violets *(Viola* spp.), bloodroot *(Sanguinaria canadensis)*, spring beauty *(Claytonia virginica)*, squawroot *(Conopholis americana)*, jack-in-the-pulpit *(Arisaema triphyllum)*, wild geranium *(Geranium maculatum)*, skunk cabbage *(Symplocarpus feotidus)*, pickerelweed *(Pontederia cordata)*, enchanter's nightshade *(Circaea quadrisulcata),* butterfly weed *(Asclepias tuberosa),* trilliums *(Trillium* spp.), and Dutchman's breeches *(Dicentra cucullaria).* Marsh and sensitive ferns grow near the shore of Churchville Reservoir.

White oak, flowering dogweed, eastern white cedar, black gum, sumac, red and white pines, red and sugar maples, apple, sassafras, aspen, American beech, and beaked hazelnut all grow here, as does bittersweet *(Celastrus scandens)* with its yellow and crimson seeds.

Get a plant guide in the visitors center before exploring the nature center's wild edible plant garden. Be warned that you must be knowledgeable about these plants before attempting to eat them, as some of these plants have poisonous look-alikes. You also must learn how to prepare them properly. Too much tansy, for instance, could be deadly.

At the lake and in the pond behind the visitors center, you may see waterbirds such as green herons, great blue herons, double-crested cormorants, and several duck species. Songbirds such as northern orioles, vireos, and ovenbirds can be seen and heard along the trails, especially in the spring. An osprey nesting platform has been erected along the lakeshore. Some of the endangered birds have roosted there, but none have nested yet.

The dragonfly, abundant around the pond, is the center's pet animal. The graceful flyer, harmless to people, benefits humans by eating mosquitos while airborne.

History. Before European settlement, the Lenni Lenape lived in a village less than two miles from the present-day nature center. Churchville Nature Center, the first of three nature centers established by the county parks department, opened in 1964. An old farmhouse served as headquarters until the current visitors center opened in 1976.

68

Silver Lake Nature Center

The largest and healthiest remnant of Pennsylvania's coastal plain forest survives in this Bucks County preserve. Delhaas Woods harbors dense communities of sweet gum, a tree uncommon outside the lowlands of the coastal plan. An endangered willow oak, now 45 feet in circumference, was a mere seedling when William Penn came to the New World.

Ownership. Bucks County Department of Parks and Recreation. The center is jointly funded by the parks department and the Friends of the Silver Lake Nature Center.

Size and Designation. 160 acres.

Nearby Nature Attractions. Peace Valley and Churchville nature centers, Ringing Rocks County Park, Bristol Marsh Preserve, David R. Johnson State Forest Natural Area, Monroe Border Fault, Bowman's Hill Wildflower Preserve, Honey Hollow Environmental Education Center, and Nockamixon, Tyler, Neshaminy, Delaware Canal, and Ralph Stover state parks.

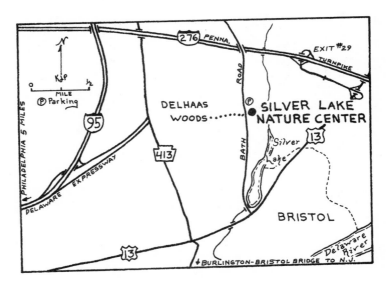

Features. At the nature interpretation building, you will find exhibits, naturalists, a gift and book shop, a library, rest rooms, and drinking water. Most nature education programs begin here. The center is open Tuesday through Saturday 10 A.M. to 5 P.M., Sunday from 12 to 5 P.M. The grounds are open daily from sunrise to sunset.

More than two miles of hiking trails lead through woods, meadows, and wetlands, and alongside a marsh. The trail to Delhaas Woods begins across the street, on the west side of Bath Road. Get a trail map at the nature center before departing, because the unnamed trails are not marked. Don't worry about getting lost, but you may get confused. High water in the swamp can make the trail impassable in the early spring.

For more information, contact the Silver Lake Nature Center, 1306 Bath Road, Bristol, PA 19007-2813, telephone (215) 785-1177.

Geology. This portion of Bucks County lies in the coastal plain, which in Pennsylvania is a narrow strip of land running along the Delaware River from Morrisville, through Philadelphia, to Marcus Hook.

Streams lose velocity entering the plain, and water drains slowly. The flat terrain partly explains the existence of the small swamps and marshes that dot these lowlands. Silver Lake Nature Center features several of these natural wetlands. The lake itself is artificial, a mill pond that grew behind a dam built across Otter Creek in the early 1700s.

Wildlife. Delhaas Woods is one of the last remnants of the coastal plain forest, which has been under siege for nearly three centuries. What spared Delhaas is its swampiness, which makes it undesirable as farmland and for residential development. Plants once widespread in these lowlands are now concentrated in this protected place.

Delhaas Woods preserves the state's last coastal plain bog. It is formed by water that has trickled into a sandy depression over thousands of years. The water is so low in nutrients and oxygen that even bacteria and fungi, the agents of decay, are virtually nonexistent. As a result, the plants that fall into the bog decay slowly (if at all), and accumulate into a kind of peat.

Only plants that have adapted to acidic conditions and Spartan rations will thrive here. Pitcher plant (*Sarracenia purpurea*), round-leaved sundew (*Drosera rotundifolia*), and bladderwort (*Utricularia* spp.) are carnivores that entrap insects for food. Bull sedge (*Carex bulata*) and spotted pondweed (*Potamogeton pulcher*), each state endangered plants, also grow here.

The wettest sections of Delhaas Woods and the other swamp forests in the park, usually spots surrounding vernal ponds (shallow ponds that dry up in the summer), are reserved for red maple, sweet gum, and black gum. Nearby are red, willow, pin, white, and swamp white oaks; river birch; hickory; green ash; silver maple; big-toothed aspen; cottonwood; and sycamore. The park's only stand of American beech grows in Delhaas Woods.

Tulip tree, black cherry, black locust, black oak, catalpa, Norway maple, elm, white pine, spruce, box elder, and gray birch also live in the park, as do flowering dogwood, American hornbeam, and sweetbay and umbrella magnolias, surviving here at the northern extreme of their range.

Shrubs and vines include southern arrowwood, pussy willow, American holly (*Ilex opaca*, PA threatened), winterberry, bittersweet, huckleberry, spicebush, catbriers, lowbush bluberry, honeysuckle, wild grape, Virginia creeper, and poison ivy.

The coastal plain forest has fewer kinds of wildflowers than the adjacent Piedmont region. Still you can find Canada mayflower (*Maianthemum canadense*), sessile bellwort (*Uvularia sessilifolia*), various violets (*Viola* spp.), jewelweed (*Impatiens capensis*), skunk cabbage (*Symplocarpus foetidus*), mayapple (*Podophyllum peltatum*), false hellebore (*Veratrum viride*), nodding ladies'-tresses (*Spiranthes cernua*), spring cress (*Cardamine bulbosa*), swamp aster (*Aster puniceus*), lizard-tail (*Saururus cernuus*), and others.

More noticeable and abundant are the ferns, represented in the park by royal, cinnamon, lady, hay-scented, sensitive, Christmas, New York, Virginia chain, Massachusetts (a rarity in Pennsylvania), marsh, net-veined chain, bracken, and ebony spleenwort. Patches of trailing and southern club mosses are also present.

The moist open fields and ecotones, the transitional zones between two different plant communities, offer some rarities, including Maryland meadow beauty (*Rhexia mariana*, PA endangered), New York aster (*Aster novi-bilgii*, PA threatened), and coast violet (*Viola brittoniana*, PA endangered). In this setting you will find Canada St.-John's-wort (*Hypericum canadense*), marsh seedbox (*Ludwigia alternifolia*), Turk's cap lily (*Lilium superbum*), slender spike-rush (*Eleocharis tenuis* var. *submuticus*, PA endangered), tickseed sunflower (*Bidens discoidea*), star toadflax (*Comandra umbellata*), and many companions.

Common at Silver Lake, but rare in the state, are slender sea oats (*Chasmanthium laxum*, PA endangered); fetterbush (*Lyonia lucida*, at the northern edge of its range); slender paspalum (*Paspalus* spp., a grass); and eastern blue-eyed grass (*Sisyrinchium atlanticum,* PA endangered). The center also features a buttonbush swamp.

Birds are the most conspicuous creatures at the nature center. In open wetlands, look for the pied-billed grebe and American coot (both PA rare); great blue, green-backed, and black-crowned night herons; great egret (PA threatened); double-crested cormorant; Canada goose; wood, mallard, and ring-necked ducks; an occasional osprey (PA endangered); spotted and solitary sandpipers; various gulls; belted kingfisher; eastern phoebe; willow flycatcher; yellow warbler; northern yellowthroat; and red-winged blackbird.

In the woods, and along its edge, you may observe the great horned and screech owls, red-bellied and hairy woodpeckers, rufous-sided towhee, yellow-bellied sapsucker, red-eyed vireo, northern oriole, yellow warbler, and wood thrush. Goldfinches, American kestrels, indigo buntings, and catbirds like the ecotone and meadows.

Silver Lake Nature Center protects other animals that are rare in the state, including coastal plain leopard frog (PA endangered) and the redbelly turtle (PA threatened). Other reptiles and amphibians found here include the black racer and northern water snakes; the musk, snapping, slider, box and painted turtles; Fowler's and American toads; and the bullfrog, spring peeper, wood, and green frogs.

Other animal inhabitants include deer, squirrel, rabbit, woodchuck, northern short-tailed shrew (look beneath bird feeders), opossum (near brooks), raccoon, striped skunk, mink (shore of marsh or pond), red and gray foxes, meadow vole, and star-nosed mole. Silver Lake has many bats—little brown myotis, big brown, red, and hoary—best observed just after sunset.

History. Before the arrival of European settlers in the seventeenth century, the native Lenni Lenape found plenty of game, medicinal herbs, and other foods here. By the time William Penn arrived in 1681, Swedish and English colonizers had already begun to subdue the forest and cultivate crops. Towns and small industries followed.

In 1701, a dam built across Otter Creek created the lake today known as Silver Lake. The lake water powered the local mills. In the early nineteenth century, Bristol became a popular spa resort with bath houses, hotels, and the trappings of the day. Bristol's fame was short-lived, but the town was revived as the southern terminus of the Delaware Canal.

The lake was hand dredged by Works Project Administration workers during the 1930s and was used as a swimming hole. In the late 1950s and '60s, the Bucks County Department of Parks and Recreation purchased the Silver Lake properties.

The Pennsylvania Chapter of the Nature Conservancy saved Delhaas Woods in 1987 when it purchased a 94-acre tract in the heart of this ecologically important swamp forest. The conservancy later turned it over to the county parks department.

◆ 69 ◆

Bristol Marsh Preserve

Bristol Marsh is a wetland under the influence of the moon. A powerful river and a meandering creek create a rare habitat—a freshwater tidal marsh—that contains rare species. Migratory waterfowl find here a safe hatchery and fertile feeding ground.

Ownership. The Pennsylvania Chapter of the Nature Conservancy.

Size. 18 acres.

Features. Two viewing platforms overlook the marsh. You also can watch the activities on the Delaware River. Make two visits to Bristol Marsh—at high and low tides.

For more information, contact the Pennsylvania Chapter of the Nature Conservancy, 1211 Chestnut Street, 12th Floor, Philadelphia, PA 19107, telephone (215) 963-1400.

Nearby Nature Attractions. Silver Lake, Churchville, and Peach Valley nature centers; Ringing Rocks County Park; Bowman's Hill Wildflower Preserve; Honey Hollow Environmental Education Center; David R. Johnson State Forest Natural Area; Monroe Border Fault; and Delaware Canal, Neshaminy, Nockamixon, Ralph Stover, and Tyler state parks.

Geology. Bristol Marsh, located in Pennsylvania's coastal plain, is one of the last freshwater tidal marshes in the commonwealth. Twice a day, like the rise and fall of ocean tides, brackish water from the Delaware River backs up three to four feet into the marsh. The freshwater of Otter Creek also flows through the marsh, before spilling into the Delaware River. These unusual hydrological influences produce a specialized and fragile habitat.

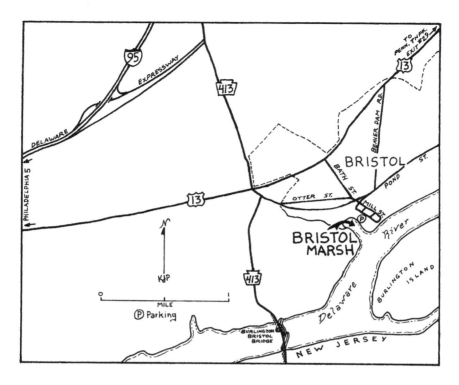

Wildlife. A tidal marsh sustains plants and animals at all levels of the food chain. During the winter, dead plant material mixes with phytoplankton. This is carried by tidal currents into the river and eventually to the ocean, nourishing many plants and animals along the way. The lavish grasses and plants in the warm months provide food and shelter for migratory birds and other animals. Here you will find plants that thrive only in freshwater tidal marshes: Indian wild rice (*Zizania aquatica,* PA rare), swamp beggar tick (*Bidens bidentoides,* PA threatened), waterhemp ragweed (*Amaranthus cannabinus,* PA rare), two kinds of arrowhead (*Sagittaria subulata,* PA rare, and *calycina* var. *spongiosa,* PA endangered), and Walter's barnyard grass (*Echinochloa walteri,* PA endangered).

Spatterdock *(Nuphar advena),* sweetflag *(Acorus calamus),* pickerelweed *(Pontederia cordata),* jewelweed *(Impatiens capensis),* arrow arum *(Peltandra virginica),* buttonbush *(Cephalanthus occidentalis),* water purslane *(Ludwigia palustris),* halberd-leaved tearthumb *(Polygonum arifolium),* marsh mallow *(Hibiscus moscheutos),* bur marigold *(Bidens laevis),* and silky dogwood *(Cornus amomum)* are also abundant. Willow, sycamore, black cherry, box elder, green ash, sugar and red maples, red and American elms, ironwood, mulberry, princess tree, red osier dogwood, and black locust rim the wetland.

The march is a haven for birds, including the laughing gull, double-crested cormorant, killdeer, barn swallow, wood duck, mallard, chimney swift, great-crested flycatcher, and American goldfinch.

The tidal marsh is a nursery for fish and other aquatic creatures, including gizzard shad, American eel, pumpkinseed fish, muskellunge, channel catfish, brown bullhead, and black crappie.

History. The Lenni Lenape (Delaware Indians) probably knew about the marsh and fished its water. European settlement began at Bristol in 1681, the same year William Penn arrived in the colony.

Bristol became a resort in the early 1800s because of its bath springs, but the town really began to flourish after the 1848 opening of the Delaware Canal, of which Bristol was the southern terminus. Lumber and coal yards developed, and mills thrived along the canal. As the businesses prospered, the marsh shrank.

By the twentieth century, the railroad had replaced the canal as the primary commercial transportation route. When the canal was abandoned in 1955, Bristol used it as a trench for sewer lines. The basin serving the canal was backfilled and converted into municipal parking in the 1970s.

In 1986, the Nature Conservancy signed a long-term conservation agreement with the borough of Bristol, preserving 11 acres of the marsh. Later, a seven-acre conservation easement that would act as a buffer was donated to the Nature Conservancy by the Rohm and Haas Company. The Gruny Foundation and the National Park Service helped conservation organizations save the marsh.

Pennsylvania's
Scenic Rivers

Pennsylvania's scenic rivers program started in December 1972. So far, 13 watercourses, totaling more than 500 miles, have been designated scenic rivers by the Pennsylvania Department of Environmental Resources. In addition, two rivers—the Delaware and the Allegheny—have earned national scenic river status from the U.S. Department of the Interior. Eight of these rivers are in eastern Pennsylvania.

The goal of the scenic rivers program is to safeguard sections of rivers that represent the state's natural and cultural river heritage. Designation is based on the level of human development influencing the flow, water quality, natural diversity, land use, and the quality of the riparian habitat. Usually, only portions of a river meet the qualifications.

Pennsylvania has five designations for protected rivers. *Wild* rivers flow freely and are accessible only by foot or canoe. They have thriving populations of native fish and wildlife, and shorelines that are pristine, forested, and undisturbed. *Scenic* rivers are free-flowing and must be capable of having water-based recreation, fish, and other aquatic life. The view from the river should look wild, but some pastoral countryside and a few roads are allowed. *Pastoral* rivers go through farming countryside. Historic and restored mill dams are allowed, but essentially the river is free-flowing and inhabited by native flora and fauna. *Recreation* and *modified recreation* rivers have readily accessible shorelines with moderate amounts of human development. Recreation rivers may have free-flowing currents and brief stretches of impounded water. Calm water, low dams, and flow-control devices characterize modified recreation waters. The water for these classifications supports native gamefish or is being restored to do so.

Scenic river status does not change land ownership, increase taxes, or increase human use of the water. Activities on scenic rivers are subject to local restrictions, for example, designated areas for launching canoes.

For more information, contact the Pennsylvania Department of Environmental Resources, Scenic Rivers Program, P.O. Box 8475, Harrisburg PA 17105-8475, telephone (717) 783-8526.

BRANDYWINE CREEK

General George Washington hoped Brandywine Creek would slow the British advance on Philadelphia, and he put his 11,000 Colonial troops on the east bank. The British attacked with 18,000 soldiers on September 11, 1777, and pushed back the Colonials.

Total Designated Miles. The Pennsylvania Department of Environmental Resources has assigned various designations to 65.85 miles in the Brandywine Creek watershed.

Watershed. The West Branch starts in Western Chester County and flows east. It joins the East Branch below Wawaset. Here, the main creek goes southeast into Delaware, flowing into the Delaware River at Wilmington. Sections of tributaries—Pocopson Creek, Valley Creek, Green Valley Stream, Broad Run, Buck Run, and Doe Run—make up the designated watershed.

Designated Portions.

1.   Starting at the Pennsylvania-Delaware state line and heading upstream to the confluence of the West and East branches (9.7 miles), Brandywine Creek is designated as pastoral.

2.   Some 6.5 miles of Pocopson Creek, a tributary of the main stem, is rated as pastoral.

3.   From its confluence with the West Branch to a railroad overpass (7.4 miles), the East Branch is pastoral. Valley Creek carries the pastoral designation from its confluence with the East Branch to the railroad bridge (2.8 miles).

4.   The West Branch is a scenic waterway from Wawaset to 1,600 feet downstream of the Modena borough boundary, a total of 16.25 miles. This rating includes 1.8 miles of Green Valley Stream and 2.2 miles of an unnamed brook in Newlin Township. The pastoral designation applies to these West Branch tributaries: Broad Run, from its confluence with the West Branch to Beacon Hill Road (4.85 miles), Buck Run, from the West Branch upstream (11 miles), and Doe Run, from its confluence with Buck Run to Fernwood Road (6.6 miles).

Nearby Nature Attractions. The Serpentine Barrens, White Clay Creek State Park, Valley Forge National Historical Park, and the Schuylkill River and Octoraro Creek, both state scenic rivers. The Brandywine battlefield has been preserved as a national historic site.

DELAWARE RIVER

The Delaware River carves a sinuous, steep gorge across the Allegheny Plateau before it flows through a gap in Kittatinny Ridge. Many waterfalls can be seen along its length.

Total Designated Miles. More than 110 miles of the Delaware River is a national scenic and recreational river, a designation bestowed by the U.S. Department of the Interior.

Watershed. Both branches of the Delaware River start in New York's Catskill Mountains and flow southwest until they merge at Hancock, New York. There the main stream heads south along the eastern boundary of Pennsylvania and into Delaware Bay. Its major tributaries are the Lackawaxen, Lehigh, and Schuylkill rivers.

Designated Portions.

1. The Middle Delaware River, a 37-mile stretch from Milford to Delaware Water Gap, has earned the national rating.

2. The Interior Department has assigned the same designation to 73.4 miles from Hancock, New York, to a few miles above Matamoras.

Nearby Nature Attractions. Delaware Water Gap National Recreation Area, Buckhorn State Forest Natural Area, Long Eddy Preserve, Grey Towers National Historic Landmark, and Bushkill Falls.

FRENCH CREEK

At the start of the French and Indian Wars, the French had a small military outpost on this creek, only 40 miles from Philadelphia. For a while, the garrison marked the boundary of French influence in Pennsylvania, but the British and Colonial armies eventually drove them away. The name French Creek stuck, however.

Total Designated Miles. The Pennsylvania Department of Environmental Resources has designated seven streams (42.75 miles) in this watershed as scenic.

Watershed. French Creek drains from Hopewell Lake, located in French Creek State Park in southeastern Berks County. It flows southeast and meets the Schuylkill River in Phoenixville.

Designated Portions.

1. French Creek is a designated scenic stream from Hopewell Lake to a mile below Snowden's bridge (22 miles).

2. The entire lengths of the South Branch of French Creek (7 miles), Pine Creek (4.25 miles), and Birch Run (3.25 miles) carry scenic designations.

3. Three miles of Rock Run (Harmonyville Road to French Creek), 2 miles of Beaver Run (Fairview Road-PA 100 to French Creek), and 1.25 miles of the West Branch of Birch Run (Shady Lane Road to Birch Run) are classified as scenic.

Nearby Nature Attractions. French Creek State Park, Hopewell Furnace National Historic Site, Great Valley Nature Center, Valley Forge National Historical Park, and the Schuylkill River, also a state-designated river.

LEHIGH RIVER

Lehigh River tumbles through a wild gorge with walls 1,000 feet tall. Thousands of boaters run the river's foamy rapids in rafts, canoes, and kayaks. Several remarkable waterfalls plunge off canyon cliffs.

Total Designated Miles. The Pennsylvania Department of Environmental Resources has classified 52 miles in the watershed as scenic and 12 miles as wild.

Watershed. The Lehigh River begins its 100-mile journey at Lehigh Pond, a glacial kettle lake on the Pocono Plateau. Below Stoddartsville, the Great Falls of the Lehigh marks the river's descent from the plateau. The river changes its southwesterly course at White Haven, where it heads south through a 30-mile gorge to Jim Thorpe. It turns east in Allentown, passes through the Allentown-Bethlehem-Easton industrial area, and empties into the Delaware River. Thirteen streams feed the 33-mile scenic section of the Lehigh.

Designated Portions.

1. The 33-mile gorge of the Lehigh River, from the Francis E. Walter Dam above White Haven to Bear Mountain at Jim Thorpe, is rated scenic.

2. The scenic designation also applies to these tributaries, heading upstream from their confluence with the Lehigh River: Hays Creek (1.13 miles); Hickory Run (to Hickory Run Lake in Hickory Run State Park, 3.9 miles); Leslie Run (1.3 miles); Mud Run (to Panther Creek, 6.24 miles); Drakes Creek (1.5 miles); Black Creek (to Quakake Creek, 4.35 miles); and Nesquehoning Creek (to Jeans Run, 75 miles).

3. Six tributaries are dedicated wild streams: Sandy Run (to railroad crossing, 1.2 miles); Stony Creek (to Yellow Run, 3 miles); Bear Creek (nearly to Bear Creek Dam, 3 miles); Little Bear Creek (1 mile); Glen Onoko (includes waterfall, 1 mile); and Jeans Run (2.75 miles).

Nearby Nature Attractions. Lehigh Gorge, Hickory Run, and Beltzville state parks; Carbon County Environmental Education Center; Pool Wildlife Sanctuary; and South Mountain Preserve.

OCTORARO CREEK

Octoraro Creek forms the boundary between Chester and Lancaster counties.

Total Designated Miles. The Pennsylvania Department of Environmental Resources has designated 24.25 miles in the watershed as pastoral and 12.25 miles as scenic.

Watershed. Each branch of the creek originates in Lancaster County. Bart Township is the source of the West Branch; the East Branch starts in Sadsbury Township. The East Branch forms the boundary between Chester and Lancaster counties. The streams merge above the Pine Grove Covered Bridge, which connects Ashville Road (Lancaster County) and Forge Road (Chester County). A dam at the confluence has created Octoraro Lake. Octoraro Creek snakes generally southwest into the Susquehanna River, just below Conowingo Dam in Maryland.

Designated Portions.

1. The stream is classified as pastoral from the Maryland border to the covered bridge (12.15 miles).

2. The East Branch is a pastoral stream from the backwaters of the lake to Steelville (8.25 miles), then it becomes a scenic course for 3.5 miles upstream.

3. From Octoraro Lake to Puseyville (3.75 miles), the creek is classified as pastoral. From there to its confluence with Meetinghouse Creek (except a stretch by a water company dam), the stream is rated as scenic. Stewart Run is a scenic stream 2 miles upstream from its meeting with Octoraro Creek.

Nearby Nature Attractions. The Serpentine Barrens, Susquehanna River Overlooks, Muddy Run Recreation Park, and White Clay Creek State Park.

SCHUYLKILL RIVER

The Lenni Lenape had several names for this legendary, scenic river. They knew the falls of the Schuylkill as *ganshowahanna.* Elsewhere, it was known as *manayunk,* a place to quench their thirst.

Total Designated Miles. 124.8 miles have been designated by the Pennsylvania Department of Environmental Resources.

Watershed. The Schuylkill River originates in Schuylkill

County and flows southeast through Berks, Chester, Montgomery, Delaware, and Philadelphia counties. It empties into the Delaware River at Philadelphia. Tulpehocken and French creeks, both state-designated, flow into the river. The Little Schuylkill River converges with the main stream at the Schuylkill-Berks county line. This tributary also is part of the designated river.

Designated Portions.

1. State designation begins at PA 209 near Pottsville. From there to Cressona (5 miles), the river is rated as recreational.

2. From Cressona (PA 183) to the spillway in Auburn (9.6 miles), modified recreational.

3. Auburn to Port Clinton (7.4 miles), recreational.

4. From New Ringgold to Port Clinton (11 miles), the Little Schuylkill is designated pastoral.

5. At the fork of the Little Schuylkill and Schuylkill rivers in Port Clinton to Cross Keys bridge (16.2 miles), recreational.

6. From the Cross Keys bridge to PA 422 in Reading (12.3 miles), modified recreational.

7. Reading to Douglassville (15.3 miles), recreational.

8. Douglassville bridge to the dam at Fairmount Park in Philadelphia (49.8 miles), modified recreational.

Nearby Nature Attractions. Valley Forge National Historical Park (trails follow the Schuylkill River) and Hawk Mountain Sanctuary (overlooks the Little Schuylkill River). The Appalachian Trail crosses the river at Port Clinton.

STONY CREEK

Stony Creek runs southwest-northeast like the two mountain ridges flanking it, Sharps Mountain and Blue Mountain. One of its tributaries, Rausch Creek, exploited a weakness in quartzite bedrock and made a gap in Sharps Mountain. In the gap, the current washes away thin layers of anthracite coal.

Total Designated Miles. The Pennsylvania Department of Environmental Resources classified 16 miles of Stony Creek and its associates as wild.

Watershed. Rausch Creek and the East Branch of Rausch Creek drain the northwest face of Sharps Mountain. The branches merge, and the tributary squeezes through Rausch Gap, then joins Stony Creek. Here the creek heads straight southwest, and empties into the Susquehanna River at Dauphin. Two other tributaries are included in the designated area: Rattling Run and Yellow Springs.

Designated Portions. From its headwaters in Lebanon

County, Stony Creek and its three feeder streams are classified as wild to the Pennsylvania Game Commission gate at Ellendale Forge.

Nearby Nature Attractions. Swatara and Memorial Lake state parks. State Game Lands 211 protects Stony Creek for most of its journey. The Appalachian Trail and the Horseshoe Trail cross Stony Creek and Rausch Creek in Rausch Gap.

TUCQUAN CREEK

Tucquan (pronounced TUCK-won) means "winding water," and for eight miles the creek winds from its headwaters in pastoral uplands to a boulder-choked conclusion at the Susquehanna River. Lush vegetation characterizes the shady glen cooled by the creek.

Total Designated Miles. Seven miles of this watershed are classified as scenic by the Pennsylvania Department of Environmental Resources. The last mile is designated as wild.

Watershed. Tucquan Creek flows southwest in southwestern Lancaster County. It travels just seven miles to the Susquehanna River.

Designated Portions.

1. Tucquan Creek is a scenic watercourse from its source near Rawlinsville to its confluence with Clark Run (4.5 miles). The same designation applies to the entire 2.5 mile length of Clark Run.

2. From River Road to the Susquehanna River (1 mile), Tucquan Creek is a wild stream.

Nearby Nature Attractions. Tucquan Glen, Pequea Creek, and Kelly's Run preserves; Susquehanna River Overlooks; Shenk's Ferry Wildflower Preserve; and Muddy Run Recreation Park.

TULPEHOCKEN CREEK

Tulpehocken Creek was a free-flowing stream before the U.S. Army Corps of Engineers dammed it in the 1970s. Before the dam, the stream periodically flooded farmland and settlements on its fertile banks.

Total Designated Miles. The Pennsylvania Department of Environmental Resources designated 20.2 miles of the stream as pastoral and 8.6 miles as recreational.

Watershed. The headwaters of Tulpehocken Creek begin in North Lebanon Township in Lebanon County. The creek winds east and empties into the Schuylkill River in Reading.

Designated Portions.

1. From its headwaters to Ramona, the creek is classified as pastoral (3.4 miles).

2. Pastoral designation begins again a short distance downstream and goes 16.8 miles to the SR 4010 bridge over the creek in Berks County, close to the backwaters of Blue Marsh Lake.

3. Tulpehocken Creek becomes a recreational stream from the Blue Marsh Lake dam to the Schuylkill River (6.6 miles). The same designation applies to a tributary, Cacoosing Creek, for 2 miles, starting at its confluence with Tulpehocken Creek upstream of SR 3023.

Nearby Nature Attractions. Blue Marsh Lake Project, Hawk Mountain Sanctuary, Nolde Forest Environmental Education Center, and French Creek State Park.

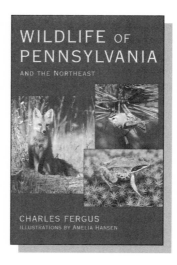